CHRIS FOXON

Chris went to Gosforth Academy in Newcastle upon Tyne before taking a first-class degree in English Language and Literature at Oxford University. He subsequently received an MA (Distinction) in Creative Producing at the Royal Central School of Speech & Drama, where he studied on an AHRC scholarship.

He has developed/produced new plays at fringe and West End venues. These have won or been nominated for a range of awards, toured the UK, and transferred internationally. He is currently the Executive Director of Papatango, and has taught at Central as well as the Universities of York and Northampton.

GEORGE TURVEY

George went to Mangotsfield School in Bristol before studying acting at the Academy of Live and Recorded Arts. He co-founded Papatango in 2007, becoming sole Artistic Director in 2013. He has directed new plays at venues including the Arcola Theatre, Theatr Clwyd, North Wall Arts Centre, Marlowe Theatre, Cheltenham Everyman and Theatre Royal, Bury St Edmunds, as well as for BBC Radio.

As a dramaturg he has led the development of all of Papatango's productions, which have premiered worldwide and won Critics' Circle, OffWestEnd, Alfred Fagon and Royal National Theatre Foundation Awards. As an actor he has appeared on stage and screen throughout the UK and internationally, including the lead roles in the world premiere of Arthur Miller's *No Villain* and *Batman Live* World Arena Tour.

Chris Foxon & George Turvey

BEING A PLAYWRIGHT

A Career Guide for Writers

NICK HERN BOOKS
London
www.nickhernbooks.co.uk

A NICK HERN BOOK

Being a Playwright
first published in Great Britain in 2018
by Nick Hern Books Limited, The Glasshouse,
49a Goldhawk Road, London W12 8QP

Designed and typeset by Nick Hern Books, London
Printed and bound in Great Britain by
Ashford Colour Press, Gosport, Hampshire

A CIP catalogue record for this book
is available from the British Library

ISBN 978 1 84842 691 7

For my parents, the family I did not choose but for whom I am thankful.

And for Hannah, for I am beyond thankful that she chose me.

Chris

For Jo and Ophelia; behind this average man are two incredible women.

And for my parents, who first introduced me to stories.

George

CONTENTS

ACKNOWLEDGEMENTS

We must first and foremost express our profound gratitude and affection for the Backstage Trust team: Kathryn, Susie, David and Dominic. You believed in us, supported us, and transformed our work.

We also wish to thank Papatango's board of trustees and artistic associates for all their hard work.

This book would not exist without Nick Hern Books, who have supported Papatango and published our writers for years. Their contribution to new writing has been immense and it is always a privilege to work with the team. We must single out Matt Applewhite for being an outstanding and merciful editor.

We are also hugely grateful to our generous, far-sighted supporters at Arts Council England, the Garfield Weston Foundation, the Boris Karloff Charitable Foundation, the Royal Victoria Hall Foundation, the Harold Hyam Wingate Foundation, the Leche Trust, the Austin and Hope Pilkington Trust, the Mildred Duveen Charitable Trust, the Derek Hill Foundation, the Fenton Arts Trust, the Mercers' Charitable Trust, the Ernest Cook Trust, the BBC Performing Arts Fund, the Channel 4 Playwrights' Scheme and the Golsoncott Foundation.

Most of all, thanks are due to those who have contributed to this book, and to all the writers and creatives with whom we have been blessed to make plays.

INTRODUCTION

To become a professional playwright requires more than just the ability to write a great script. This runs counter to many of our cultural reference points, which perpetuate the romantic image of the writer as a lone genius, penning something of such outstanding wisdom and artistic worth that the world falls into line to accommodate them. Think of the wonderful story of George Devine rowing out to John Osborne's little houseboat, where the writer was literally stewing nettles to survive, so eager was Devine to announce that *Look Back in Anger* would headline the Royal Court's next season. But this story is wonderful because it's so exceptional. Usually the myth of the sudden 'breakthrough' is just that – a myth. Most playwrights have to labour for a very long time on a lot of things besides their script before they achieve success.

That's one of the reasons British playwriting still has significant failings in representation; if talent were truly all it took, we'd see new playwrights emerging from every avenue of society. Instead, the writers who make a professional career in theatre are, disproportionately, from more privileged, insider backgrounds. This is for many reasons – cultural capital, confidence, education, wealth to fall back on – but perhaps the most crucial is having the connections and know-how to navigate the business, not just the art, of playwriting.

Successful playwrights have to understand how to promote their script, how to build relationships with venues and companies, how to collaborate with different practitioners, how to navigate different deals and production opportunities, and how to maximise the impact of such opportunities. These are just a few of the practical realities that writers must master if they are to survive within a competitive, often flawed, theatre industry.

Since 2007 our theatre company, Papatango, has worked to discover new playwrights, develop their writing, and support them in building careers, focusing on artists who might otherwise struggle to access professional resources. We have time and again been asked the same questions, faced the same uncertainties, resolved the same complications.

Hence this book. If each writer who emerges, blinking, from the creative sanctuary of the bedroom/garret/studio faces the same challenges as the writer before them did and the writer after them will do, then it seems there is a need for an accessible, unpretentious guide to the business of playwriting. And maybe, just maybe, that will help to diversify playwriting and open up pathways into theatre.

This book therefore shares our experiences and the experiences of the many brilliant writers and theatre-makers with whom we have been lucky enough to work, both through Papatango and independently. It is the result of thousands of conversations with hundreds of artists. In that sense it is a collaboration, as any work for theatre must be. It would not exist were it not for all the individuals who have had the desire and daring to ask how to be a playwright. We will make it clear when we are referring to a particular writer's experiences. Huge thanks to all who have shared.

The book is structured in three acts to work through the main stages of an emerging writer's career, from getting started to making a production to capitalising on a show's run. Each act addresses the situation of a writer at a different level of experience. If you've never attempted to write a play before or need some guidance on how to reach out to companies, start at Act One; if you feel fully equipped to write a script and share it, but are keen to know more about how to turn it into a production, then check out Act Two; if you've already had a full professional production and are looking to capitalise on this, then you might decide to go straight to Act Three. The appendices contain some useful lists and expand on the references outlined in the book.

Regardless of where you are in your career right now, we trust this book will prove a useful resource. By tackling the recurring questions and challenges encountered on a writer's journey, we hope to enable playwrights to flourish – especially those who would otherwise lack the knowledge or contacts to overcome the barriers of what can be a monolithic industry.

What It Offers

This book is not an academic analysis of playwriting or the theatre industry, nor is it a guide to writing a play. Instead, by distilling our experiences as producers at the coalface of new writing, we attempt to explain in clear terms what being a playwright means, how the business of playwriting often works, and some of the ways you might go about it.

New writing is a changing industry: in recent years we have seen the rise of more playwriting awards (often in place of commissioning); moves towards devising and collaboration rather than traditional text-based practices; and a shift of public funding away from the focus on new writing that characterised the decades either side of the millennium. All of these impact on how playwrights navigate their place within British theatre today. Rather than be drawn into discursive reflections on the reasons for these trends, we focus on the practicalities of how playwrights can carve out successful careers within this landscape.

The proviso is that Chris is a producer and George an actor and artistic director (we'll explain these terms in the chapter on 'Working with Collaborators'); neither of us are playwrights. While we have both taught playwriting within drama schools, workshops and universities, we do so from the perspectives of our different disciplines. This book therefore is categorically not a guide to writing a play. There are already several impressive books on that subject (we recommend some in the chapter on 'Training'). Instead, this book outlines how to make the most of any play that you have written, because even Shakespeare would never have gone very far if his manuscripts remained trapped in a drawer.

Nor is this book designed to advocate any ideal process. Something as personal as writing stories cannot follow any fixed route. Instead, we consider all the elements that affect a playwright's career, so you can navigate the best pathway for yourself.

What is a Playwright?

This seems an easy question, no? The answer appears obvious: someone who writes a play. But it's not quite that simple.

Firstly, 'writing a play' covers a vast range of approaches, from an individual scribbling away on a literary masterpiece, to a devising ensemble with one person nominated to turn collective ideas into a single text-based story, through to teams of writers coming together to edit verbatim material into a script – and many more practices besides.

Secondly, even if the writing is a solitary pursuit, plays are never individual enterprises. For a script to become a play it needs to be performed, meaning actors, directors, producers, designers and stage managers will get involved. The script will almost certainly evolve according to their contributions. That doesn't (at least, it shouldn't) diminish the playwright's role, but it does take us beyond the apparent confines of the title.

Thirdly, etymology muscles in to reveal that 'playwright' is a compound word which has no linguistic basis in the word 'writing'. It is comprised of 'play', which derives from the Old English *plega* meaning 'brisk movement' (remember that next time you're entering the fourth hour of a Trevor Nunn production), and 'wright', deriving from the Old English *wrihta* meaning 'worker'. We rather like this: it's a reminder that a playwright is someone who works to make movement happen, and that their play is wrought, hammered, beaten into shape – however it's done. That seems a far more inclusive concept for all the different forms that playwriting can take than the initial assumption from which we started.

(On a sidenote, the word 'writing' itself comes from the Old Saxon *writan* which means to write and also to tear. So tearing your hair out is an honourable part of writing.)

The point is that being a playwright is not just something you decide to do, it's something you decide *how* to do.

For the purposes of this book, we're assuming that 'playwright' means someone with at least a partial creative stake in a text-based script that they want to see performed, and who has an interest in continuing to make more text-based scripts for performance. We don't champion any particular creative process but just explain various approaches in how to build a career as a playwright, informed by the principle that certain practical challenges recur regardless of individual artistic practices.

The most important thing to remember is that you are a playwright if you call yourself a playwright; no one has the right to dispute that by picking holes in your CV, training or process. We trust that this book will help your plays to be successful, however you choose to make them.

We've worked with hundreds of new writers, who have gone on to win BAFTA, OffWestEnd, RNT Foundation and Alfred Fagon Awards, and had their work premiere worldwide as well as in the West End. They've all been very different, as people and as artists, except for one thing: every one of them built a career from nothing more than an idea for a play. So can you.

Papatango's motto has always been: 'All you need is a story.' We hope we can now add: 'And perhaps also this guide.'

Good luck.

ACT ONE:
STARTING OUT

This first act is aimed at writers at the beginning of their careers. Wondering how to learn about playwriting? Sent off scripts to a few companies but never heard back? Don't know what producers want to see in a theatre script? It's all explained here.

Respective chapters discuss: options for training and how to acquire the skills of a playwright; how to shape your script for the stage, addressing the formal and practical concerns of decision-makers; techniques to redraft and hone your script; and the best ways to share your finished script with maximum impact.

These cover everything it takes to give your script the best possible chance of being produced. We discuss the pragmatic factors that influence script readers, and detail tricks of the trade that may help your script overcome the hurdles of programming.

Acts Two and Three will discuss what happens after your script has been accepted for programming.

TRAINING

This chapter covers what 'training' for playwrights means, its potential benefits and its limitations. It explains the various forms training can take, including accredited higher education programmes, industry development schemes and private courses. We weigh up the pros and cons of each of these, and outline alternatives.

There is no right or wrong route to learn about playwriting. Everyone has different needs, financial and personal as well as artistic. We therefore do not promote any single approach, but describe the different resources available as objectively as we can, so you can research, reflect and decide.

Can a Playwright Be Trained?

In recent years the provision of education in creative writing, including specialist playwriting courses, has exploded. It is now common (but by no means expected) for playwrights to undertake some form of training.

Yet training is a vexed concept in relation to any artistic practice. One can instruct people in mechanical or technical skills with relative ease, and certainly elements of the playwright's toolkit may be regarded as technical, such as: narrative and scenic structure; character arcs; stagecraft; formatting. These all operate according to certain basic principles that can be taught (although artists often break, and occasionally revolutionise, such rules). Playwrights are judged, however, on their conceptual, imaginative, storytelling qualities as much as on technical virtuosity (see the case study of *An Oak Tree* at the end of this chapter). The extent to which these creative assets can be taught is less certain.

This is perhaps misleading: technical skill and creative vision shape each other and are usually inextricable in the best plays. Nonetheless, any course that aims to teach playwriting must operate according to a set of principles about what makes a 'good' playwright. This is especially true of any that award accredited qualifications, as they have not only to teach but also to evaluate. Thus, training programmes break playwriting down to its elements in order to teach and assess. The obvious truth is that some of these elements will be more suited to being taught and assessed than others. These tend to be the more technical skills.

You can reasonably expect any training programme to equip you to research ideas, plan an effective structure, map satisfying character arcs and use stagecraft and theatricality. You should not expect it to give you the ability to generate superb ideas, conceive truthful characters, or write witty and moving dialogue. Good teachers and supportive peers may sharpen your abilities in these areas, but they cannot instil them. Training should improve your writing in every aspect, but it is limited in the skills it can actually impart.

Training programmes may enrich a playwright in many ways; being part of a structured series of discussions and tasks, and having a framework within which to write, should stimulate the creative imagination. Joining a group of peers, likely with a wide range of interests, backgrounds and skills, plays a huge part in the development of any playwright. Good training will enable you to have conversations about ideas, share work-in-progress, have a support network to help solve problems or provide fresh inspiration, and access industry professionals for insight and guidance.

It may, therefore, sound as if training on a dedicated playwriting programme could not be other than beneficial, but as with any structured course aimed at meeting the needs of a potentially very diverse group, there can be no guarantees. We have seen learning environments at their worst as well as at their best. Perhaps the group dynamic becomes hostile or competitive; maybe the deadlines are appropriate for someone writing a short monologue but not someone attempting an ensemble musical; possibly the course leader has a fixation on theory when you would prefer practical exercises; perhaps the inflexible structure of modules perversely cuts down on your time and energy to write.

The point is that playwriting is personal and subjective; no course designed for multiple participants can recognise and respond to everything that distinguishes you. The question then is whether the likely benefits outweigh the potential frustrations for you as an individual.

Remember, there are plenty of alternatives to formal training. It is not de rigueur for a playwright to have qualifications; many of our most successful writers never trained. Don't be unduly influenced by the increasing trend for aspiring playwrights to train, but decide carefully what is best for you.

What Kind of Training?

Formal training for playwrights tends to fall into one of three strands:

- Accredited programmes at institutions of higher education that award a qualification.

- Courses within the theatre industry.

- Private courses led by tutors with professional experience.

You don't have to confine yourself to just one of these; many playwrights undertake all at different points (or none). You can reflect on what each offers and decide what suits you best at the present time, without compromising future opportunities.

Higher Education Programmes

Institutions offering formal qualifications in playwriting are usually either universities or drama schools (often affiliated to a university). There are several important differences between these which we will discuss shortly, but both normally offer:

- A programme for undergraduates, awarding the equivalent of a Bachelor's degree (BA), studied over three years full-time, or longer part-time.

- A programme for postgraduates, awarding the equivalent of a Master's degree (MA, MPhil, MFA, etc.), studied over one or two years full-time, or longer part-time.

Some institutions may also offer doctoral degrees (PhDs) in playwriting. These are not taught training programmes but are conducted through independent research. They tend to be more academic than vocational. We therefore only discuss Bachelor's and Master's degrees.

The BA

If you have not already got a degree or you find the undergraduate lifestyle irresistible, or you wish to retrain, then you could apply for a BA degree. These usually require qualifications at A level or equivalent in appropriate subjects such as English Literature or Drama. You may also be asked for a sample of your writing, but this depends on the course and the institution. These requirements are not set in stone. If you have alternative experiences or qualifications then approach the institution to discuss these before making an application.

Few undergraduate courses offer a specialist focus on playwriting. Instead you are likely to study playwriting within a mix of disciplines. The title of the course you enrol on is likely to be Creative Writing or Theatre Studies (or some variant). There is a difference between these. In the former you will probably experience playwriting alongside modules on other literary forms, such as prose fiction, journalism, poetry, literary essays, and so on. In the latter you are likely to experience playwriting alongside related theatre-making disciplines such as directing, producing, performing and designing.

Choosing between a Creative Writing course and a Theatre Studies course will impact on the nature of the training you receive in playwriting. Do you want to hone your literary skills across the board and experiment with your writing in different forms? Or are you clear that you want to write specifically for the stage and want to focus on gaining a strong understanding of all its components?

Whichever you choose, the breadth of learning covered under an umbrella undergraduate degree is wonderful. It can be a great way to broaden horizons and think in more depth about the kind of writing you want to pursue. Equally, writing to a structured series of exercises will force you to examine your process, and figure out *how* you write. Up to this point, especially if you're fresh from school, you may well have only experienced short-form writing (one-act plays, short stories, articles, etc.); having to complete large ensemble plays with two acts, or write a novella, will prove a new challenge. A good undergraduate degree should stretch your range and compel you to interrogate what new skills you need. The chance to work with students interested in different elements of writing and/or theatre may prove invaluable in enabling you to envisage all that makes up a script.

BAs are mostly taught through a mixture of lectures and tutorials. The former are large-scale presentations, the standard teaching method at most universities. They tend to be mostly one-way, so be prepared to take notes and absorb ideas. Tutorials are less common outside of Oxbridge (which does not offer creative writing or theatre studies at this level), and mainly occur in the last year of study. They are usually one-to-one and intended to review final pieces of work before submission and assessment. The onus will therefore be on you to carve out your own learning programme; good teachers should stimulate not spoonfeed.

A big advantage is that the breadth of an undergraduate degree results in a very flexible qualification that can support your future. A friend of Chris's who studied Creative Writing at Northumbria University is now pursuing postgraduate study in medicine! Keeping your options open is sensible. Few writers make a living solely from playwriting, and having a broader qualification could help to sustain your writing by making other jobs possible (see the chapter 'Moving On').

Be aware that a BA qualification will only be the initial stage on a long journey in playwriting. Even a starred double-first-class degree with whipped cream and a cherry on top won't command much attention outside of academia; after all, you are only being measured against a handful of students of similar experience on your course, rather than the vast numbers of writers within the industry. Equally, end-of-course showcases are not guaranteed to draw in industry movers and shakers. There are simply too many undergraduate degrees for professionals to keep an eye on graduates from every course every year.

Don't be disheartened by this; depth and range of study over several years provide an excellent foundation for recognition in the future. Having a 'safe' space alongside other committed creative people in which to learn, try things out, and perhaps fail and therefore change your approach, is a golden opportunity.

Case Study: Arthur Miller

Consider Arthur Miller's *No Villain* (George played the lead in the world premiere at the Old Red Lion Theatre/Trafalgar Studios). It's the first play by one of the greatest playwrights of the twentieth century, written when he was a nineteen-year-old student but only discovered and produced after his death. As a piece of juvenilia, it's hardly surprising that it's an interesting rather than a great play.

Miller is flexing his dramatic muscles. Many of the ideas and characters that would go into masterpieces like *All My Sons* and *Death of a Salesman* are apparent in embryonic, often crude, form. It's probably for the best that this play went undiscovered for eighty years, and was not staged until Miller's brilliance was already understood. He is palpably not a complete playwright in this script, but writing and learning from it will have been the crucible (forgive the pun) in which his genius was forged.

Modelling yourself on Arthur Miller sounds sensible to us: treat an undergraduate degree as a place to grow without the pressure of critical or professional scrutiny.

If you feel ready for a more public platform, already have an undergraduate degree, do not want to commit to multiple years of study, or want to specialise solely in playwriting, then a BA is probably not suitable. Instead, you could consider:

The MA

Master's degrees are shorter, more intensive and more specialised. They are intended to build on pre-existing skills. Usually you will be expected to have an undergraduate degree. The Creative Writing or Theatre Studies courses mentioned above are obvious fits, but truthfully you could argue that any subject is relevant. Playwriting, after all, can be about anything and demands many skills. Normally any undergraduate degree is sufficient to apply; ultimately your portfolio of writing will be the most significant factor in whether you receive an offer.

If you don't have an undergraduate degree, you won't necessarily be excluded. Some institutions accept relevant experience instead. So if, for instance, you have worked as an actor and performed in new plays, but never went to university, you could still make a good application. Your professional experience is easily as valuable as, say, an undergraduate degree in English Literature. If in doubt, contact the institution.

A Master's degree will be focused on playwriting. That being so, you won't mix with the range of artists you would on a broad undergraduate degree. It's an environment in which you are likely to be pushed harder on your writing choices with more in-depth perusal of your work. This comes at the cost of having fewer opportunities to explore different sides of theatre-making or creative writing. Conversely, your peers will probably be a more mixed group in terms of ages and backgrounds than the students on an undergraduate course.

Most MAs do not rely on the rather didactic method of lectures common at undergraduate level. Instead, courses are based around small group seminars, in which topics are discussed and practical writing tasks set or scenes reviewed. These have much more scope for individual input. Tutorials are infrequent, and tend to be scheduled to discuss drafts of a play being written for submission and assessment; they give a taste of the one-to-one dramaturgy you can expect in a professional context.

MAs usually culminate in a showcase. Goldsmiths has often hired Soho Theatre for this purpose, and other institutions book out similarly prestigious venues. This, and the fact that the teachers

TRAINING

on MA courses tend to have closer links to the industry than the leaders of BA degrees, who are more rooted in full-time academia, makes professional interest more likely. Recognise that this will not be the safe, padded dojo of the undergraduate years; it is a public arena and you will be expected to produce work that can withstand proper scrutiny (take comfort in the fact that anyone attending a showcase yearns for students to succeed).

As most MAs last for no more than one or two intensive years, they require proactive input. You will be suited if you have a good idea what you want to learn, are ready for the challenges of in-depth feedback, and are not fazed by exposure to industry figures.

Insider's View: Luke Owen

I did an MA in Creative Writing: Scriptwriting at the University of East Anglia. I had always been interested in scriptwriting but had only a self-taught understanding. My plays were okay but had never really had success or been noticed by the industry.

During one year my writing progressed further than ever, partly due to superb tuition but also because it got me thinking about scriptwriting in ways I hadn't even considered. We studied Christopher Vogler's concepts of character archetypes, plot types, story structure, dialogue, genre and adaptation, and broke scripts down into their constituent parts, analysing why one script worked and another didn't. There was a strong emphasis on 'round table' writing, giving constructive criticism. Though occasionally difficult to hear, this helped prepare me for industry feedback.

Within months of finishing I had been invited onto the Young Writers' Programme at the Royal Court and had a meeting at the BBC. While at the Court I wrote *Unscorched*.

Luke won the 2013 Papatango New Writing Prize, and has since developed new plays with Headlong. His winning play Unscorched *was translated into Italian and performed in Milan.*

Drama school or university?

Universities, as the name implies, are intended as places in which a universe of subjects is studied. You will have access to thousands of students on hundreds of courses, which can only be intellectually and creatively stimulating. Equally, the vast range of extra-curricular opportunities provides a valuable release from the pressures of study.

Universities are oriented towards academic discourse; you will study plays, read criticism and examine theory, and write essays. If a course specifies playwriting then there should be a practical element, but this will be in conjunction with academic work. This arguably gives you stronger critical appreciation, builds analytical skills, and fosters the ability to write clearly and concisely. If you are interested in the theory of playwriting as well as the practice, and have an eye on an academic career either on its own or in conjunction with practising as a playwright, then university is a good base. It also makes you more attractive to employers, assuming at some point you will need to find paid work outside theatre.

Drama schools are often affiliated with universities, but their roots in vocational training are readily apparent. Courses are focused on the practical rather than the academic side of playwriting. You will complete some essays, but do far more of your own writing. One of the big advantages of a drama school is access to people training to a high standard in a wide range of different theatre disciplines. It makes finding talented collaborators much easier. Likewise, drama schools have superlative resources including theatres, rehearsal rooms and libraries of plays. They tend to attract industry professionals as visiting teachers, a useful way to connect with high-quality theatre-makers. No university can compete with the specialised nature of a drama school, but being in such an environment does mean that the intensity and pressure can be overwhelming: everyone will be obsessed with theatre.

It is important not to pick between a university or a drama school for the labels; successful playwrights with brilliant understanding of practical theatre emerge from universities, and academics with profound philosophical and theoretical insight train at drama schools. Your place of study will not define you. Just reflect on the different environments, and pick a course that excites you. If you are studying the right material, you'll be in the right place.

I lead the MA/MFA Writing for Stage and Broadcast Media course at the Royal Central School of Speech & Drama. The course offers vocational training in writing drama across different media contexts. It aims to equip students with the key skills to succeed as dramatists, help them develop their unique 'voice' and build confidence in their own writing. Students study the principles of writing full-length drama for film, radio, stage and television. They also develop ideas for shorter pieces. While the focus of the course is on developing each writer's individual voice, students also have the opportunity to work collaboratively on developing a television series, giving the experience of working on someone else's idea, as is often the case in television writing.

Alongside developing students' writing, we think it's important for them to understand the theories that underlie dramatic writing and its current place within the cultural environment. The course includes a module exploring the history of dramatic writing. Students also take part in a group research project into a contemporary issue related to dramatic writing that interests them.

A crucial element is that students have the opportunity to be taught by and to engage with a range of industry professionals, and eventually work with a mentor to develop at least one full-length script. This kind of exposure to professional scriptwriters is often very hard to attain outside a course.

In my experience, students embark on a dramatic writing course for a combination of three reasons: to learn the fundamentals of dramatic structure; to finally finish that full-length script; and to gain some insight into how to succeed in a professional context.

No course can guarantee a career, but it will equip you with the skills of a professional writer. With talent, passion and hard work, it is possible to succeed once you have these skills and a sense of how the industry works. Our graduates have had their work produced nationally and internationally, and been commissioned by organisations including the Royal Court and BBC. They include winners of the George Devine Award, Tinniswood Award, Evening Standard Best Play Award and Bruntwood Prize, and BAFTA and Olivier Award nominees.

STARTING OUT

Sarah is a multi-award-winning playwright, dramaturg and academic. Her work has been produced at the Finborough Theatre and in Sydney and Toronto, and she was Associate Artist at Headlong from 2012 to 2016. She teaches playwriting and supervises PhD candidates at the Royal Central School of Speech & Drama.

Industry Courses

If you are not looking to earn a qualification or do not wish to embark on a prolonged period of formal study, then an excellent alternative is to undertake training within the theatre industry. This is substantially cheaper (not necessarily the same as being better value, of course) than degree study, and brings you into contact with professional theatre-makers.

There is a plethora of courses available, although some close and others emerge every year, so careful research is recommended. A good place to start is your local theatre(s); see what they offer and, if nothing is listed, get in touch and ask. They may at the very least point you in the right direction. Remember that non-venue-based companies – like Papatango – also provide training, so check what these organisations offer.

Industry training usually takes several forms: short introductory programmes; one-off workshops or writing events; and online resources.

Introductory programmes

These are usually structured to deliver sessions focusing on different writing skills at regular intervals. They're a great way to get to the heart of playwriting and learn what programmers want. Excellent examples include the Royal Court Young Writers' Programme, the Playwrights' Programme at Liverpool Everyman & Playhouse or the free GoWrite courses that Papatango run.

Each course will have its own idiosyncratic structure, but as a rough guide you might, over a certain period, take part in fortnightly or monthly sessions with the venue's literary department and visiting professionals. Groups tend to be small and the emphasis is on practical exercises to stimulate your writing. Some programmes culminate in a showcase; as these are validated by coming from within the industry, they attract attention.

Leaders are often keen to read your work – every course dreams of uncovering a home-grown success – and it can be a great way to nurture a relationship with a theatre, as well as meet other writers and establish an enduring support network. You may also get discounted or free tickets to performances, to build your experience and understanding of new writing.

There are a surprising number of opportunities along these lines. That's not entirely altruistic; venues and companies often develop participation and training schemes as part of a wider artistic programme in order to attract funding. Lest that sound overly cynical, be assured that no one goes to the effort of devising these schemes without also wanting to develop their own talent pools. They may even have an eye on future commissions.

Nonetheless, these opportunities are often not well advertised. If they are to be affordable (ideally free), then marketing budgets will be limited. Never assume they don't exist just because you haven't heard about them. Be proactive and seek them out (note the irony that courses to make playwriting accessible are often only discovered by those with advanced detective skills).

Before you start the search, be aware that only certain venues or companies will offer such courses. Usually those that produce a lot of new plays (rather than revivals or musicals) will have a literary department. Of these, relatively few will have the resources to run training programmes. Competition is therefore fierce. Have a writing sample ready and be prepared to wait before a place is available.

In general, it is hard to think of reasons why you shouldn't take up such courses if you are able; they are usually free or reasonably priced, constitute a relatively small time commitment, offer an introduction to industry professionals who are in a position to advance you as a writer, and provide the stimulus and networks to sustain your practice, potentially well into the future. And, of course, they should improve your writing.

Workshops

Often companies that cannot commit to extended introductory programmes will instead provide one-off or short-term training in the form of workshops. Workshops tend to be sessions for a half- or full day that focus on a particular skill, often led by industry professionals.

The term 'workshop' implies practical contributions and working as part of a group to trial things; they aren't lectures or Q&As (though do ask questions!). They suit people who feel ready to write and are confident sharing work, even if it has been composed impromptu. If you're looking for gentler introductions or want a theoretical overview, consider other training first, and build up to an industry workshop. If you are ready for public writing tasks, then workshops are worth a try: at best they provide excellent stimulation and refresh or renew your writing and your confidence; at worst you waste a few hours and probably still meet interesting people.

That said, be careful before you hand over any money. Some unscrupulous companies charge an exorbitant fee for workshops run by people with wobbly CVs for an absurd number of participants. Often the best workshops are free or cost-price, because they are run by organisations with the credibility and motivation to secure funding for a genuinely accessible, worthwhile opportunity. If you are contemplating paying for a workshop, do your research first. Look at the track record of the workshop leader and don't be afraid to question the organisers about participant numbers or subjects covered.

Whether free or not, make sure your expectations are appropriate. Only apply for a workshop if the topic or the leader interests you. Come prepared to contribute and try new things. A one-off workshop will obviously have limited impact and is not a substitute for in-depth training. Nor should you believe that participating in a series of discrete and unrelated workshops will provide a comprehensive playwriting framework. If you wish to train, then workshops are excellent supplements, not complete programmes.

Online Resources

The days when you had to be in the same room to learn from a teacher are long over. Venues and companies increasingly share materials online. This keeps costs down and makes learning accessible to anyone. Fantastic online courses include those by Newcastle upon Tyne's Live Theatre and London's Bush Theatre, as well as Papatango's captioned GoWrite workshop videos.

Of course there are limitations attached to online courses. It is up to you to find the motivation to work through exercises, while you won't build any relationships with peers and teachers or benefit from the showcases that accompany face-to-face courses. Equally, completing an online course won't offer much validation; they are not as selective, nor assessed with as much rigour, as programmes with limited physical places.

Nonetheless, what's not to like? They can be a great catalyst for learning and writing at your own pace and according to your own needs. It may be particularly worthwhile to access these if you are drafting writing samples for other opportunities and need to test them against industry standards. They can also refresh your thinking and build confidence.

Private Courses

As well as industry courses and higher education, there are private courses offering training. These do not work to the predetermined goals of accredited courses, which need to assess students for qualifications or industry programmes, which need measurable results to show funders. Instead, they cater to a limited number of select participants and respond to individual needs. Their USP is therefore to provide a more personal programme of study than other training opportunities – especially as participants pay for and expect a satisfactory customer experience. The fewer the participants, the more the costs rise, and the better equipped the course should be to accelerate your writing with precise, tailored insights.

Private courses attract writers for many different reasons. Some are keen to work with a particular teacher; some hope to supplement training elsewhere; some seek preparation for a particular project; some are struggling to get on to competitive industry programmes and want to build skills and a stronger portfolio; some merely want the structure to write and the chance for feedback.

This variety reflects the chief advantage of undertaking a private course: you should receive meaningful personal attention from someone with a superlative background in developing plays. Make sure the teacher has the CV and relevant skills to justify their position. You should be convinced that you will receive proper expertise in exchange for hard-earned cash.

The drawbacks are that, as commercial and unaccredited enterprises, private courses do not lend particular validation. Places are costed and a certain number need to be filled, so emerging from a private course does not in itself mean anything more than that you could afford it (although this is increasingly also true of our higher education sector). Of course, certain courses are more competitive and have stronger reputations, but even these will not guarantee you recognition in themselves.

Moreover, private courses function behind closed doors. These are specialist playwriting courses, and do not generally present the chance to become involved in playmaking. Don't expect to learn too much about writing with collaborators or performers, or to gain new insights into theatricality, nor to have a public platform to share your writing. They are more akin to sustained retreats to develop individual playwrights.

Private courses benefit people who know what they need to improve, who are not seeking collaborators or a showcase, and who are willing to take guidance from a teacher who should have genuine expertise. Provided you understand what a private course is designed to deliver, can afford it, and choose carefully, it can be a rare chance to hone your practice.

Insider's View: Fiona Doyle

I don't believe a playwright has to do a course. All a playwright has to do is read and write as much as they can, and want wholeheartedly to commit to it. So I understand why some might be a little suspicious of the multitude of writing courses on offer these days, but each writer's journey is highly personal and individual. For where I was in my life back in 2012, I needed a little kick-start. I had zero experience of writing plays but a strong feeling that this was for me. In hindsight, I guess I was looking for guidance and someone with experience to signal that I perhaps wasn't completely hopeless.

I had been offered a place on a full-time MA but failed to secure funding so couldn't afford to take it up. Instead, I undertook a private course with John Burgess [former Head of New Writing at the National Theatre]. John's course is structured in a way that allows people to work while they're on it, and he was kind enough to let the more financially strapped students (like me) pay in instalments.

The set-up was simple: a two-hour class once a week, where we would focus on something specific like rhythm or use of silences or exits and entrances. There was a lot of reading, listening to and learning from other people's work, practical writing exercises in every class, and eventually bigger tasks were set, like having to write a ten-minute play using three acts. These tasks accumulated and became more challenging as the course progressed, so that by the end we were expected to have completed, or be close to completing, a full-length play.

We were encouraged to discipline ourselves and get into the habit of writing regularly. John is an experienced director of new plays – one of the most important things he taught me was all the talking and thinking and theorising in the world won't make you a writer; you are not a writer until you start writing. Other advantages are small class sizes and mentorship that sometimes continues long after the course has finished. John still reads my work and he'll always find time to meet for a coffee when I'm in town.

I'm not sure I could ever have written a play without first spending a year in his company. That course unlocked something and I've not looked back. But that's just me. Writing courses aren't for everyone so my advice would be to listen to what your gut is telling you – it rarely lets you down.

Fiona won the 2014 Papatango New Writing Prize for Coolatully, *which Papatango produced at the Finborough Theatre and which has since been performed in the USA. Her subsequent plays* Deluge *and* The Strange Death of John Doe *premiered at Hampstead Theatre, and she joined the National Theatre Studio on attachment. She has also written for NT Connections. She has received a MacDowell Colony Fellowship, won the Eamon Keane Full Length Play Award, and been nominated for the Susan Smith Blackburn Prize.*

Should I Train?

So, you're deluged with options and opportunities. But are any of them right for you? Let's consider the arguments for, and the risks of, training.

Pros:

Learn the craft

While formal training alone won't make you a successful writer, it should give you a good grounding in fundamentals such as structure, characters, genre, form, dialogue, and so on. A solid technique may prove invaluable in realising your stories.

Test your ideas

Training programmes often enable you to work with practitioners in other disciplines, either as an integral part of the process or by organising your own events with fellow students. Learning how your script develops when staged by directors and actors, in a safe and supportive environment, can be an important learning curve. Equally, having your script interrogated by people with different perspectives will teach you a lot about writing, collaboration and production.

Build a network

Writing is often solitary, and can tip into loneliness. It is a tough gig. Debilitating nerves can strike when you ponder sharing the play you've spent months polishing. Training is a great opportunity to meet other writers who can act as a sounding board, give constructive feedback, and provide support. It's always nice to know you're not alone; sometimes it's vital.

Guaranteed feedback

Feedback can be harder to come by than tickets to *Hamilton* (or whatever sold-out West End show comes to mind at the time of reading). The sheer number of scripts in circulation means that giving a personalised response to your submission isn't necessarily on the agenda of agents, literary managers or producers. Training usually guarantees that your work will be read by someone with a decent knowledge of theatre, and the feedback you receive should have the sole purpose of improving your writing.

Meet industry professionals

Training is usually run by industry professionals who should bring genuine insight. Their guidance could set you on the right path. They may also have connections to venues and companies, so you may gain access to these. Because…

New relationships

…'It's not what you know, it's who you know.' Terrible cliché – never use it in your writing – but keep it at the back of your mind. Building relationships is going to be vital to your progression as a playwright. If you are attending a writers' group at a venue, you might be able to get your scripts read by the literary department. If you are on a more formal writing course, you could introduce yourself to the guest speakers, who often represent leading organisations. Training is one of the easiest ways of making these connections.

Even if you are already involved in a playwriting network, it may be that you joined because it's run by people with similar tastes or background. You could shake things up by getting involved in a training programme that connects you with people with different experiences. Access to industry decision-makers or artists with different perspectives is a privilege.

Showcase your work

Many playwriting courses culminate in a showcase of your work. This often takes the form of a rehearsed reading or a staged performance of certain scenes (we discuss these in detail in the 'Getting Noticed' chapter). These tend to be performed for an invited audience including agents, producers, directors, etc. It's a great chance for your writing to be seen.

Showcases of training programmes are likely to have more impact than any private showcase you might arrange on your own. The course leaders will ask personal contacts, and it's more efficient and appealing for busy theatre professionals to take in work from several writers on a single trip.

Confidence

Confidence plays a big part in writing. Feeling secure in what you are doing and in your ability to do it is key. Training can help you to feel that you have a legitimate case for calling yourself a playwright, that you have a set of skills to rely on, that you can solve that tricky second act. At the very least it gives you something to say to *that* family member the next time they ask, 'What exactly do you do again?'

Have a reason to write

This may sound silly, given you are reading a book about your desire to be a playwright, but being part of a course gives you a structure and motivation to write. If you have the desire but lack the discipline, training can be the perfect way to bring potential to fruition.

Funding

Many accredited training programmes at universities or educational institutions have funding available. It's worth investigating whether you might be eligible for a student loan, although bear in mind this will count as a debt you will be liable to repay. You should also see what grants are available. Bursaries for those from particular backgrounds or in financial need are relatively common, and sought-after grants are worth an application. Even some private courses offer scholarships or discounts.

Chris received a grant for tuition fees plus a year's living costs for his postgraduate degree, so be like any gumshoe detective and follow the money. Look up what grants or scholarships are attached to particular courses or institutions, and their eligibility criteria. In Chris's case, his scholarship came from the Arts and Humanities Research Council, so he had to prove academic merit and ongoing scholarly potential. Other grant programmes will have different values. You will always have to make a formal application, inevitably with steep competition, so be honest: do you have a realistic shot at an application and can you provide what the funder wants? (See the chapter 'Moving On' for tips on applying for funding.)

You may find yourself paid to write – but don't bank on it until you've actually received an offer.

Cons:

Cost

Nobody goes into theatre for the money, so the cost of training has to be a consideration (unless you land a funded place). Industry courses attached to venues or companies are sometimes free of charge or offered at cost-price. Accredited courses at higher education institutions or private courses, however, may charge thousands of pounds in tuition fees before you even contemplate living costs.

Moreover, this may be compounded by the need to turn away work and sacrifice income in order to give your training sufficient attention to justify the fees. This is all money you won't be able to put into your work in future. Decide whether the training is worth this investment.

Time

The timescale of training may be a factor. If you have finished formal education and can't bear the prospect of dusting off your satchel, then a year or longer at a university or drama school may seem like a long stretch. Introductory playwriting courses, one-off sessions or private playwriting courses with limited terms may be good opportunities to test the water before you commit to any long-term programme.

Moreover, the time demanded to make a success of training may adversely affect your personal or professional commitments. Drama schools tend to run a full working week. Universities and industry courses are generally more flexible, but will nonetheless demand regular attendance. Consider your professional schedule and personal life before signing up.

Location

Most training opportunities rely either on your proximity or your willingness to travel, as they are usually conducted on a face-to-face basis. Unless you live locally, you may have to endure a lengthy commute. This will cut into the time available for extra-curricular benefits like networking or seeing shows. Of course, you could move to be near the training, but such a relocation will entail costs and disruption. If you do decide to relocate, make sure it's to somewhere you want to live – uprooting can either stimulate or swallow your writing.

Don't make these decisions lightly, and never let the location of training dictate your life. There will always be other options, and there are excellent opportunities in every part of the country. Alternatively, a few training courses are low-residency, meaning most work is done remotely, and these may prove a blessing.

Location and accessibility should be important considerations if you are to maximise the opportunity, justify any fees, and play a full part in the programme.

Pressure to conform

You may feel that training isn't for you because you don't want to write to somebody else's criteria. While some find training expands their ability, others find it constricting. If you are attempting something radical, this may not be catered for in a formal programme, especially if a standardised system of assessment is involved.

That said, to succeed professionally you will need to work with collaborators and share your work with audiences, so it would be a shame to be unduly suspicious of professional teachers of playwriting. Maybe your ideas would benefit from exposure to and interrogation by more conventional approaches?

It may also be that deadlines and scrutiny are not conducive to your best work. There's no point putting yourself in a pressurised or rigid environment if it will impede your writing or well-being.

Getting a place

'What do you mean, I can't just show up?' Getting on to a playwriting course can be tricky. Industry schemes usually only open a couple of times a year and are very competitive. Many of the more prestigious university or drama schools are heavily oversubscribed.

Entry is usually based on a sample of your work and/or pitching an idea in an interview. To choose a good sample or pitch, consider what best represents you as a writer. Don't try to ape someone else's style. Pick work that you feel encapsulates your voice and interests. Showing range is also advisable; try to convey that you have more than one story to tell and can inhabit different characters, genres or situations. Of course, that shouldn't compromise the first point, about being true to your own voice – but any writer should have more than a single perspective to offer. Lastly, make sure that whatever you submit makes sense; it's fine to take a short extract from a bigger work provided it is clear on its own. Chopping a short, witty duologue out of a full play may mean the jokes fall flat and the characterisation is hard to follow.

These applications can be gruelling – but no more so than competing in the industry. Every successful writer has experienced knockbacks. If you want to take part in a course but get rejected, persevere, learn from the experience, and make a stronger application in future. Just be prepared to be bruised.

Pieces of paper

Many training programmes offer some form of qualification upon successful completion. Cue mortarboards flung in the air, downing of shots, weeping grannies – and the deflation next morning of realising that being a certified playwright won't get you anywhere. Venues and companies only trust a writer when they read or see their work. So while completing any course that tests your creative limits is an immense achievement, be aware that your CV alone won't take you to the Olivier Awards. Hopefully everything you learned in gaining that qualification will produce a script that does.

Key Questions

Weighing up the pros and cons and understanding what you want from training is vital before deciding whether to take the plunge. Ask yourself:

- Do I need help with the technical side of writing (e.g. do I struggle to structure a play? Am I finding it hard to research ideas?)?

- Do I struggle for motivation and would a structured set of deadlines help?

- Would gaining qualifications and feedback make an important difference to my confidence?

- Do the course leaders have genuine expertise?

- Is the course affordable?

- Are the time commitment and location amenable to my professional and personal life?

- Would access to a network of peers able to read/perform/direct/critique my work be a new experience?

- Would the course connect me with the industry and reach influential professionals otherwise outside my ken?

If the answer to most of these is yes, then some form of training is probably right for you. If you answered no to most, then you might consider alternatives.

Alternatives to Training

It's becoming increasingly common for playwrights to train, but don't feel under pressure to do so. You may decide that formal training is not for you for any one of a dozen valid reasons. Don't be disheartened by this. Training for playwrights is a relatively new phenomenon; for most of history, playwrights have learned on the job. If we abandon that, then we resign ourselves to a future in which new plays come from a narrow selection of those fortunate enough to access training opportunities. This would be absurd, a criminal neglect of talent and potential. Fortunately, there are still manifold routes for the self-taught playwright to emerge, and some of our most exciting voices come through these. Never be abashed to declare yourself an autodidact.

Write

There is no better way to improve your writing than to write, as much and as often as you can. Don't prejudge your work; get it on paper, and get the whole story on paper. Don't agonise over small details; create the whole and don't worry about lapses or weaknesses. After all, whole always contains a hole! Only once it's complete can you review it, and if you see the holes, the flaws – well, congratulations. You've developed the critical faculty that will enable you to improve. If you can't see any failings, then look again; no one ever pens a perfect draft on a first attempt.

Only through writing and rewriting can you discover your 'voice'. Don't expect to crack this with your first draft, or even your first play; if you learn from mistakes, you'll get stronger.

We are big believers that all you need is a story. Don't let yourself be intimidated by the idea of being a playwright. Essentially it's just storytelling. We spend our lives telling stories, whether recounting something that happened to us in our day or entertaining friends with a joke. For the most part we don't struggle to structure our story correctly, nor do we forget the punchline. If you think you have a story to tell that will work on stage then get writing. It's the first and most important step. Just be prepared for it to take a while.

In the words of Samuel Beckett: 'Ever tried. Ever failed. No matter. Try Again. Fail again. Fail better.'

Set deadlines

Procrastination is a writer's worst enemy. Set deadlines, whether it be to write a scene a day or to have finished your play by a certain date. Try to be strict.

If you aren't sure what deadlines to aim for, then there are some great writing challenges you can sign up to. The Space's *28 Plays Later* runs online every February, and provides stimuli for you to write one short play a day throughout the month. Commitments like these are tough but worthwhile. However you do it, devise a schedule and a structure that keep you writing. (We offer more advice on how to find your writing process in the next chapter, 'Writing for Theatre'.)

Turn to friends

Once you've written something, there is no point keeping it locked in your desk; you can only learn and improve by testing it. This is daunting, but feedback, from whomever it comes, is the only way to discover if the story in your head has made its way to the page. (See our discussion of this in the chapter on 'Redrafting and Editing'.)

The key thing to remember when getting feedback is that it's only one person's opinion; whether it be your mother or the most experienced of literary managers, not everything they say is necessarily right. A good general rule is that if one person says something then it may reflect personal taste, but if five people say it, then it's probably reliable. This is true of both positive and negative comments.

Seek feedback from friends – ones you can trust to be honest – before rushing to share with industry figures. Non-professional readers will pick up on obvious things that you can polish or fix, and as people outside of theatre, their feedback will tell you a lot about the potential audience's response. This can be invaluable in redrafting before you share within professional circles, who will judge your writing very quickly. Remember, a good first impression is golden.

Once you've ironed out the flaws of the first draft, a good trick to test the new version before dispatching it far and wide is to invite friends to read it for the cost of a couple of bottles of wine. This allows you to hear your words in a stress-free environment and gives you access to instant feedback. Often, writers believe that the first time their script is read should be with a professional cast, in order to give it the best realisation, but a talented actor can disguise a bad line whereas an amateur will reveal every clanger. You'll hear them, excise them, and then share your work more confident in its readiness.

Learn from the pros

Getting professional tips or feedback is not simple. A dozen years ago most companies had literary departments primed to respond to unsolicited submissions, but these are now increasingly rare. Papatango are unusual, perhaps quixotic, in giving feedback on every submission we receive, but it is always worth checking to see who else will do so. Most companies state their literary policy on their website.

As well as theatre-makers, you might consider sending your script to a literary agent. They do accept unsolicited submissions, as they are always on the lookout for new clients. However, they are under no obligation to provide feedback. (See our discussion on the role of agents in the chapters on 'Working with Collaborators' and 'Making Deals'.)

You can also pay for feedback with organisations which offer script-reading services, like New Writing South, or with individuals with professional experience. In return for a fee of around £60 to £150 depending on the length of your script, you will receive professional, objective feedback. This is a great way of finding out what an experienced industry professional might think of your writing, but rapidly becomes expensive, so try not to rely on it. Only invest in it if you trust the service.

If you are not having any success with unsolicited submissions, you may need to build a relationship with a company in another way. If you become known personally to the team, you are more likely to get a response. (Look up our suggestions in the 'Getting Noticed' chapter on how to establish such a relationship.)

Even if you do manage to get an unsolicited submission accepted with the promise of feedback, this may take months. Don't wait for a response. Get started on a new script!

Learn by doing

There are always opportunities for new playwrights to learn on the job. In particular, many venues or companies offer informal or improvisational writing events. They usually challenge a small group of writers to complete a short play either individually or collaboratively within a brief period, often in response to particular material. This play is then read or performed for feedback, with the possibility of developing it in the future and the prospect of having some industry bigwigs take note.

For instance, scratch nights (which we'll talk more about in the 'Getting Noticed' chapter) offer the chance to see short samples of your work performed before an audience. Theatre503 in London currently organises a Rapid Write Response initiative, in which one night of every production includes performances of short plays penned in response to the main show. Other popular formats include twenty-four-hour plays, in which theatre-makers write, rehearse and perform plays inside one day.

Events along these lines are usually a rich learning experience but have their limitations; there is only so much you can do in the allotted time and your actors and director won't have much chance to rehearse. It is difficult to deliver a good play within such stringent parameters, and your work will be scrutinised by collaborators and audiences. But they give you an immovable deadline and the invaluable opportunity to see your work in action. They are also widely recognised as great platforms from which to keep an eye out for new talent.

Only sign up if you feel ready for the exposure and the technical challenge, and keep your expectations in check. Be willing to learn and don't resent it if an important guest gives you critical notes; any attention is a sign you must have done something to catch the eye.

Or you might join an amateur theatre society. Often these companies are really keen for new plays; everyone loves to initiate a role! Becoming attached to such a group can be a great way to pen new plays and see them tested across every stage of a production, without the pressure of professional scrutiny but with the input of passionate and knowledgeable theatre-makers.

Never be afraid to hustle or hawk your work; just make sure you understand what the benefits and limitations are.

Join a writers' group

Playwriting is a collaborative venture, and joining a writers' group can give you an opportunity to meet like-minded people and share work.

Writers' groups are more relaxed than formal training; some are free, while others incur a small membership fee. They consist of regular sessions in which samples of work are read out to receive constructive feedback. If you prefer, you can simply listen and feed back, to learn from others.

Some groups will organise workshops and talks with industry professionals. Overlying all of this is a sociable, supportive environment. They're a great way to sustain a trusted network, gain access to industry figures, build confidence, and earn vital feedback.

Examples of writers' groups devoted to theatre are Player Playwrights and Actors & Writers London. There are also online communities that organise events; look at Playwriting UK on

Facebook or the London Playwrights' Blog (despite the name, it lists national opportunities). A superlative list of opportunities is also maintained by BBC Writersroom.

Who knows, you could even establish your own writers' group!

Read

You don't need to be enrolled on a training programme to learn from masterly playwrights. Fantastic books on the artistic and technical sides of playwriting include:

- *How Plays Work* by David Edgar
- *The No Rules Handbook for Writers* by Lisa Goldman
- *The Secret Life of Plays* by Steve Waters

Each gives a different angle, and you can absorb at your leisure and with repeated interrogations. (There is a Select Bibliography in the appendices.)

The best way to understand how plays truly work, however, is to read as many scripts as you can. Challenge yourself to read a play each week for an entire year, covering as wide a range of periods and genres as possible. This needn't cost the earth; most decent charity shops have a drama section, as do libraries.

Don't read passively; study the text. Read a scene or a section at a time, get the general sense of it, then re-read it to test the purpose and dramatic/thematic function of each line. In a fundamentally economical form like drama, the heart of good writing is that nothing is superfluous, so don't move on until you understand why every feature is as it is. Try to answer this question: why has the writer done this and what is the effect on the audience?

Explore what is going on in one of Pinter's pauses, or delve into Chekhov's use of subtext. Look at a playwright's early work and track their development through to their later plays; what changes or improvements occurred in their writing?

Have a pen in your hand and a notebook at your side. Scribble down thoughts, responses, queries, or anything that you find striking or memorable. Build a journal full of private inspiration.

Watch theatre

Probably the best way to learn how playwriting works is to experience it live. By seeing productions of everything from the classics through to the freshest new writing, you can find out first hand what works – or, just as valuably, what doesn't.

Again, take a notepad and record your impressions at the interval and immediately afterwards. Then, a week later, look back over these notes and see what you remember and what you have forgotten. That will reveal a huge amount about the writing.

A useful exercise after watching a show is to pen a short scene in response; discover how the characters feel in your hands, how you'd use the setting and design, and what creative choices are available that the original playwright didn't make. Perhaps reflect on why that is.

You may also think about writing scenes to explore the wider world; what is happening offstage, what narratives may spin out (think of Stoppard's *Rosencrantz and Guildenstern Are Dead*)? Do whatever you can to test the writing against your own tastes and skills, and to experiment with new techniques.

Of course, the theatre can be an expensive endeavour, but there are ways you can avoid bankruptcy. If youth is on your side, most theatres run schemes that are very affordable. For those of us over twenty-five it's a little trickier, but there are still options. Follow www.theatremonkey.com for a round-up of the best deals available.

Moreover, papering agencies like Audience Club enable producers anticipating empty seats to give away free tickets, which you can book for a small donation. Many theatres also have an allocated number of cheap tickets; these are usually in high demand but if you have a keen eye and are quick on the draw you might snap them up. With luck, people will do the same for your plays in future.

Case Study: Can Writing a Good Play Be Taught?

The aesthetic principles of what makes a 'good' play have changed throughout history. In Shakespeare's day, the so-called Golden Age of English Literature, Aristotle's Unities of Time, Place and Action held sway (albeit, in practice, these were broken with cheerful abandon, including by the Bard himself). Literature was informed by the notion that art was the representation of universal truths long since identified by classical authorities; the role of contemporary writers was not to express new ideas but to deliver established truths in fresh ways – the spirit of Renaissance (literally 'rebirth') endeavour.

Thus, writers were primarily judged – at least by the self-appointed intelligentsia – not on creative vision but on such skills as rhetoric, structure and 'moral truth'. Hence the bitter complaints of Robert Greene that Shakespeare, the grammar-school parvenu, was an 'upstart crow' with no appreciation of these refinements. Ben Jonson also commented that Shakespeare had 'small Latin and less Greek', as if this were an important critical point on his work in the vernacular. Jonson was at least partly rebuffing establishment snobbery; even so, his line now seems strange. It is no longer a prerequisite for a writer to embed themselves within an ancient tradition.

Arguably, since the complex and multifaceted movements now retrospectively dubbed with the catch-all label 'Romanticism', our critical precepts have undergone a revolutionary shift towards creative vision. As Wordsworth put it, a writer is 'impelled to create'. A century later, the modernist Ezra Pound exhorted us to 'make it new' (although ironically – and weirdly – he borrowed that phrase from a Chinese Emperor's four-thousand-year-old wash basin).

The point is that the criteria for judging a play, or any art, have never been fixed; in all likelihood, if someone were to read or see your play in a hundred years, they would assess it very differently from a critic today. The best that anyone teaching playwrights can do is to make them aware of the contemporary criteria that the industry and the public tend to abide by. It's up to you if you want to conform to these standards.

So when training programmes emphasise technical virtuosity or the vital importance of an original idea, it's worth remembering these are values for our time, not for all time. You need to decide on the principles that deliver your story in the best way: if that means breaking with received opinion on technique, or at the other end of the spectrum borrowing ideas currently deemed old-fashioned, then do so. Training programmes should empower you to make such choices and to understand your place as a playwright as part of an evolving and changing artistic landscape; they should not teach prescriptive rules.

We would argue that the only timeless test of a play can be its story, its emotional heart; it's hard to name any play that has lasted that does not excel at telling a story, however that is done – even *Waiting for Godot* or *4.48 Psychosis*.

Let's consider one of the most successful new plays of this century, Tim Crouch's *An Oak Tree*. It premiered in 2005 and is regularly revived over a decade later, having toured the world.

The premise is that a stage hypnotist (a profession with interesting parallels to a playwright), originally played by Crouch, has accidentally run over and killed a young girl; at one of his shows – this show, the one the audience is watching now – her grieving father appears to confront him. The final piece of this self-referential puzzle is that for every show a different actor, of any age or gender, plays the father, having neither read nor seen the play before. It's a perplexing conceit that works brilliantly in performance. Crouch highlights all the conventions and contrivances of playwriting in order to wring shock and impact from them.

While critics uniformly praised the technical skill behind the concept, opinion was divided on the show itself. Lyn Gardner in the *Guardian* in 2007 wrote that:

> It is a fascinating excavation of process. At its worst it feels contrived; at its best it feels like sheer bloody magic. This might just be all so much clever game-playing, but *An Oak Tree* is saved from disappearing up its own philosophical arse by its emotional underpinning. It is like watching your own heart being mugged.

Speaking of the 2015 revival, Henry Hitchings in the *Evening Standard* broadly concurred:

> The slightly jarring cleverness is matched by real emotional density.

In the same year, however, Paul Vale in *The Stage* found the experience hollow:

> Crouch's touching drama remains a deeply moving piece [but for the second actor] there is an understandable reticence at letting go emotionally with a script you have never seen. Ultimately it remains a distinctly unsatisfying and vaguely schizophrenic experience... the drama and emotion are invariably overpowered by the method.

We are not suggesting that the responses from these critics define the show's worth (see the 'Going into Production' chapter on handling reviews); we simply regard these as the views of three audience members. It is clear that, ultimately, whatever its undoubted technical depth and precision, they each measured the play's success in terms of emotional impact.

This is a helpful illustration for any playwright considering training: you will, ultimately, be judged on the story you tell as much as, or more than, how you tell it. Of course, the technical wizardry is integral to *An Oak Tree*, but whether this enhances or detracts from the story has been the acid test for most, with no consensus. Probably no play has ever been met with universal praise or unmitigated disdain.

Therefore, training should give you the skills to use form and technique as brilliantly as Crouch does, but it should not dictate what form and technique you choose, and nor should any of the aesthetic yardsticks we use at the moment determine the work you want to make. Indeed, training may not be necessary to realise the stories you wish to tell. If you are to write well, you should first and foremost write for yourself. Do this, and the chances are that others will respond.

WRITING FOR THEATRE

Once equipped with the skills of playwriting, the time comes to write your own script. Unsurprisingly, this is where many budding playwrights come a cropper. Not necessarily because of the quality of their writing, but because their script flouts the basic principles of a stage play. Many ostensibly theatrical scripts read more like film or TV treatments, or are confusingly formatted, or rely on sleights-of-hand or huge ensembles that are unlikely to work convincingly on stage. Any of these can mean the end of that script's journey.

This chapter therefore outlines what is required of a theatre script, at least in the mind of a producer, literary manager or other decision-maker. We do not attempt to tell you how to write your play; as we have mentioned, there are several excellent books on the art and craft of playwriting. Instead, we explain all the factors separate from the quality of the writing itself that may determine the eventual success or failure of your play.

Try not to think of these as restrictions upon your storytelling. Most of these principles are based on very sound experience and knowledge of what makes a script triumphant on stage; if you wish to break them, then understand how you will do so in a way that still works in performance. As noted in the Introduction, it's a charming myth that artistic worth can bend all to its will; in practice (or unless you are a genius *and* lucky), pragmatism and practicality hold sway. If a producer is to spend many thousands of pounds on staging your play, they need to know you've written with an eye on practicalities and respect for the needs of actors, directors and designers.

We also describe the various forms that playwriting may take. Often there's an assumption that a playwright works alone until their mission is accomplished, at which point a creative team and producer swoop in and take over. This is a traditional model, and many writers excel at it, but it's not necessarily the best way for everyone, especially those still honing their practice. In order to make sure your script meets the requirements of producers and has the best shot at being staged, you may want to follow more flexible or collaborative approaches. We explain different approaches to playwriting and how to make them work for you. There is also a section on beating writer's block, so that the technical challenges of playwriting don't stump you.

What Counts as 'Playwriting'?

Don't assume the only way to create a story for the stage is to tap away in splendid isolation (though it's perfectly respectable to do so). Such assumptions are not necessarily conducive to creating good scripts, but they are how we've tended to model the creative process for the last couple of centuries, since Wordsworth's ponderous declaration that a literary artist is:

> endued with more lively sensibility, more enthusiasm and tenderness, who has a greater knowledge of human nature, and a more comprehensive soul, than are supposed to be common among mankind.

How comprehensive is your soul feeling today? Such pronouncements are problematic for our conception of an artist. Wordsworth imbues the artist with mythic qualities, a lone creative visionary far beyond the reach of collaborators. Frankly, it's small wonder that his long-suffering associate Coleridge resorted to opium (which fuelled a different kind of Romantic myth of creativity, from semi-divine or hallucinatory inspiration – this is also not recommended).

Let's be clear. Great writers need not work in a vacuum; their genius does not place them beyond the compass of mere mortals. Yet such rot informs many of our cultural touchstones. No one in theatre thinks like this, but many artists starting out have no reference other than these outmoded assumptions, and this hinders their development. We should never burden someone developing their art with the demand that they must do it alone or otherwise compromise their vision.

It's only relatively recently that scholars have recognised the role that collaboration played in the greatest English writer, a William who surpasses even Wordsworth; that is, Shakespeare. For centuries we assumed our national bard was so glorious as to be totally beyond his peers, but recent research has revealed that many of his plays were, to a greater or lesser extent, collaborations. Indeed, one could argue that the fact he wrote for a company of actors, tailoring roles to specific talents, was itself a form of collaboration. Rather than diminish his glory, the contributions of others enhanced it.

It may well be that you do write best working alone. Certainly many great playwrights did and do write independently, spending no more time with those peculiar beasts, the director or cast, than strictly necessary. The point, however, is that the nature of your writing process should be your choice. It's as respectable to create your script alongside others as it is to work alone. Doing so may mean you have a script that's informed by collaborators and takes into account the practicalities of staging.

Consider these different approaches. Which one, or which combination, will enable you to deliver your script with the best chance of success on stage?

Write It

This is the traditional model. You sit down and, erm, write the thing.

That simple statement elides a multitude of issues. Bashing out a play at will clearly favours people who have the time, space and money to dedicate themselves to solo creation. Models of playwriting that assume a playwright works alone to turn in a great script therefore narrow our bracket of artists considerably.

Theatre is perhaps getting a little better at enabling people outside this small slice of relative privilege to write plays. It's always going to be true that affluence will make writing easier – but that doesn't mean it makes it better. We won't speculate further on this, but consider it all as one, whether you write by hand or by dictation, whether on a grimy night bus or on a marble table in a house by the ocean – but we hope our tips will level everyone's chances of success.

Reflecting on who is able to write alone matters, because this is how most playwrights in British theatre are expected to undertake most of the writing, at least at the initial stage. Text-based theatre usually relies on a playwright having the initial concept and completing a first draft, however rough and ready, before others contribute. That has perhaps changed a little in recent years, with the role of dramaturg and the notion of devising as an ensemble filtering through from abroad, but the majority of our new writing remains not merely writer-centric but writer-led. Where dramaturgs do cast their spell, or workshopping does occur, it tends to be later in the process. The playwright remains the starting point.

The reasons for this are varied. Obviously it's cheaper for producers to commission one writer to pen a script than to pay a team of artists to devise. If that script looks promising, then the purse strings may loosen sufficiently to bring in others – and if it doesn't, then the lost investment isn't so substantial. Commissions are therefore usually for an individual playwright. So, as you start to turn playwriting into a living (hopefully), get used to the prospect of writing independently and individually, at least at the start of the process. If you rely heavily on a devising process, chances are you will build your career as part of a company ensemble funded by means other than writing commissions.

This is not a problem for many playwrights, who cherish retaining sole control over the script (although as we touched on in the 'Training' chapter, most will seek out feedback and notes from others). Changes may be mooted during pre-production or rehearsals, but in essence the script has been given its shape by one person alone: the playwright.

This is a process that works for many but not all writers. If you relish it, then congratulations – you'll slot well into the prevailing model of British playwriting. If you're not entirely comfortable writing alone, but you recognise that doing so is likely to be fundamental to making a living as a playwright, then you might find these tactics helpful:

- Work out whether you need a structure…

  Some writers can't get stuck into a script without knowing the plot. If you like planning, then map out the journey(s) the characters will go on. Write the 'objectives' of each scene on separate pieces of card. Work out the arcs of each individual character as well as looking at the overall plot; summarise each character's role in each scene on yet more pieces of card, then read these together. Do they develop or stagnate? It's often the case that the protagonist has a brilliant journey but supporting characters only enable that, which isn't always noticeable until someone else gets involved. Break your story down into its separate components, to test your ideas and make writing alone more effective.

- …or whether you prefer to figure it out as you go along.

  Dominic Mitchell, the winner of the first Papatango New Writing Prize (he's since notched up a couple of lesser trophies called BAFTAs) talks of a 'spew draft'; get your ideas out, meet your characters, don't worry overly about details. Spew it all out. Then return and tease out plot and structure. Over multiple drafts, you'll arrive at the final story. This model works for writers who prefer to explore the dramatic world before constructing plots, feeling their way into how characters behave and what they want. This is likely to prove a labour-intensive and time-consuming method, but if it's how your writing flows, and you prefer not to be tied into a pre-determined plan that you'd only stray from, it's worth trying.

- Act out moments or scenes.

  If you're not confident creating dialogue 'cold', then improvise conversations. Speak aloud, recording yourself, and play it back. It's likely to be much more natural than struggling to construct dialogue artificially on the page; you may find a few humdingers that you can then write around. Writing alone doesn't mean you can't devise or improvise!

- Set a writing schedule.

  One of the biggest challenges to working alone is finding motivation and endurance. Having clear goals is important, provided you tailor these to your situation. If you're young, free and loaded, you'll be in a great position to work fast; if you're a parent with a full-time job, you'll probably go more slowly (although sometimes being under time pressure is a great boost to efficiency). You need to make sure you have an appropriate framework for your writing.

- Try different things.

  Pick up one of those guides to playwriting we recommended, or read interviews with other playwrights, to collect new tricks. If you find writing alone a struggle or stultifying, it may be you haven't discovered your best process yet.

Regardless of whether writing alone is just your starting point or your entire process, you must never lose sight of the principles of what makes a good stage play. Writing alone should not mask any attention to the needs of a prospective production. Even if you plan to bash out a rough first draft and then convince a producer to fund some R&D, that's far more likely to be successful the more practical your thoughts have been from day one. Check over the points to consider in the next section on writing for the stage, and test your writing, scene by scene and line by line, against these.

Collaboration and Co-writing

Collaborative writing has been relatively rare in British theatre but is becoming more common. There are various forms it may take, but in general anything that means someone else is working with you at every stage of the process, from conception to planning to writing, is a form of collaborative writing, and may affect how credit/fees for the script are designated. This ranges from working with a dramaturg through to sharing full writing duties with a formal co-writer. We wouldn't consider getting feedback from a producer or director to be the same as collaboration on the actual writing (we reflect on how to manage relationships with the people who critique your writing in the chapters on 'Redrafting and Editing' and 'Working with Collaborators').

The chief benefits of writing collaboratively are that it helps with motivation, enables you to play to your different strengths, and widens the network of potential collaborators/funders/producers you can reach. The chief downsides are that you'll likely have to split the same sum of commissioning money as if you were working alone, may well encounter creative differences that prove insuperable rather than constructive, or may grow frustrated if your partner(s) makes slower progress than expected.

That's very much the key to a collaborative writing process – managing expectations. You should make sure you can answer these questions before committing to such a process:

- Have we outlined a clear plan for roles and responsibilities that we are all happy with?

- Have we been rigorous in settling on the identity of proposed collaborators, finding people whose skills are needed and not just people we regard as friends? How effective has the recruitment process been?

- Have deadlines and goals been mutually agreed and are they practical for everyone?

- Is everyone happy with agreed credits, rights and remuneration?

- Perhaps most importantly, has everyone discussed the creative vision and is there a sympathetic understanding that will make the writing constructive?

These should be written down and signed off before the process starts. It may seem unduly formal, even suspiciously legalistic, but a proper agreement with clear principles will lay the foundations for a successful collaboration. Without this there is the real possibility of disputes arising that cannot be adequately resolved and which can sink the whole project. So don't be intimidated by the notion of a 'contract'; drawing one up does not need to be confrontational or antagonistic, and can be as simple as laying out who the parties and signatories are, supplemented with a few bullet points answering the above questions. (We give further advice on this in the chapter on 'Making Deals'.)

The nature of these answers will depend on who the co-writers are. Some potential relationships include:

Writer and dramaturg

A dramaturg seems to bring a little thrill with them, as a relatively new phenomenon in British theatre. Having had dramaturgical input gives a script a rakish air. But it's a role that is actually quite tricky to pin down, and the term is not used consistently.

Often when people speak of a dramaturg, they really just mean someone who reads a script and provides feedback, but properly understood it's far more than that. A dramaturg should be proactive, not reactive; they should shape the play from an early stage and have significant input into the creative process, without actually doing much if any of the writing.

Usually a dramaturg will research the subject, develop the thematic and structural shape of the play, and help devise characters and narrative arcs that convey these. It remains the playwright's role to do the actual writing, such as penning dialogue, but within a framework mutually worked out with the dramaturg. Should the script enter R&D or rehearsals, the dramaturg usually remains involved, acting as a mediator between the playwright and the production team, helping refine choices and proposing changes that reflect their superlative insight into the script and the overall creative vision.

A dramaturg, used properly, can be invaluable. They should have a real stake in and knowledge of the project, but be sufficiently detached from the writing to detect flaws and offer continuous constructive criticism, helping guide it from start to finish. The playwright normally retains the sole authorial credit and rights; a dramaturg usually receives a fee and/or royalties in recognition of their contribution, but not any hold over the script itself.

Dramaturgs are more common outside the UK. If you find the right dramaturg, however, and are happy to work with that person for the long haul, it could make a big difference to the success of your writing. (See the chapter on 'Working with Collaborators' for more discussion of this.)

Co-writers

It's a quirk of British theatre that the most collaborative of our literary arts is one of the least likely to stem from collaborative writing. How many co-authored plays can you name?

The relative dearth of such work in comparison with screenplays or novels (or books like this) is probably a reflection of the limited money within theatre; canny playwrights are reluctant to split meagre commissioning fees. The same writers will often co-write television series or films, so it's not like collaborative writing is anathema to them. Of course, the structural separation of an episodic TV show makes incorporating different voices a little easier, but ultimately the writing still needs to be as coherent and consistent as a one-act play.

There are various reasons to co-write: a longstanding creative partnership that is now being expressed in theatre; lacking the time or a specific skill to complete a script alone; simply to avoid the loneliness and doubt of writing in a vacuum.

Whatever the reason, and however rock-solid you believe the mutual respect underpinning the endeavour may be, you still need to have that agreement drawn up before you start – especially making clear the division of responsibilities and how credit and rights will be shared. You should discuss an exit strategy: if things don't work out, or one of you becomes involved in another project, how will you extricate yourself? Can the script survive?

The nature of your partnership will be up to you. Some co-writers physically work together, discussing dialogue and talking over lines, perhaps with responsibility for particular characters divided up; others map out a structure and then allocate the writing of particular sections, so that someone with a knack for romance pens the climactic love scene while someone with a wicked sense of humour drafts the witty opening. The advantage of the former is that the authorial voice will be more seamless; the advantages of the latter are probably a swifter process and the chance to play to your separate strengths, at the risk of a fragmented tone.

Make sure you have good reasons for co-writing and understand how the process will work. It will be a challenge and you will sacrifice a good chunk of any commission and royalties.

Writer and subject, including verbatim theatre

Some writers involve themselves so heavily in research that elements of the script may be understood, in a way, as co-written with its subjects. Sometimes that's literally so – verbatim theatre, like Alecky Blythe and Adam Cork's musical *London Road* (also an interesting example of co-writing between a playwright and a composer), draws on the actual words of interviewees.

Even without being strictly verbatim, any script rooted in real events or a real area will, consciously or subconsciously, incorporate phrases and happenings uncovered in the research process. It's a fascinating and vexed question whether any dialogue can be understood to be original, even in ostensibly fictitious stories; much of it probably draws on snippets of interviews, overheard chats on the bus, or half-remembered conversations. The spattering of intertextuality is integral to all writing.

There's no need to be anxious about using the words of others; unless a research subject or interviewee is involved in the actual writing, they won't be due a credit or share of the commission or royalties, however much you draw inspiration from their accounts. It is nonetheless important, ethically if for no other reason, that subjects are made aware that their lives, experiences or words may be used. A writer must establish that a contributor or interviewee consents to this, with the option of fictional identities if they wish. If you are working from second-hand material, something that's been recorded in a news item or report, then that's not so pressing – it's already in the public domain – but it would still be ideal to reach the source for approval of the new use in a play. Also, make sure you are free to borrow it without trespassing on copyright (approach the original publisher and/or the Writers' Guild of Great Britain, and seek legal advice if in any doubt).

If a subject has made significant contributions to a script, it's up to you how that is acknowledged. Courtesy would suggest that an invitation to the press night and acknowledgement in any published script are in order; if they have been the sole or major contributor, and their words and time have truly shaped the script, then more may be due. This is unusual, however; verbatim theatre is mainly considered a form of collaborative writing only in the loosest sense.

Even if a subject is not so significant that they could claim to be a co-writer, it may be worth formalising their involvement in a written agreement (clarifying control of, or entitlement to, finances, rights, or differences of creative opinion). Always exercise sensitivity in how you obtain permission to use, and how you deploy, the words of the subject.

Case Study: *The Fear of Breathing*

Chris produced a verbatim play called *The Fear of Breathing*, edited by Zoe Lafferty, Ruth Sherlock and Paul Wood. It premiered at the Finborough Theatre in 2012 and was translated and restaged at Tokyo's Akasaka Red Theatre in 2013.

The Fear of Breathing was drawn from interviews and film footage collected by Zoe, a theatre director, and Ruth and Paul, award-winning journalists, operating in secret in Syria at the start of the revolution. The subject is, palpably, highly sensitive – several of the contributors have since suffered torture or been murdered – and there was a heavy responsibility incumbent upon reshaping the material into the form of a play.

It was because the subject felt so important, and the need to relate the actual experiences of those living through it so urgent, that a verbatim approach drawing on true testimony was deemed appropriate – and yet the paradox was that in making this into a play, the objective 'truth' of the testimony was inevitably affected. There needed to be a narrative, and emotional development of character, yet crafting that from hundreds of interviews and archive material demanded cutting chunks from an interviewee's statement, or juxtaposing different interviewees as if they had cohabited the space or shared an experience.

Imposing a sense of narrative meaning on to separate and individual lives carried three principal risks. Firstly, changing the nature of the experience related by the subject could compromise the inherent purpose of the verbatim project. Secondly, prioritising their words according to theatrical concerns might be to dismiss the dignity of their lived experience. Thirdly, might the project distort their perception to fit with a different or counter-truth belonging to the theatre-makers? It is the irony of verbatim theatre that in pursuing the actual experiences and perceptions of its subjects, it must fabricate, or less cynically construct, drama that in some ways distorts or alters these perceptions. Zoe, Ruth and Paul undertook multiple drafts in order to decipher how best to balance the dramatic narrative with the subjects' own voices and experiences. Fortunately, at least some of the interviewees were available for consultation, to help ensure the integrity of the process.

These concerns are probably inevitable. All that a responsible maker of verbatim theatre can do is acknowledge them, to the subjects as well as to the audience, and strive to be as respectful as possible. It is here that the distinction between the subject and the playwright lies. The subject provides the material, but the writer remakes that as a narrative. It would be misleading to present the subject as a writer, as that lends a false sense of authenticity to what is ultimately a theatrical construct. Zoe, Ruth and Paul chose the title of 'Editors' rather than 'Writers' to express this relationship between themselves and the subject.

Devising

There is a thriving branch of British playwriting that creates new plays from a devising process. Devising may take a range of forms, from a writer bringing a clear structure and characters into a room and asking actors to improvise scenes based on these, through to an ensemble spending weeks growing ideas from scratch with one or two people responsible for recording these and turning them into a script.

Don't be misled by the abstract concept of 'devising'; it's actually a well-established part of playwriting. For decades playwrights have taken drafts of scripts into a workshop process and tested them, or rewritten based on actors' suggestions or improvisations during rehearsals (see the chapters on 'R&D' and 'Going into Production'). Formally designating an entire process as devising simply relocates this common late-stage practice to an earlier and in some ways more constructive form of input. Don't let the term intimidate – there's no magical dividing line between devised practice, playwriting workshops, and testing scripts in scratch nights and readings. They're all on the same spectrum. It just depends to what extent, if at all, you wish to base your writing on these.

If you choose to work within a devising process you will usually do so in one of two ways. You will either be part of an ensemble company which collaborates to create stories through improvisation and discussion, that you as the nominated writer then formalise as a script, or you write alone but bring in actors and directors to trial ideas. It's quite rare for a writer to have the resources to do this; usually, as mentioned already, it comes later in the process after a first draft has been successfully pitched.

Ensembles

Let's talk about devising within an ensemble. Companies like Scotland's Vanishing Point and Bristol's Wardrobe Ensemble have produced fantastic plays. The exact process will vary with every company and every artist, but generally they spend a few weeks together to explore a pre-agreed starting idea. Through exercises like storyboarding, hot-seating characters and improvisations, they refine this idea and take it from concept to story to structured plot.

In a successful ensemble, everyone should know their role (without this being oppressive or restrictive); usually someone will take on the mantle of director, others the roles of actors, some may have a dramaturgical capacity, and others will contribute suggestions for design and staging. Not all ensembles will nominate a writer, but often the most successful recognise the importance of letting one person exercise some order over, and lend technical shape to, the free-flowing ideas. This may take place within the room or occur afterwards.

This is an incredibly exciting and stimulating practice but it presents several challenges for a playwright. Firstly, writing commissions usually go to playwrights not companies, and it's increasingly hard to raise the money to fund one person on a new play, let alone an entire ensemble. There has been a shift in recent years towards funding more collaborative models of new writing/theatre-making, but the competition remains intense and the pots of money small. Secondly, your identity as a playwright will almost certainly be subsumed by the brand of the ensemble. You will be one of a company, affecting how you build a writing career.

Insider's View: Tom Brennan

I make devised (or 'collaboratively written') shows with The Wardrobe Ensemble. It's always strange to me when The Wardrobe Ensemble's shows aren't classed as new writing. Almost all our shows are original stories with scripts full of words we care about. Devising has no thematic, stylistic or tonal restraints. It is a merely a mode of creation. It could be comedic, tragic, documentarian, or include text, movement, music. Making theatre in this way can be incredibly difficult. My old course director at Rose Bruford once described a Martin Crimp play we were working on as '4D Chess'. Devised productions feel like '4D Chess', but Chess where you're building the board as you play. It's not one person quietly writing. Instead it's a sweaty group desperately trying to make a play. The Wardrobe Ensemble and I have learned several lessons:

1. Build a production schedule that suits you

Work-in-progress performances have been vital. They give us a chance to understand how challenging elements of our story or formal language work in front of an audience. Similarly, we like to build in lots of time between phases of development so we have a chance to reflect on our decisions.

2. Everyone is a writer. It's everyone's play

A fundamental principle for us is that the stuff brought to the group is communally owned. Some members of the group write more scenes in a traditional way. But it would be a disservice to those who write less to suggest that they are not co-writers. Their improvisations, performances, feedback, movement, choreography and off-the-cuff edits are just as fundamental to the work.

3. You are the best artist in the room

It's important to have faith in your ability. Of course, you should work with the best people you know. But equally you should believe in your ability to make consistent and valid offers to the group. 'I can write that' is far more useful in creating a productive work space than 'I'm shit at writing dialogue.' Any self-effacing behaviours deaden productivity.

4. You are not the best artist in the room

When watching or reading the work of your colleagues, respect their skills. Take stock of the things they do better than you. This balance between greediness and generosity, between your desire to impress and an absolute respect for your peers' skills, is vital. In best cases, your ideas, your particular creative ambitions and your ego all melt away. Instead, it is the show that becomes paramount. You find yourself asking – What does the show need? What is the voice of the company as opposed to your voice as a playwright? Sometimes you will be aware of a problem with the play or with a scene you have written but will not have the skills to fix it. It's a liberating experience to realise that you are not the best person to fix that problem. The weight of the show is not on your shoulders alone.

5. Listen

Although devising does not force style, subject matter or form, the work you make is often informed by the particular dynamic of the group. In our case, devising has been a conducive technique for making performances with particular comedic qualities. I find making funny stuff is easier. When writing plays alone, I'm hypothesising about an audience's reaction. But in the devising room a joke either works or doesn't. Even if you want to make a deadly serious play, listening to the group will open up a new set of qualities and ideas that you would not have discovered alone.

6. Get real

What's difficult in a devising room is understanding the difference between what exists in the play and what your company have just talked about. I find that there's a tendency to create work that is theatrically exciting but shallow in ideas and story. The lesson is, if you are interested in creating a full and engaging piece of work, be rigorous in sorting out the story. In other words, treat your script like any self-respecting playwright would.

7. Fail together

If the show is bad, remember it's your fault as much as anyone else's. In moments of creative failure it's easy to blame those around you. Working in a devising company can feel more intense, insular and emotional than traditional theatre rehearsals, so it's important to remember: it's just a play.

Tom co-founded The Wardrobe Ensemble, for whom he has written and co-directed several plays which have toured internationally. As a director he has worked at the National Theatre, Almeida Theatre and Soho Theatre, among many venues in the UK and US.

Early-stage workshops and improvisations

A route less likely to compromise your identity as a playwright, but that still confers the considerable benefits of devising with skilled collaborators, is to base your writing practice on early-stage workshops and improvisations. Usually these involve the playwright bringing character notes, outlines for plotting and narrative arcs, and research material, which are then used with actors and possibly a director or dramaturg to stimulate discussions, improvisations and ideas. It's worth recording these for later reflection. As the playwright is very much the driving force for the entire process, you should retain all credit and control over the material.

This process requires the resources to hire a space and pay actors, and bring materials to make the most of your time. You need to raise money or in-kind support beyond your commission, or risk ending up out of pocket. It may be tricky to convince producers or funders, but it is possible. Chris has received Arts Council funding for several commissions on this model; you just need to demonstrate how the process will work and why it's appropriate (see the chapter on 'Moving On' for tips on raising this funding).

Many playwrights would envy an opportunity like this. If you are fortunate enough to make it a reality, don't squander it. Make sure you understand what will happen in the room. Arriving without plans to explore is a sure-fire way for this precious opportunity to degenerate into a rambling chat. Break the day(s) into sessions with clear focal points and aims, understand what you need the actors to do in order to advance your ideas, and be prepared to hear irrelevant or desperate improvisations in the search for a golden moment. (We discuss detailed techniques in the chapter on 'R&D'.)

Adaptation and Translation

A form of playwriting that often does not carry the cachet it deserves is adaptation, including translation of plays originally written in other languages. Adaptation and translation are arts in themselves; to reconfigure a text to work in a different medium, culture and/or language requires exceptional creativity and technique. That's why writers like Helen Edmundson are so sought after; she is among the few playwrights who can be relied upon to render something that was written for another form or language for our own theatre, still alive, fresh and new.

You may adore adaptation; even if not, cracking it can generate income and commissions that support your own original writing. Producers are often more willing to fund adaptations of popular books or films, classic plays or scripts already proven in other languages than they are untested new writing. Equally, audiences and critics are perhaps more amenable to trying such work. It can be a useful and strategic way to build a following for your writing through a sustainable financial model.

Ultimately, however, you should only venture into adaptation if it genuinely excites you. Uncovering work that may not otherwise reach English-speaking audiences, bringing modern relevance to a classic or adapting an existing work for the stage should be a creative thrill. If it isn't, then this form isn't for you.

There are manifold practical as well as artistic challenges to adaptation. Firstly, you need to find an original work, or a producer who will ask you to adapt a work of their choice. Finding a producer who will commission an adaptation is far trickier than uncovering a text in need of adaptation! The best way is to woo producers with your own writing. Only once they have a flavour of this can they responsibly entrust another's work to you. So, if adaptation is a route you would like to explore, make yourself known to producers who specialise in this kind of work (see the chapter 'Getting Noticed').

If you want to find a text to adapt or translate, try keeping an eye out for reviews of new plays abroad, if you are fluent in that particular tongue. If you aren't bilingual, then research old classics or neglected plays. A good rule of thumb is to search out lesser plays by successful playwrights, or explore the catalogue of playwrights now out of fashion, and identify which have the potential for a modern updating. Of course, famous plays like *The Seagull* are ripe for adaptations, but these tend to be done relatively frequently by big-name writers. Finding a less familiar text may bolster the appeal and the sense of rediscovery.

Or ask yourself, what novels, films or poems do you love that have never had a life on stage? What deserves to reach a different audience and has the potential to work in a three-dimensional, live medium like the stage?

Bear in mind that for any work by an author who is still alive, or who died within the last seventy years (sometimes longer), you will need to contact their agent or estate to obtain the rights. Negotiating rights can be convoluted and full of jargon, especially if related to a different medium like novels or films over which more than a single person often holds different rights. It may be worth having a producer attached beforehand to provide financial support and validity. Few agents will sign rights over without the prospect of production. (See chapter on 'Making Deals' for more guidance.)

Whether you find the material or the producer first, the process of adaptation will be challenging. You need to identify what makes the original text suitable for a contemporary stage production, and what must be jettisoned. Don't slavishly or literally translate; be an active artist. Of course, the main body of the characters and plot are unlikely to change much (though they may well be different in some ways), but the details of their depiction and the world they inhabit are surely going to be overhauled.

If you are working on a novel, then some subplots will probably need to be compressed or cut (the RSC's famed eight-hour *Nicholas Nickleby* may be an exception, but its devotion to Dickens's many-splendoured narrative prompted Michael Billington to complain that it was 'like being force-fed on peacock'). If you are staging a poem, then how can a (usually but not exclusively) monologic or lyric form be given a physical and dialogic expression? Even if you are adapting an existing play, some choices will be needed to adjust to the modern world. These decisons are potentially without end; each adjustment will affect many other elements.

Technically, adaptation is perhaps even harder than writing a brand-new play, because you are more circumscribed, and audiences will bring pre-existing expectations and affections. Be sure that you are adapting a text because you love it, not simply because you need the activity or hope to land a production. Without a real sympathy for and an innate understanding of the existing work, adaptation or translation can become a bind; with these, they can be a joy and the bedrock of a writing career.

Writing for the Stage

No matter what process of playwriting you undertake, it is impor-tant that you understand the fundamentals of stagecraft. Otherwise, whether writing alone, devising or adapting, you will not have much chance of seeing your script become a play.

Decide carefully what medium is best to tell your stories; each has its own benefits and limitations. Radio relies on igniting the imag-ination through sound alone, while television and film present a series of images that collectively tell a story. Theatre is different, again, in that the audience experience it live; it unfolds in front of us and relies on our participation for its magic. It connects with us in a way that is entirely unique. Successful playwrights recog-nise and exploit this, factoring in the opportunities as well as the restrictions of sharing a space and time with an audience.

Consider the following topics:

Cast size

Recent years have seen a spate of one-person shows. This rise has been in inverse proportion to cuts in arts funding, as they are cheap to produce and represent a low risk for producers. Don't rush to conclude, however, that penning a one-person show is the easy way to production; the market can feel saturated with such work, and audience fatigue is a genuine concern. Because of this, the competition to get one-person shows into good venues is often fiercer than to get a large ensemble piece accepted.

Decision-makers read for quality first and foremost, before any practical considerations. A play with a cast of six that feels complete will have a better chance of production than a one-hander full of holes. Of course, an equally accomplished one-hander may be more likely to be staged, but a season will not bear more than a couple of such shows, so your script may miss that slot in any case.

The point is that cast size is an important consideration in writing for stage but it's not the be-all and end-all. Don't try to second-guess decision-makers or bend your story to fit preconceived assumptions; they're constructing a varied programme and you have no way of knowing what their other options are. Write the cast size demanded by your story.

Moreover, at a time when many emerging writers are serving up a diet of one-act plays for only one or two roles, it can be immensely cheering to encounter a playwright who can meet the challenges of a large ensemble. The largest and most financially challenging play Chris has produced was *Donkey Heart* by Moses Raine, which premiered at London's Old Red Lion Theatre before transferring to the West End. It had a cast of ten, including two child actors who required a chaperone. Chris still took it on because of the quality of the script – if it's good enough, trust that someone will take the risk.

It is nonetheless important to consider the practicalities of production when deciding on the number of characters and the size of the cast (which are not necessarily the same thing, thanks to the possibilities of doubling). Make sure every character earns the right to be there. If your script feels indulgent, producers will be wary. They need to see the scale justify itself.

Let's say you have written a character in their fifties who comes into a scene, utters three lines, then disappears. If it's impossible for this character to be doubled with another role, it means a producer has to hire an actor especially. Financially it's galling: at the time of going to print, Equity/ITC (Independent Theatre Council) minimum wage is £471 per week before pension contributions, NI contributions, sick pay, holiday pay or VAT are considered, so over a four-week rehearsal and a four-week run those three lines cost an absolute minimum of £3,768. Artistically it's also problematic: few good, experienced actors of that mature age are going to want to sign up for a meagre role, and a director may have to compromise on quality. It's also less satisfying to see characters with limited function; audiences want to engage with the personalities they encounter. That's part of the charm of theatre, especially for new plays which tend to be in smaller studios in which the audience are close enough to feel the physical presence of the actor. So, pragmatically and aesthetically, are those lines justified? Is there an alternative?

Don't be bound to preconceptions of cast size, but shape your story with an eye on extracting every ounce of value.

Length

With the caveat that your play should be as long as it takes to tell the story, you should keep an eye on length. It's hard to estimate the equation between number of words on the page and time on stage. It will depend on how many stage directions or complex physical 'business' there are, or whether moments of silence are frequent and prolonged. The only way to be sure is to get it up on its feet with a stopwatch. As a rough yardstick, however, assume a playing time of ninety minutes per 15,000 words, or around seventy-five seconds per page.

Sometimes you have to write to prescribed timings. Short plays for a scratch night might have a limit of fifteen minutes, while Edinburgh Fringe slots tailor to forty-five to sixty-minute pieces. Perhaps because many writers learn within such parameters, it is increasingly common even outside of constrained slots for new plays to be relatively short, one-act pieces. These are undoubtedly popular; everyone loves the chance to drink and dissect afterwards rather than rush for trains.

As with small cast sizes, however, there is concern in the industry that emerging playwrights are losing the technique to tell big stories. There is something to be said for being ambitious. Two-act plays are rarer; that may make yours stand out.

If your script is coming in at a Shakespearian four hours it might be time to make cuts, but otherwise don't chop from a misguided notion that brevity will find favour. Of course, neither should you inflate your script to make it impress by virtue of length alone. Sometimes writers pad plays out to justify an interval, in the belief that venues are desperate to sell drinks and peanuts. Intervals are indeed a boon to venues, but most decision-makers are not the people overseeing the merchandise or bar, so don't allow this kind of thinking to affect your script.

The audience

Having a live audience interact with your work affects its length and structure. People who have just been caught in the rain en route to the theatre, or who dashed in panting after dreadful traffic, might not give the first five minutes their full attention. You need to capture them quickly. Which openings to plays do you remember most vividly? Why?

Similarly, an interval may be necessary out of respect for bladder capacity (after ninety minutes, most people will be grateful for the chance to pass water as well as judgement on Act One). You will then need to earn the audience's attention at the resumption; don't rush to deliver a revelation while the ice-cream cartons are still being scraped clean.

Learn the rhythm of a show. Consider what affects your comfort and concentration when you are in an audience – and let this inform your writing's pacing and structure. Remember, the audience is who we make theatre for. You mustn't lose them along the way.

Writing for the medium

EXT. OUTSIDE OF SHOP. NIGHT.

CU of a man smoking a cigarette. A car drives by.

If your play opens with the above then you are writing for the wrong medium. The notions of 'exteriors' or 'interiors', of a 'close up' (CU), all belong on screen, not on the stage.

It sounds obvious, but a good crop of the scripts we receive are written in this way. It is inescapable when a writer has shoddily passed off a film script as a play – and it almost inevitably signals poor quality and/or disinterest in theatre. What works brilliantly for one medium may be impossible, or deathly, for the other.

Theatre doesn't have the benefit of a close-up to see a specific facial expression; your story should be as clear at the back of the gods as in the front row of the stalls. Ensure stage directions and scene locations are appropriate to being in a theatre. Avoid frequent short scenes in multiple locations. TV can cut straight from a police station to a hospital bed to the inside of a car, with only two lines of dialogue in between, but in theatre this tasks both stage crew and the audience's imagination beyond endurance – someone's likely to have an aneurysm. Let your scenes have time to breathe, and revel in the intimacy and subtlety offered by sharing a close space with actors and design. Embrace being in a theatre.

Of course, innovations in technology allow us to soar beyond the stage's physical limitations. Camera feeds can be used in performance. But this should still be theatrical, not a substitute for a frustrated film-maker.

Lest this sound like theatre is the poor cousin of johnny-come-lately media, remember that theatre can be free of the literalness that dogs so much screenwriting. Scenes in plays can run concurrently or leap back and forwards in time. An audience, so close to the action, can be swept up in a theatrical vision. So seize that opportunity.

Stage directions

Keep stage directions simple. Only specify things that are really vital. Trust your director to bring their vision to the piece. Even if you are planning to direct the play yourself, make this part of the process in the room rather than imposing it in rigid written rules. A good cast can often enrich ideas during the rehearsal period.

Remember that plays are ultimately meant to be performed, not read, so express the narrative within your dialogue rather than through stage directions. We should learn who a character is by what they do (or don't) say, not in a lengthy description that will never be available to an audience. Indeed, sometimes writers convince themselves their script achieves clarity or poignancy, only to realise this all resides in superfluous prose. Overlong stage directions can distract from effective dialogue.

If you have information that an actor, director or designer needs, make it as concise as possible; the likelihood is that they'll be freed up to provide fresh interpretations. Oscar Wilde famously introduced one of his characters in *An Ideal Husband* with 'she is really like a Tanagra statuette, and would be rather annoyed if she were told so'. Memorable and entertaining, but an actor and costume designer probably draw more inspiration from her dialogue and actions.

Similarly, when describing the set, lighting or soundscape, only go into detail if something is integral to the story. It is a designer's job to interpret the world of the play, and the best designers do so in a way that most of us probably couldn't dream of.

In essence, stage directions need to be functional and appropriate. Resist the urge to pen a novel (or write a novel instead). Trust your collaborators and empower them to do their jobs.

Props and costume

While it's good to be ambitious, it's also important to be realistic. A character finishing one scene and then having to start the next in a completely different costume means getting that actor changed incredibly quickly. Not impossible, of course, but is there a way to avoid it? Write with an eye on how things will be realised in performance; it will save headaches in rehearsal and disappointment on stage.

Equally, having a car speed on stage, crash and burst into flames might be incredibly original but is it achievable? George starred as Batman in the World Arena Tour of *Batman Live* (making Chris Robin, minus the tights), and sometimes the show had to be halted to deal with technical issues, despite its formidable budget and even more formidable crew.

Respect the medium, draw on your experiences and desires as an audience member, and write with forethought for the directors, designers and actors who will make your vision a reality.

Process and Progress

Whatever route into playwriting you have taken, and no matter how strong your knowledge of stagecraft, you will need to develop a resilience and a method to drive your playwriting forward. Don't just plan your story, plan your process.

Here are some suggestions to help you formulate a path to success.

Plan your process and set goals

Sometimes the mere prospect of writing a play can prove so daunting it kills the project off before it begins. The first step in developing your process is to set manageable goals. We suggest that you nominate:

- A deadline for completion of a first draft.
- A friend to check up on your progress.
- A daily writing target (in words or scenes, not time).
- A routine/schedule of when and where you will write (decide what hour of the day – or night – is most productive, or most free of distractions, for you).

These help to break the project down into smaller, more achievable targets, while keeping an eye on the inspirational finish line. Aiming to finish one scene per week, or to write three hundred words a day, doesn't sound like much, yet would mean you complete a full-length play within three or four months. It also means you are inspired to stick to the task. This is especially so if you make others aware of your goals. Professional playwrights will be set deadlines, by agents or collaborators or publishers. If someone expects you to deliver, the process is less likely to disintegrate.

These goals will be the bedrock of your playwriting process – and it will be yours. They should all be particular to your situation. Don't imitate other people's schedules, but design a process that suits you. Setting unattainable targets will be no help – but make them challenging. And why not give yourself a reward for each goal met?

Get something on paper

Transitioning from planning to practice can be tricky. Process and goals should empower playwriting, not swallow it. Avoid the schoolchild error of spending more time concocting an intricate revision schedule than actually revising. So, however much care you put into a tailored schedule, it's important to get started quickly.

A useful exercise at the outset of a project is 'automatic writing'. It helps release your creative energy, and gives expression to your ideas, however rough and ready. It can stimulate the process and ensure you always work to your goals. Follow these steps:

1. Think of a strong emotion in your life (a fear or an aspiration work well).

2. Set a timer for five minutes and force yourself to write anything and everything that comes into your mind on this topic, in prose, as a constant stream-of-consciousness, until the timer buzzes.

3. Read what you've scribbled down and underline any striking phrases or ideas. What recurring motifs underpin your writing? Devise five words that encapsulate the theme(s) of this writing.

4. Pick one of these words as a central theme. Set the timer for another five minutes, and write about all the emotions you associate with this theme. Be as florid as you like.

5. This theme and its emotional reservoir are going to be the fuel for a short scene between two characters. Character A is emotionally affected by the theme. Character B, conversely, has a professional relationship to the theme. So if your theme was 'theft', A may be the victim of a burglary and B may an investigating detective. This creates an emotional gap, a form of tension, between them. Now write a dialogue in which A tries to make B understand their feelings, while B tries to complete their job. Give yourself twenty minutes to conjure up that pressure.

There – you've written a scene in less than an hour. Chances are that it relates in some way to the play that's at the heart of your process; basing your writing on a fear or aspiration taps into such concerns. Automatic writing won't produce a masterpiece, but it can get you into the swing.

We also often advocate the importance of exploratory writing. That is, writing about the wider dramatic universe rather than just the small part of it contained within the play. It's the difference between story – which is everything that's happening to every character – and plot – which is what the audience see. It can lend inspiration to your playwriting and make planning a practical writerly experience, not a refuge from really getting stuck in.

Try writing a part of the story that would never make it into the plot. What happened to a character ten minutes after the end of a scene? Can you write down one key detail about every year of a character's life? How would it be to try to write a letter in the voice of one character to another, and answer it in the other character's voice? These explorations will liberate you from the pressure of writing for an audience or worrying about quality, will sharpen your grasp of the dramatic world, and make your planning and process much more hands-on.

Once you've kindled your creative drive, follow your process and goals and get stuck into the script. Write character lists, plot out your structure on note cards, invent ways for problematic characters to be dispatched, whatever it takes to get material down on paper and the brain churning, to move from planning to playwriting.

Rule over your process, don't be ruled by it

For all designing a process for your playwriting and sticking to goals are important, you must not become enslaved to a plan. If you are struggling, then you might need to adjust your process. After all, playwriting is creative, and you should allow yourself scope to find fresh inspiration or try new things. Retain a degree of flexibility – this is where some of the exercises mooted above might help.

In a study conducted by Mike Rose, detailed in 'Rigid Rules, Inflexible Plans, and the Stifling of Language: A Cognitivist Analysis of Writer's Block', ten undergraduates were interviewed on the subject of writing process. They were a cross-section of the student community in class, grades, gender and attitude towards education. The only thing connecting them was that they could all write competently and regularly penned significant amounts for their course. Five of the group wrote with relative ease, while the other five suffered from writer's block to varying degrees. The one noticeable difference that Rose detected between the two groups was in their approach:

> The five students who experienced blocking were all operating either with writing rules or with planning strategies that impeded rather than enhanced the composing process. The five students who were not hampered by writer's block also utilised rules, but they were less rigid ones, and thus more appropriate to a complex process like writing.

Examine your process accordingly. Is it conducive to good work for you? If it isn't meeting your needs, then ditch it and set new goals. Just be honest about this: is it the process itself or your approach to it that needs to be changed? You may find that altering your work environment or ethos unlocks the ability to meet those goals. If it doesn't, then we've some tips to really vanquish that block.

Beating Writer's Block

The autumn 1974 issue of the *Journal of Applied Behavior Analysis* includes a wonderfully satirical blank page: 'The Unsuccessful Self-Treatment of a Case of "Writer's Block"'. This encapsulates a feeling most of us have experienced.

However successful your process and however sound your plan, writing for as rigorous and technical a form as theatre is likely to beget some form of block at some point. The sheer number of elements to juggle, with an eye on practicalities as well as art, can lead to turmoil, contradiction and doubt.

Don't force yourself to write if you're heading off-track. If this is happening, stick to your goals but write about something else – whether that's starting a new play or penning a rant about the pain of writing! The key thing is that you are maintaining the discipline and habit of writing regularly, and not abandoning your process; forcing your mind to try new things can be an effective way of spotting fresh solutions to embedded problems.

Here are some tips to revive your process and keep your play alive:

Reset the plot or character

Written yourself into a hole? Characters behaving erratically, main plot overtaken by a distracting sub-narrative, or scenes confused or meandering? Don't force yourself to write through it, as that will only compound the problem. Instead, consider working backwards from the stumbling point, to see where any misdirection began. Make a list of all the plot points or character decisions that preceded this moment. Consider the ramifications of each. What led to this situation arising? It may be as simple as tweaking one line, so that a different course of action is set in motion, closer to your original vision.

A tip from novelist and screenwriter Neil Gaiman is to print the text out, sit down with a pen and highlighters, and scribble all over it as you read. Break it down, figure out what works and what doesn't. Interrogate every line and every choice, answer why you've made each one and how it feeds into the overall success of the script. You'll discover that some judicious editing and cuts can get you back on track, without having to sacrifice large chunks of your work – or give up.

Eliminate distractions

Noël Coward may have had to deal with the decadence and moral ambiguities of the Roaring Twenties, a tricky personal life, and a homophobic society, but at least he didn't have to cram his witty aphorisms into a tweet. Any task, let alone something as complex as writing, has become harder with the advent of social media. If, for every five minutes spent writing, you fritter away ten minutes online, be strict and disconnect the internet. You might revive an ailing process.

If you aren't falling prey to clickbait, and instead have the classic distraction of the neighbour cutting up bongo drums with a chainsaw, you must find a better environment in which to write. Most professional writers end up with a knowledge of all cafés and libraries within a ten-mile radius that would put a minicab driver to shame.

Think therefore you are

Never underestimate the power of the mind to break free of a deadlock. Malcolm Gladwell's bestseller *Blink* cites Dutch researchers who asked students forty-two questions from the board game Trivial Pursuit. Beforehand, half were asked to think for five minutes of everything it would take to become a professor (a role synonymous with half-moon glasses, books weighed by the tonne, and being 'smart'). The other half were asked to imagine behaving like football hooligans (a role synonymous with smashing chairs, crude chants, and racism). There was little measurable difference in IQ or academic pedigree between the groups, but having merely thought about the qualities of being perceived as 'smart', the first cohort answered 55.6 per cent of questions correctly while the second managed only 42.6 per cent.

It may sound a tad silly, but the next time you write, spend five minutes visualising yourself collecting the Olivier Award for Best New Play. It can only help conjure a more constructive mindset.

Rest or change

However important it is to stick to a schedule, and to have a clear sense of when you will write and where, this should not be punitive. Everyone needs a break. Often a block stems from a prolonged period of overwriting, of exhausting your imagination. That in itself can make a minor block seem more significant than it is; cropping up in mid-flow, the eddy currents are more disruptive than if you were churning out only a little every day.

You might just need some time away – and if a complete break sits uneasily with your creative impulse, switch to a different project to refresh your ideas. Philip Larkin broke his writing block by resorting to some rather dubious fiction about schoolgirls. We wouldn't suggest that, but the principle's sound.

Go for a walk

Beyond the physical benefits, research has shown that walking can enhance creative thinking. A 2014 study by Stanford University found that the creative output of their participants increased by an average of 60 per cent when walking compared with sitting. With such compelling statistics, beating your writer's block should be a walk in the park.

Bounce ideas around

We've hammered this point home several times but it bears repeating – playwriting depends on others for success, whether that's the contributions of a director or the reaction of an audience. If you're going in circles, share what you have with someone you trust (look at our notes on finding feedback or collaborators in the chapters on 'Training', 'Redrafting and Editing' and 'Working with Collaborators'). Even if their notes aren't spot-on, they may trigger new ideas to break the impasse. Hopefully consolation and support will be forthcoming too.

Insider's View: Tristan Bernays

My schedule and process is:

1. Routine

Ray Bradbury said 'Just write every day of your life'. This isn't always possible – everyday life and earning a living get in the way – but when you are starting on a play or project, aim to have a routine. Ideally, when I'm starting a new play, I aim to write Monday to Friday, 11 a.m. to 3 p.m. Beforehand, I try to do some exercise and work admin; afterwards I'll go off to my day job, teaching. After that, I usually have enough spare time in the evening for leisure.

I don't always achieve this, but it's a routine I aim to stick to and the consistency helps.

2. Working hours

It's very easy to feel guilty that you aren't doing enough work – that there are people out there writing more and doing it better.

I try to write for three hours a day, maybe four if I'm lucky. Anything I write beyond that usually isn't very good – and spending more than four hours alone in my head is frankly more than anyone deserves. But I know some writers who do nine to five, like an office job; others roll out of bed at 7 a.m. and immediately hit the computer in their pyjamas for two hours before heading out to work; some start work at midnight and go on till 4 a.m. I have tried all of these methods too, and in the end, there is no right way to work – just the right way for you. Try each way out, see what fits you and your life, and then try and stick with it. If you can only do an hour a day – brilliant! That's sixty more minutes writing than if you weren't doing any at all.

3. Environment

I literally put on a suit, leave my house and commute to a library to work. I leave my phone in a locker and use a laptop without internet connection. I find a formal environment helps me to focus – there are too many distractions at home and seeing other people working encourages me to work.

On the other hand, I know wonderful writers who write brilliant plays sat alone in their bed in their pyjamas with toast crumbs in their belly buttons. I know one writer who goes round and round on a bus route back and forth across London, computer on her lap, tapping away. Experiment and see what the best environment is for you.

4. Goals and deadlines

A little pressure can help. Organise an informal reading with a few trusted friends at home or in the back room of a pub. Not only will you get invaluable feedback, you actually have a deadline to aim for – something to give you drive and purpose.

When I wrote my first ever play, *Coffin*, in 2010, I booked a room above a pub for £75, invited fifty friends to watch and asked five others to read it – and this was before I had fully finished it. That bit of pressure was a real help – if I turned up on the day with nothing, I would have looked like a right fool and wasted my time and money.

5. Get off the computer and crack out the stationery

If you're blocked, try leaving your computer and plotting the story out on paper. Lay out the story like an explorer charting a route on a map. Stick it up on the wall, use coloured pencils and highlighters, bits of string, Blu Tack, Post-It notes, flashcards, scraps – whatever. Changing the physical way you write and look at your writing will give you a (literal) new perspective on your story and may help bust a block.

6. A play takes as long as it takes

My play *Teddy* took two weeks to write. My play *Old Fools* took two years. It takes as long as it takes to write a play – some pour out of you, others have to be dragged out kicking and screaming. Don't beat yourself up about it. Be patient and stick with it. If it is meant to be, it will be. If it isn't working – try something else and come back to it later. Time and distance, as well as a new perspective, always help.

Tristan is a playwright and winner of the OffWestEnd Award for Best New Musical. His work has been performed at Shakespeare's Globe, Soho Theatre, Southwark Playhouse, Bush Theatre, National Theatre Studio and the Roundhouse, and toured the UK.

When you've completed your process and overcome any blocks, you'll have a script. Then comes the task of checking it has been properly formatted – it's always best to do this as you go, and double-check at the end.

Formatting

This should be nice, straightforward stuff. Don't worry unduly about arcane points of presentation. All anyone on the receiving end of a script cares about is that it's easy to read and the margins are sufficient for ample note-making. Don't be afraid to adjust the guidelines suggested here if others will serve the play better.

Specialist playwriting software is available, like Final Draft, but it's fine to knock your script together in Microsoft Word or similar. A good free package, designed for screenwriting but applicable for most playscripts, is CeltX.

It's amazing how many writers make baffling choices that render their script incomprehensible. No reader wants to wade through reams of diagrams or endure Comic Sans; that may constitute a crime against humanity. We suggest the following are safe guidelines to guarantee your script is read, not read out in a deposition at The Hague.

Cover page

Keep it simple. The title, your name and contact details, and those of your agent if applicable, are ample. There's no need for a synopsis or your CV unless requested. The play won't be read any faster just because you've summarised it (indeed, any synopsis may give a reader an excuse to reject it based on plot alone, whereas opening the document and reading the dialogue is a fairer assessment of your writing). Equally, if your CV is strong enough to command special attention, then you shouldn't need to send it; the name alone will be sufficient. The only exception may be if you boast a stellar record in some field germane to the play but little known in the theatre industry.

Character list

This is useful as it gives a sense of the show's scale and complexity. Keep character descriptions brief; name, age, gender (if required) or ethnicity (if required) are sufficient. It's also more than fine not to specify these attributes; directors will welcome a free rein in casting. As previously noted, the dialogue should be enough to convey personalities or motivations, so don't rely on extra-textual information in a character list.

Notes on the text

These can be useful, but keep them strictly necessary. Usually they consist of information about the pronunciation of non-standard words, identify any particular symbols that denote a speech habit, or suggest when and where to include an interval.

Resist the temptation to proffer instructions on matters of staging or design unless there are specific requirements to guarantee a plot point or thematic symbol is effective. Trust in the director or designer in these regards; keep your focus on the script and don't worry about signposting how it should be staged.

Epigraphs

If you must – but make sure they are relevant to the play, witty and unpretentious. If in any doubt, excise. Not having referenced Suetonius cannot possibly count against you.

Page numbers

These are welcome. Put them in the bottom middle or bottom right corner.

Font and colour

The choice of font doesn't matter, as long as it's clear, doesn't obtrude, and isn't 'quirky'. We suggest Times New Roman or Arial. Remember, safe isn't boring. Safe is safe. Ditto for colour; stick to black.

Size

There's no need to fiddle with font sizes. Keep them consistent and at a legible but not enormous scale; 12 or 14 are perfectly sufficient. If you feel it imperative to signal a character is SHOUTING then use uppercase or italic – or better yet, note it as a stage direction.

Act or scene titles

These usually go at the top of a new page, bold and underlined.

Denoting the speaking character

It's vital to designate which character speaks which line. Put the name, in bold and uppercase, either in the left margin level with the dialogue or centred above the dialogue.

Dialogue

This should be in normal font. No bold, no italics, no uppercase, unless you need to emphasise some specific moment. Make sure it is either to the right of or underneath the relevant character name.

Stage directions

These are usually in italics to distinguish them from dialogue. If they are separate actions, they will have their own line, with the relevant character name in bold and uppercase for ease of discernment. If they denote an action during a speech, then enclose within brackets inside the line of dialogue.

Spacing

This is an important consideration. Don't cram the lines together! This can be illegible, and reduce space for notes. Usually it's best to leave a single line space between lines of continuous speech by one character, and leave double line spacing after a speech by one character and before the start of the next speech or stage direction.

Submission

A PDF is preferable if submitting online, as this retains all your formatting choices. Different versions of word-processing programmes can sometimes scramble the layout and render all your efforts to follow these guidelines wasted.

If you're submitting a hard copy, then check it's printed properly before sealing that envelope.

These guidelines are suggestions, not prescriptive. You should represent your play on the page as seems best to you. It's always handy to open up modern playtexts and examine their formatting – you'll see that there are degrees of variance. Some writers really exploit the possibilities of the page to represent their play. Small details can make a big difference!

And that's about it on how to build a playwriting process that enables you to craft and deliver a story that is fit for stage. There's no single pathway, but answering the questions or bearing in mind the points covered in this chapter will help your script become a play.

REDRAFTING AND EDITING

You've got your first draft! Congratulations. Now the real work can begin.

Perhaps the most important part of writing a play is redrafting it. Opinion is divided as to whether this is the most excruciating and joyless ordeal or the easiest and most satisfying reflection. It probably depends whether you find bashing out the first draft so easy that making corrections seems tedious, or such a strain that the chance merely to tweak is a welcome relief. Either way, it's virtually certain that your first draft will be just that – an initial step, with more to be done.

Redrafting is crucial because your script is going to be scrutinised again and again. First by producers and programmers, then by directors and actors, and finally by audiences and reviewers. It's vital to iron out as many of the creases and fill in as many of the holes as possible before you approach people asking them to invest time and money.

Frankly, as producers receiving around two thousand submissions a year, we're looking for reasons not to take a script forward. It isn't enough to be well-written; it needs to be airtight. Of course, we usually find it necessary to undertake several more drafts, because stories can always be improved and structures honed, but the more compelling the first version we read, and the more we believe the writer has made every decision with reason and care, the more we will trust them and the easier it is to envisage and programme a production.

This chapter therefore sounds a warning bell: never be satisfied with a first draft. It discusses questions to ask of your script and practical tests to apply to it, ways to seek out and handle feedback, and how to undertake revisions. All of these should give your script the best possible chance of meeting with success. Neglect these at your peril, because your script will be competing with thousands of others that have been rigorously road-tested.

The mantra often parroted to emerging playwrights is: 'Don't get it right, get it written.' That may be so. But it's important to add: 'And then get it right.' This will show you how.

What Is It?

'Redrafting' means making changes to a script in order to redress pre-identified weaknesses and tackle areas for improvement. How extensive the redrafting is depends on the needs of the script. Some redrafts may change the ending, chop three characters, add a talking dog, and relocate the play from New York to the Outback; others will involve only superficial changes to a handful of lines.

This is why we've paired 'redrafting' with the less drastic 'editing', because significant changes or experiments aren't always necessary – it all depends on the shape of the first draft. Sometimes a script is so strong that to tinker with it would be foolhardy. This is relatively rare, but the point is that producers should adapt the process of redrafting to suit the script and the writer, rather than impose a dogmatic one-size-fits-all approach.

Usually the writers we are producing will undergo at least a couple of big redrafts, to fix any issues, try different ideas, and make sure the story is understood properly. Subsequent redrafts should then, hopefully, consist of progressively smaller tweaks and nudges, ultimately comprising only gentle edits, as we close in on the production draft.

The Stages of Redrafting

Never convince yourself that this version of the script is the one, the final draft. There is always a chance that more work will be called for at some point. Instead, the ambition with each redraft should be to get the script ready for the next stage.

Think of it like scaling a mountain. You'll never reach the peak in one mad dash. You have to find a safe route, establishing a series of base camps from which to make the next ascent. Each draft brings you a little closer to the summit.

First off, you want to make sure the script is in strong enough shape to impress programmers and producers. Don't rush to send them your first draft; go through it yourself initially, and then show it to friends for advice. Redrafting at this point should focus on cutting any clunky exposition, making the timeline tight and the story clear, and ensuring the script showcases its virtues, with an eye on the practicalities of stagecraft. Then you can be confident it's ready to be shared with decision-makers.

Once accepted for production, redrafting will focus on preparing the script for rehearsals. You may have the luxury of some R&D, workshopping the script with a director and actors, but even if you don't, you should sit down with your collaborators and ask for notes (you aren't obliged to act on them). You'll probably find that they have suggestions for improvements; you may be surprised by their value or you may consider them misguided. Even if no one raises anything substantial, you should still consider whether there are elements of your play that aren't clear for a director or actor. Try to guarantee that, when rehearsals begin, the script will withstand weeks of examination.

Lastly, once rehearsals are underway, you will probably find that cuts or rewrites are mooted. Try not to be oversensitive; when collaborators make suggestions, it's usually with goodwill. Rather than an aspersion on your writing, it simply reflects that theatre is about discovery.

That said, not all suggestions will be good, but there will probably be some gems. And it's not just the cast who might make incisive comments. Don't be afraid to make further changes during previews based on what you see of audience reactions or overhear in the loos. Spying on audiences is a must, although bugging a urinal is taking it too far.

At each stage, the redrafting should be less substantial and more straightforward; by the last few days, it's hopefully a matter of tweaks and edits. Though don't hold us to that…

This chapter focuses on the first stage of the redrafting process, to get your script ready for others' eyes. (The subsequent stages of redrafting are variously covered in the chapters on 'Working with Collaborators', 'R&D' and 'Going into Production'.)

Insider's View: Rachel De-lahay

Before beginning any redraft, I try to have as much time away from the script as possible. Without this, I find I don't truly re-read the script. The story is so fresh in my head I struggle to differentiate between what I wanted to write and what is actually on the page, and not only do I overlook plot holes and structural problems but also the most basic of typing errors.

Only once space and distance have been given to the text am I able to read it properly. Then the story feels almost new to me; I'm no longer skimming paragraphs assuming the work's there, but am forced to read everything rigorously in order to find and follow what feels almost like someone else's story. I can then note what I enjoy, where I get bored, and any sections that feel inactive.

In an ideal world I would also allow others to read my work in order to get second opinions. A perfect reader to me is a friend whose opinion I trust and whose taste I regard highly. They probably would not be a writer, director or actor. I would want them to be excited to read a new story, not fatigued with the task of reading yet another script.

Rachel's plays have premiered at the Royal Court Theatre, Birmingham REP and the Tricycle Theatre. She has also written for radio, TV and Netflix. Her plays have won the Catherine Johnson Award, the Alfred Fagon Award, the

Questions to Ask Before Others Do

Finishing a play is a real achievement, and it can be dispiriting to contemplate rewriting. You'll be glad you did, however, once collaborators start interrogating you about every line. Find improvements yourself, before others put you on the spot, and you'll enjoy workshops, rehearsals and press nights far more.

That said, it's best not to dive straight back in immediately after scribbling the direction for lights down; take a few weeks to distance yourself from the script and gain some perspective. Once you feel rejuvenated, able to look at the script afresh, try the exercises below.

Where is exposition hiding?

Unnecessary exposition is the bogeyman of new writing. It's when dialogue serves a crude explanatory or didactic purpose. It makes a character feel artificial and suggests the writer either doesn't trust their audience to piece clues together or isn't skilled enough to convey ideas with subtlety. Exposition kills a script. It's why 90 per cent of the plays we read are dismissed.

Of course, not all exposition is bogus. Any story needs some explication of character and situation, lest it leave the audience behind. This should be conveyed as much through subtext and implication as possible; exposition only becomes unacceptable when it's couched as bald statements with no other merit than information.

Writing clunky exposition doesn't mean you're a bad writer; leaving it in situ does. It's natural that in a first draft there will be some lines that you wrote for your own edification, rather than because they are necessary for an audience's understanding or true to that character. After all, you're still figuring out who these characters are. Once you've discovered that, however, you need to excise any clumsy statements in favour of more nuanced and natural speech and behaviour.

As a starting point, any line in which a character reminds another character of something profoundly obvious to them both, asserts a biographical fact apropos of nothing, or explains something that just happened, is probably a clanger. Consider this sample exchange from our (less than mighty) pens:

> TITMUSS. Lousy day *at work. The wrapping paper factory* is really busy because we've had *lots of orders for Christmas*. It's a bloody nightmare. I gave up on lunch, all I could taste was elves.

> LAKER. I had a shocker too. Lock is a pain in the arse.

> TITMUSS. Lock has only been *your line manager for two months, since they promoted her from the floor against your wishes*. Give her time. At least she doesn't wear a pointy hat.

The italics indicate the bits that are probably exposition. After all, surely both characters know Titmuss has been at work and where that is, understand that Christmas means lots of wrapping paper, and know that Lock is an unwelcome new manager. Editing these bits makes the exchange tighter and more natural, yet still conveys the important ideas:

> TITMUSS. This month's always a bloody nightmare. Orders are through the roof, especially for the rolls with the bloody penguins. Even my lunch tasted of elves.

> LAKER. I had a shocker too. Lock is a pain in the arse.

> TITMUSS. Give her time. At least she isn't an Antarctic fowl.

These examples might seem egregious, but many of the scripts we receive really are this laden with clumsy information. Be ruthless in challenging every line for superfluous exposition.

Is it dramatic?

> 'Bore an audience for five minutes
> and you've lost them for an hour.'
> John Mortimer

Wariness of melodrama is laudable, but not at the cost of drama itself. It's surprising how many plays are well-written but boring. Lots of playwrights seem to have a knack for dialogue yet indulge this at the cost of narrative tension. This can be especially true of first drafts; often the focus is so much on pinning down key plot points and characterisation that the drama of the story is overlooked. This is as fatal to your script's chances as exposition.

Of course, good dialogue and nuanced characters are always engaging whatever the plot, but just because they're enjoyable to write and rewarding to read does not mean they will hold an audience's attention for a full performance. At some point, you need to approach your script as a detached audience member would.

Try to read it through at a canter. Don't agonise over small details, but give yourself the experience of the story as a whole. Does it grip you? Perhaps jot exclamation marks down whenever there's a moment that carries tension or makes you sit up – are there enough of these throughout the script?

A term commonly bandied around by theatre-makers is 'stakes'; this means that pressure/risk/importance is attached to each event for at least one character. Rehearsals often contain more talk of stakes than a Hammer Horror vampire film. Does your script carry genuine dramatic weight? This is one question that feedback from friends can often help answer; you don't need to be a theatre professional versed in the lingo of 'stakes' to say whether a plot holds the attention.

Now, stakes don't need to be melodramatic. They just need to matter to the characters. Duncan Macmillan's play *Lungs* is a great example of this: two nameless people agonise over whether to have a child, apparently without any major financial or personal crises. A first-world dilemma that would be horribly earnest and self-important were it related by a friend in the pub becomes riveting simply because the characters are so well-drawn and the play so skilfully structured. So, never apologise for your story; if it

REDRAFTING AND EDITING

interests you, it will others. Just make sure that it has sufficient narrative drive.

You could try plotting the stakes on a graph. Break the script down into 'units' (a section that has its own distinctive drive, purpose or subtext, which can be as short as a single word or as long as a scene). Assign each unit a number from one to ten, corresponding to how much is at stake for the characters. Marking this on a graph represents the play's narrative drive visually, and might pinpoint any areas that meander or lack tension.

Does the timeline work?

It's a prosaic consideration, yet many scripts are marred by mysterious contradictions or leaps in chronology. More than once we've dug into an exciting script and found that the entire structure unravels once the timings are totted up.

Say there's a terrible event looming. Character A reveals this to Character B, who then flees on her motorbike. That would be fine, except that Character B was the only person with the key to a locked room, yet later Character A opens it to find the solution to the terrible event hidden inside. So why didn't Character B know about it if she had the key? How did Character A get inside? To fix this, we need to change either the time at which Character B flees or the information about the key. It's not insurmountable, but it's a silly slip that should be caught early on.

Who knows what, and when, and who does what, and when, must be infallible. Lapses are never going to ruin a script, but they may require a good chunk of effort to fix. Best make sure the timeline's tight from the off.

Do the gaps between scenes make sense?

It's easy to overlook what's not happening on stage. Out of sight doesn't necessarily mean out of mind for the audience, however; if a character disappears at the end of the first scene, and then re-appears at the start of the fifth, some bright spark will wonder how in the interim they've managed to learn something that's only just been revealed in their absence. Ensure that whatever happens on the stage corresponds to events or time offstage, and vice versa.

Remember that every character's journey must make perfect sense, whether or not we see all of it. A good tip is to lay out all the scenes featuring a certain character in order, and follow them through, treating each character as if they were the protagonist in their own story. That way, you'll see what their narrative arc is, without being distracted by the scenes they aren't in. Do this for each character, and you'll quickly discover any non sequiturs in what people are doing, saying or thinking.

Another trick we use is to write a one-sentence summary of each scene on a piece of card, then read through these, to check that each scene adds something new without the gap between it and the previous scene being unclear or contradictory. If you can plan this in advance, so much the better!

Is it credible?

When wrestling an early draft into shape, it's usually the plot and structure that are the most pressing challenges. To fix the shape, sometimes writers have to contrive certain things. Characters may make decisions or say lines that are a little forced, in order to set up a crucial event for the plot. Once you have the overall story down, any such contrivances must be replaced with more elegant solutions.

Make a list of all the key decisions made by each character. Then look at them one by one, in the context of that individual character at that point in the play. Does each decision make sense? That doesn't necessarily mean it has to be rational, but if it isn't emotionally truthful the audience will see through it.

Will this work?

This is the big question that most producers ask. No matter how brilliant the script, if you demand a cast of thirty-seven perform entirely in Latin, with a dozen costume changes per scene, it's not very feasible. There's something to be said for being big and bold, but it must be earned and justified. Check the list of things to watch out for when writing for the stage in the previous chapter and make sure your play is stageable.

These questions should help identify any problems in a script, and redress these, before you share it with anyone who really matters. Of course, the hardest part is to fix the problems – which is where feedback may help.

Feedback

What makes a script into a play is performing it in front of an audience. The response of your audience matters as much as that of professional reviewers, especially in an age of social media, which has levelled the critical field. This means that obtaining non-professional feedback on your script is valuable; you'll be hearing what your potential audience think.

Deciding whom to approach for feedback and how to handle the process is not always easy. Here are some tips on how to get the best from feedback.

Do:

- Share your script with five or six friends. They should preferably have some theatregoing experience, so you can trust them to read with an understanding of the basic form, but not be heavily invested in the script. They should read with a fresh eye. You want a wide sample of responses, but not so many that you're bombarded; be selective. This is where enrolling on a training course or writers' group can be valuable.

- Encourage readers to be honest. Make it clear that you intend to redraft and are looking for constructive notes, not unquestioning emotional support.

- Be patient. Allow readers a few weeks to respond. If you hassle them, you may compromise the quality and effort that goes into their notes.

- Be open. Receiving notes is hard, but try not to be defensive; resist the urge to explain or debate individual points. Let your reader speak, without interruption, and focus on listening and absorbing. A Dictaphone to record their ideas may be useful, for further reflection. You could also ask the reader to email their thoughts in lieu of a face-to-face meeting.

- Allow readers to focus on the points that occur to them. Don't interrogate them or ask leading questions; that only curtails the ideas they may offer and precludes unexpected insights.

- Ask your readers to feedback individually, not en masse. You want to hear a range of opinions, not just those of the loudest person in the room. It's very easy for a dominant voice to overshadow or influence others.

- Ask your readers to express in a few sentences what they get from each scene. This will reveal any places where the story isn't coming across clearly.

- Know your own mind. Remember that when you ask people to read a script, they are under pressure to find something to say. Even professional readers often latch on to something just for the sake of justifying their input. So reflect carefully on all notes, don't accept them on principle.

- Be grateful for readers' time and effort, whether or not you intend to act on their notes. You want to build up a trusted cadre of informal readers you can return to, rather than huffily dismiss people who are only trying to help.

Don't:

- Give your readers an exhaustive synopsis of the play or your themes. They shouldn't be influenced by what you think it's about; they should judge what the script actually is. The field of literary criticism has long been aware of the 'intentional fallacy' (a memorable term coined by the even more brilliantly named Wimsatt and Beardsley); put simply, it means that an author's intentions are irrelevant in judging a text. Not just because a writer may have failed to execute their vision, but also because there may be virtues in the text of which an author is not consciously aware. You'll gain far more from hearing your readers' unadulterated personal responses than by priming them to address your preconceived ideas.

- Despair when readers comment negatively about aspects of the script. That's much more useful than generic praise. Don't be put off even if it sounds brutal. A professional reader will usually shape their criticism into constructive language, but an amateur may, with all goodwill, simply make a devastating statement. Train yourself to translate seemingly harsh criticism into constructive suggestion, so that 'it's utterly unbelievable that the character would do this' becomes 'it needs to be clearer why the character does this'. It may appear superficial, but when you are on the receiving end of a volley of notes, such delicacy can be vital to morale.

- Rush to make corrections or cuts based on one reader's feedback. You've shared the script with several people for a reason. Wait until you've heard the full range of thoughts, and assimilate these carefully, before picking up the red pen. One reader may give a note that reflects personal taste, or is simply a misreading; several readers concurring on a note mean it's probably worth acting on.

- Make piecemeal revisions. Working on particular issues separately will result in a patchwork script that may lose coherence; you may even be pulled to and fro by conflicting feedback. Wait until you have a complete list of notes and then address them all together, so that the play retains a clear structure and tone.

There is a curious balancing act required when taking notes on a play. Whilst it is essential to absorb the notes you are given (they are invariably identifying something that isn't working about your play), at the same time, you also need to hold on to your own artistic integrity; you know best where you ultimately want the play to go and if a note takes you away from your intended destination, then that note isn't the right solution. It will still have been useful because it helps you to define what your destination is.

One thing that I have noticed about writing plays is that for a long, *long* time, you will get a disparity of feedback from the people you give your play to. Often that feedback will be confusing: the notes will contradict one another, your readers will disagree about what needs fixing and how to fix it, someone will point to an area of the play you are happy with and away from an area that you think needs work. What eventually happens, however, is that at a certain point, this polarity of views disappears and instead, everyone who reads or sees your play will pretty much say the same thing about it; they will like it for the same reasons, they will tell you that they understood from your play the thing you were trying to communicate. When you reach this point, you know your play is ready. It's wrong until it's right, basically. Until then, gratefully receive any notes you are given and have faith that you will get there in the end.

Sam was Papatango's second Resident Playwright. Her first play, Mucky Kid, *premiered at Theatre503 and was nominated for an OffWestEnd Award for Most Promising Playwright, and her play* Hanna *toured with Papatango across England and Wales. She has been commissioned by the Tricycle Theatre and Oxford North Wall, and was formerly Literary Manager at Out of Joint and Creative Associate at Headlong. As a director, she has worked at the National Theatre, the RSC, Hampstead Theatre and Glyndebourne Opera.*

REDRAFTING AND EDITING

How to Redraft

Once you've interrogated your script and received feedback from trusted readers, you should start the business of redrafting. The key is knowing what to accomplish. Reflect carefully on all your notes and then draw up a list of targets. You aren't (hopefully) starting the script from scratch, and you aren't looking to write for the sake of getting to know your characters or explore the story. That's been done. Now, you must be strategic. Focus on what is needed to improve the script.

No redraft will be quite like another, because the nature and the scale of the changes needed will vary every time. This means it's worth treating every redraft as a new experience. Draw up a schedule for tackling your targets. Don't rush in headlong, however confident you are that you now understand the script, or however energised you feel by the prospect of getting to grips with it, because you may end up confusing things further.

It's sometimes the case that a first redraft brings excellent progress and a second redraft ruins the play! This is because many writers are initially tentative about changes and approach redrafting carefully and methodically, but then, emboldened by initial success, plunge enthusiastically into the next version and thrash their way to a confused mess.

Truly, trying to fix one issue can generate a dozen more, because it knocks the structure or timeline out of kilter or because you unintentionally repeat dialogue or introduce inconsistencies or contrivances. It can be a case of out of the frying pan, into the fire! You therefore need to exercise rigorous control over every redraft; it will save you time and effort in the long run. Consider setting out your plan for each redraft in a table:

Note	Scenes Affected	Proposed Revision	Consequences	Potential Issues
The opening feels flat and uninteresting.	Scene 1	Open with the boy in hospital, rather than his parents driving there.	The argument between his parents over the responsibility for the accident may need to occur in a new scene, as they wouldn't argue in front of their son. Where would this fit in?	Will this make the first act too long? Check running time.

Such a table enables you to track how all the changes in combination will affect the script. It means that knock-on effects or possible contradictions are easier to identify and resolve. Proceed cautiously. If one change has wider ramifications than anticipated, stop to reflect, and trace what parts of the script will need to take account of this. You may decide the change isn't justified, in which case, look for another, less destabilising, solution to the initial problem. This holistic approach to the whole script is key.

You need to allow yourself time to get the redraft right. Often writers regard a redraft as a straightforward, swift exercise and commit to knocking it off in a few days. Don't put yourself under that pressure unless you have to; err towards generosity and give yourself the best chance of making this redraft the final one, or as close to it as possible.

Once you think you've addressed all your targets, and the script remains clear and coherent, it's advisable to pass it back to your readers, if they're generous with their time, to see if they agree that their concerns have been met. Just be wary of this turning into an endless cycle; make it clear that you're asking them to comment on the changes in relation to their initial notes, and they should only make new suggestions if they really feel it's vital. Otherwise you could be redrafting and sharing and redrafting and sharing forever!

It may also be worth asking at least one completely fresh reader to cast their eye over it, following the same principles as before, to hear their verdict. This will reveal whether the story is now sharper and the weaknesses resolved – or if new ones have been introduced to the mix.

When to Stop?

Redrafting is dangerous. It can rapidly become a compulsion, then an addiction. Many playwrights struggle to break free of the saga. It takes a lot of nerve and courage to send a script off to a stranger to be assessed, so the temptation to do one more draft, to try to make it even more perfect, can be irresistible.

Again, this is where starting the redrafting process with a clear list of targets, formulated in a no-nonsense table, helps. Once you've struck off the targets, are convinced that all the consequences across the script are seamlessly integrated, and your readers have agreed, then you have no excuse to continue tinkering.

The challenge comes when new notes emerge in response to new drafts. It's almost inevitable that they will, however many redrafts you undertake, so when is enough enough? There is no definite rule, but once the comments from readers tend to be of a small scale (e.g. focused on individual lines or stage directions rather than structural changes), you are probably in a position to sign off. Relatively trivial issues are not going to sway any producer against you, as these can be dealt with easily. So, once you're no longer getting 'big' notes from readers, it means this stage of the redrafting is done. Take the plunge and share your script.

We'll discuss how to approach producers and programmers in the next chapter, the final part of this act. There are reflections on later forms of redrafting during R&D, rehearsals and previews in Act Two.

GETTING NOTICED:
THE ROAD TO BEING PROGRAMMED

Most successful playwrights have to be savvy about championing their work, as well as being talented writers. Many of us have a natural reticence about promoting ourselves, but a playwright simply cannot afford this (though pushiness should never spill over into immodesty!). Only fortunate, probably well-connected, writers find advocates within the industry at an early stage of their careers. For the majority of emerging playwrights, their first champion must be themselves.

This is well understood; no one will resent you for standing up for your work or regard you as unduly pushy for asking them to read your script. After all, if you don't believe in your play enough to promote it, why should anyone else? Stiffen your resolve. Remember, your script submission will be one of thousands. The more you can do to attach value to it in advance, the more likely it is to fare well.

This chapter discusses how to achieve this. It outlines ways to catch attention, how companies programme plays, strategies by which writers can promote their scripts, and whether representation from an agent is advantageous.

Catching the Eye

The majority of playwrights only earn notice once they have a complete full-length script to circulate. Most of this chapter therefore discusses how to make the most of such a script. However, it can be worthwhile to establish relationships with companies before your script reaches them, to render them more receptive.

Indeed, if you are labouring on a script but nowhere near ready to submit, that doesn't mean you can't lay the foundations of a writing career in other ways. Relatively few playwrights break through as a completely unknown discovery; most debutants are already familiar names within the industry in one way or another. That's not sinister or nepotistic (most of the time); the most promising writers tend to have actively learned and experimented for quite a while before writing a script that is ready for production.

Following are some suggestions on how to introduce yourself.

Scratch nights, short-play festivals, writing events

No one gets too excited about a writer until there's a full-length play to get stuck in to, but becoming involved in the 'shorts and scratches' circuit can build a useful profile. If people in the industry are familiar with and fond of your ten-minute skits, chances are they'll want to read your hundred-page magnum opus.

There are lots of companies that specialise in mounting shorts, as these are relatively cheap and easy to stage. They will take the producing burden, often pairing a writer with exciting creatives. Companies include Little Pieces of Gold (usually found at Southwark Playhouse or Theatre503, both in London), The Miniaturists (London's Arcola Theatre), Alphabetti Soup Commissions (at Alphabetti Theatre in Newcastle upon Tyne), Birmingham REP's scratch nights, Traverse Theatre's Words Words Words (in Edinburgh), and many others nationwide.

Seeing your short play programmed as part of a wider line-up can be educational, is a great way to meet collaborators and effectively introduces your writing to professional theatre-makers. Moreover, there is a Venn diagram between companies who facilitate short plays and those who mount full productions; while not every producer of shorts and scratches has the resources to scale up, many do – and bigger projects often evolve from this initial platform.

If you aren't comfortable writing shorts – and they are quite a specific skill; as with prose, some writers are better suited to long-form stories – then you can still make yourself known. Participate in local writing workshops or join writer-oriented events. (We have already discussed some industry courses and workshop options in the 'Training' chapter, so won't repeat ourselves here.) Even if you don't feel the training itself has much value, it may prove hugely beneficial to attend and establish yourself as a writer in the minds of decision-makers. Warm them up for your script.

Residencies or networking schemes

Another way to get noticed is to apply for a writing position within an organisation. Residencies offer resources to develop new plays, usually via some combination of a bursary or commission, dramaturgy and rehearsal/R&D facilities. Many writers benefit from a deadline to work to and a more productive, focused environment in which to write, while the companies get to know a writer's work without the risk or financial outlay of a production.

Resident writers are usually embedded within organisations, so benefit from long-term relationships as well as gaining enormous validation. The more prestigious the host organisation, the stronger the prospects for the resident.

Sometimes residencies are not attached to a producing company but are granted as part of a bursary or artist development scheme. These are more common in America than the UK, with initiatives like the MacDowell Colony, open to international artists, providing funds and space simply to write (it boasts an alumni list crammed with Pulitzer Prize winners). Schemes specific to this country include Bristol University's Kevin Elyot Award for a writer-in-residence. We recommend signing up to the London Playwrights' Blog mailing list to receive alerts on these opportunities. The advantage of these kind of residencies is that there's no obligation to meet a specific programming ethos or work to a producer's remit; it's purely about your writing, and an appropriate production can be sought later.

Residencies with good companies or esteemed retreats are the holy grail of industry opportunities, so inevitably they are also the most rigorous and selective. Nonetheless, it's easier to get your work seen by applying for a slot as a resident or writer-on-attachment than it is to win big on an unsolicited submission. There will inevitably be fewer applications for these positions than there are scripts cramming the inbox. Papatango get around two thousand submissions a year, mainly to the Papatango New Writing Prize, compared with five hundred applications for our Resident Playwright scheme. The odds are still stacked against you, but it's more favourable. Moreover, where companies may not be enthused by unsolicited submissions, they actively seek applications for these positions.

The best residencies are fiercely competitive, and won't go to writers without a strong track record, so build your writing portfolio at scratch nights or workshops before you expect to be considered. Generally, residencies go to writers with proven experience of working with collaborators and completing scripts, or who have a particular connection with the host organisation. Getting involved with local theatres through introductory programmes, workshops and writing events is an important preliminary step. Very few writers land such lucrative opportunities 'cold'.

If a residency feels out of reach, then also common within the industry are schemes designed to promote collaboration. Like residencies, these normally provide some degree of resources to develop new scripts, but unlike residencies they focus on connecting artists from different disciplines rather than prioritising an individual playwright to work within the organisation's own team. Examples include Ferment at Bristol Old Vic and Furnace at Leeds Playhouse. The benefit is that playwrights gain a network to support future work, and like residencies there is immense validation in being selected. Competition, again, is fierce, and you will need to have built up a track record through other opportunities before applying.

Tough as landing places on these schemes is, applying will put you on the company's radar. Even if you aren't successful, it establishes your name, which can only benefit future approaches. If you are successful, then you will be in an advantageous position to exploit interest in your writing.

Sidestep theatres and find other routes

Residencies aren't the sole property of theatre companies or venues. Organisations in related sectors like public education or literature often fund playwriting positions. You might find that libraries or universities, sometimes even schools, have writer-in-residence positions available. Examples include Gladstone's Library in Flintshire or the collaboration between Northumbria University and Live Theatre on a playwriting position.

While perhaps not as prestigious as an industry position, they are still heavily competitive, so any script or showcase that you produce while attached to/funded by such institutions will carry more clout than if you were just writing alone. Moreover, these institutions usually have strong connections to local theatres, so getting an 'in' with them can lead to opportunities within the industry itself. (We discuss these routes further in the 'Moving On' chapter.)

Become a reader

Companies that accept new plays are always stretched, and willing readers are sought after. Some will pay while some rely on volunteers (not the best policy in terms of guaranteeing consistency or quality). Either way, if you have experience of theatre, and can spare a few hours a week, you may be welcomed on to the team. This serves a dual function: you will foster valuable relationships and gain insight into programming policies.

What qualifies someone to be a reader? Put simply: experience. Being a budding playwright will certainly not hurt your case. Many playwrights emerge after a period cocooned in the dark rooms of literary departments; many literary managers are themselves writers. The disciplines clearly inform each other. Nonetheless, you will be required to demonstrate your skills as a reader. Usually this involves a reading test and proving an ability to write clear, concise script reports. Prepare by reading plays recently produced by the company, so you understand the tastes and artistic remit of the team you're applying to join. (Look at the 'Writing for Theatre' chapter for detailed guidance on how readers assess scripts and what they base their verdicts upon.)

Join a company's team

The bars, box offices and backstages of theatres are staffed by and stuffed with aspiring actors, directors or writers. It makes sense as a recruitment policy. Not only do these people have an infectious enthusiasm for theatre, they are likely to strive hard to impress the management. In return, it's understood (not too wearily) that these staff members would value a little mentoring and invest-ment. So, if you happen to be looking for work while awaiting your big break, seek it within the industry. It's surely no coinci-dence that one of the very few debut playwrights to reach the Royal Court stage in recent years was their PR manager; quality remains key, but being in a position to show that quality off is a huge advantage.

This may seem cynical. Papatango insist all submissions are anonymous, to actively guard against the very real risk of personal or unconscious bias. Nonetheless, provided you are trying to con-nect with and learn from experienced professionals, not just curry favour, it's not dubious practice. We all learn from colleagues. Go into a job with this attitude, rather than with false, even syco-phantic, expectations of unprofessional favours, and you may reap the benefits.

Social media

Once budding playwrights had to flag down a hansom cab and brave the heart of the city to reach a producer. Now you just tweet.

Social media has irrevocably changed the way artists, audiences, funders and producers converse. Nearly everyone is accessible on one platform or another – generally, Twitter and LinkedIn are the more professional sites through which to start a conversation; Facebook (unless it's an official or organisational page) is relatively more personal.

Joining the buzz online can be a great leveller, enabling sixth-formers to invite Hollywood stars to their showcase or am-dram writers in the Highlands to chat with Olivier winners in Avignon. Gloriously, the former wrestler Dwayne 'The Rock' Johnson once tweeted about a show being performed at London's VAULT

Festival. Even if you can't engage with a company in person, social media can help nurture a valid relationship.

But it can also intimidate. Sometimes, more established – or at least cocky – artists hold forth, spouting endless assertive comments that are ostensibly part of a public conversation but really consist of in-jokes amid a closed circle that make everyone else feel excluded from and ignorant of theatre. Ignore these bozos. If they put half the effort into playwriting that they did tweeting, they'd genuinely be leading the industry, not just posing as doing so. Most influential theatre-makers are too busy to be a constant social-media presence, but will usually respond to queries or share thoughts.

Engaging with companies on social media is welcome, and can make your name memorable. Be more tactful about contacting individuals, but not inhibited. Be positive, be polite, build a two-way, generous chat – just as you would in person. The conventions are no different.

Just send a good play!

However you do it, establishing your name as more than just a by-line helps ensure that when the time to submit a full-length script comes, it gets a more tailored response. Don't obsess over forging a personal connection, however; leaving aside the questionable moral perspective, back channels only speed up the process, they won't determine how your script fares. A dreadful play remains dreadful, no matter that it was scrawled by the producer's favourite barista, while a quality piece stands out, even if penned by a complete stranger.

So if you lack the resources or nerve to sidle up to decision-makers, or aren't comfortable writing shorts for scratch nights, don't despair. The most important thing is to concentrate on submitting your script in the canniest way.

It's important to read and see as much as you can, not just new writing but also classics. If you meet a literary manager/director/producer, they will probably ask what writers, recent productions and artists you like. So be aware of the world of theatre and who is within it. This will help you understand what you can offer and how to shape a pitch.

My first three theatre commissions after the success of my Papatango play *After Independence* came from the Traverse Theatre and the National Theatre of Scotland (NTS). When I met with the artistic management of NTS they were clear that what they wanted was a play which combined Scottish themes with international resonance. I therefore successfully pitched an idea about the first slave to successfully free himself in the Scottish law courts during the Scottish enlightenment.

Conversely, the Traverse plays came about after I made a mistake, approaching the company with another period play. I hit it off with Orla O'Loughlin, the Artistic Director, but she didn't feel the play was right for the theatre. Nonetheless, because of that initial meeting, soon after telling me the Traverse wouldn't take the play she called and set me a challenge. 'May, I want you to write me a play that speaks directly about how we live today or how we might be living tomorrow.' I accepted, and ended up writing about the complex relationship between the agricultural industry and human trafficking, as well as a play about the effect on immigrants of the Scottish Government's integration policy. As important, therefore, as the subject and quality of your work are, I would say this: never, never, never underestimate the importance of good relationships.

May was Papatango's first Resident Playwright, and won the 2016 Alfred Fagon Audience Award for Papatango's production of his play After Independence *at the Arcola Theatre, London, which May then adapted for BBC Radio 4. He has received a BBC Performing Arts Fund Legacy Award, been extensively commissioned across theatre, TV and radio, including for National Theatre Scotland, Theatre Royal Stratford East, Scottish Opera and the BBC, and is a trustee of The Writing Squad. He teaches on the MFA in Playwriting at Edinburgh Napier University.*

Where to Target

Playwrights, like rats, are everywhere, and like rats they often feel unwanted at home. Innumerable writers have lamented that their local theatres are not interested in new plays. London, in the common imagination, shines forth as a beacon of new writing. This myth needs busting.

London is indisputably the theatre capital of the UK – the biggest venues and, as importantly, the major press outlets are there. But while the concentration of new writing in the wen may be denser than anywhere else on the planet, that doesn't mean that the regions are a barren desert where only the plays of Alan Ayckbourn cling to life.

New writing thrives across the country, at least in most cities; tackling the dearth of theatre and indeed wider culture in smaller conurbations or rural areas is another matter. Nonetheless, most people have new-writing opportunities within reach – it's just that the press don't cover these adequately and the cultural conversation, deplorably, tends not to stretch beyond the M25.

Don't rush to take your writing elsewhere; start by looking locally. And really look. Don't just turn to the nearest producing house; very few emerging playwrights will have any shot at waltzing into a big venue. Seek out the fringe venues, festivals or networks that feed the bigger companies, but which may not be as well reported. For instance, in Manchester, try the Hope Mill Theatre as well as the Royal Exchange; in Liverpool, the Hope Street Theatre alongside the Everyman & Playhouse; in Cardiff, The Other Room as well as the Sherman Cymru; in Nottingham, Fifth Word as well as the Playhouse. And so on.

A vital fringe ecosystem thrives in most regions, and parochial pride means that plays from local writers always have cachet. So don't assume you have to plug your play further afield – and if you do, don't assume that therefore means London alone. There is a wide producing network throughout the country. The more you can explore this, the better chance you will have of getting a foot in the door, wherever it may be.

That said, sometimes writers do not have access to local theatres, or local companies simply aren't interested or their programme is oversubscribed, forcing people to turn elsewhere. And ultimately writers need to be produced as widely as possible to earn a crust. But there's not an unavoidable obligation to turn to London from the very first. Be rigorous in looking beyond the obvious names; respect the *national* new-writing scene and widen your opportunities.

How Plays are Programmed

Companies have traditionally selected the plays they produce through three main channels: commissioning, unsolicited submissions, and transfers from fringe or scratch showcases. Recently, playwriting prizes have also become common. We launched the Papatango New Writing Prize in 2008, at which point it was the only award to guarantee a full production and publication, but since then several others have followed suit (although we remain unique in running every year, offering a follow-up commission, and giving feedback to all). These channels are explained below.

The importance of understanding how to sell a script via these channels and navigate the tricky field of programming has been exacerbated in recent years. Due to funding cuts, literary departments have shrunk. Fewer in-house readers means there is now less provision for unsolicited submissions and capacity to attend showcases has been reduced. Many companies therefore concentrate their dwindling literary resources on programming commissions from established playwrights. Those who remain open, at least in theory, to unsolicited submissions are deluged, so the competition is harder than ever. This is especially true of playwriting prizes. To break into professional theatre as a new writer, it's not enough simply to have written a good script; the onus is on you to ensure it shines out.

Understanding how to approach companies depends on appreciating the ways that programming works. Once you are attuned to the process your script will undergo, you can be strategic in sharing it.

Commissions

Commissions are when a company hires a playwright to create a new script. Often, as well as a fee, the company pledges a level of support and resources, such as dramaturgy or workshop facilities, to help realise this script.

Commissions are usually offered to a pre-selected playwright rather than available by application. Nonetheless, sometimes an open-entry opportunity includes a commission. Papatango's annual Resident Playwright position, for instance, is a year-long programme that supports an emerging writer through mentoring, R&D and a commission. There are other initiatives like this – but the truth is that the majority of commissions go to established playwrights whom a company has in mind from the start.

This is because commissions are increasingly the main source of programming; cuts to public subsidy have made companies increasingly dependent on box-office success, so to mitigate their financial risk they are drawn to tried-and-trusted artists with bankable names. Such established writers quite properly expect a commission, and once a company has made this significant investment they are more inclined to stage the final outcome and recoup their money.

The vision behind a commission, however, is not always production. Sometimes companies knowingly take a punt on a project without being certain of its viability. Sometimes they commission playwrights as part of a development programme. This may be altruistic, or simply because specific funding streams are available to develop talent but not necessarily produce it (a constant bugbear of ours; playwrights learn best from seeing their work performed).

Correspondingly, the amount of money paid, the resources available, and the rights and control over the script all vary according to the nature of the commission, as well as the experience and commercial prospects of the playwright. (We discuss how to approach different commissioning opportunities and contract negotiations in the chapter on 'Making Deals'.) The main thing to understand for now is that a commission comes with the obligation to write a play in return for a financial and sometimes artistic investment.

Inevitably playwrights need to have proven talent and a capacity to deliver before commissions materialise. This can be a Catch-22 situation; as commissions are now the staple source of programming, there are fewer production slots available for emerging playwrights. This means it's harder to prove writing credentials to a sufficient degree to earn that elusive commission – hence the difficult spiral of getting started. The pool of playwrights regarded as ripe for commissioning is stagnating, even shrinking.

That's not to be fatalistic. You may be fortunate enough to land a development opportunity that includes a commission, and then be talented enough to pen a script of such quality that a producer takes a risk on an unknown artist. Only a minority of writers follow this route, however; it's more likely that you will first be programmed by catching someone's eye through an unsolicited submission or showcase.

Unsolicited submissions

An unsolicited submission refers to the practice of submitting a script without being asked. Usually such submissions are done online through the miracle of email attachment, much cheaper and easier than entrusting a hefty parcel to snail mail.

Particular companies have particular guidelines for submissions (at Papatango, they need to be anonymous; at Paines Plough, they must be accompanied by an equal opportunities monitoring form), so make a tailored submission for each rather than a mass email out. Obviously, the more personal the submission, reflecting the reasons you are sharing it with this company, the more favourably it will be received. It's time-consuming but worthwhile.

As well as reading the guidelines, it's also worth researching the companies. As important as it is to get your work staged, it is just as vital that the style and artistic philosophy of the company matches your play. If they have recently programmed a play tackling similar subjects, they are unlikely to consider your script for production (although if it's well-written, it may still earn their attention); equally, if they only produce comedies, they are unlikely to be receptive to a hard-hitting drama. Think about who and where would be the best fit.

In writing something that you envisage will be sent out as an unsolicited submission, be true to yourself and your story; don't chase after the zeitgeist or try to bend your writing to some pre-conceived notion of what a faceless producer wants. Write for yourself, and then decide whom to approach; anything else will probably not result in a good play.

If you already know someone at an organisation, it is possible that you will be able to send your script directly to them – this is why we discussed ways of making yourself known. In a best-case scenario, you will have impressed someone with artistic clout who will advocate for your writing.

Don't assume that this is the case, however, without careful reflection. Have you earned the right to approach them and will they welcome your message? If you only met them in passing five years ago, or had to trawl the internet for their details, they may feel used, even persecuted. And if they would welcome a message from you, is it relevant to send them a script? Your neighbour may be a theatre's finance officer; that doesn't mean they have any say in literary matters. Be careful not to seem to be exploiting an angle, especially if it isn't really there! Better to be transparent and trust the designated system than wheedle for an 'in'.

Once a script is submitted, it goes into a pile that the literary team will work their way through. It takes months for this to be completed, as readers will prioritise commissions. If an unsolicited submission is put forward by someone who already knows your work, or is submitted by a reputable agent or theatre-maker on your behalf, it may go to the top of the pile since someone has vouched for it. This speeds up the process but doesn't make a favourable response any likelier.

As you have taken a chance putting your script forward, you are under no obligation of exclusivity to the company. You don't have to wait for months and months to hear back before sending your script elsewhere. Share it as widely as seems sensible, and if you end up the subject of a bidding war, all the better! Equally, you are not obliged to permit the company any rights over your play; the act of submitting it does not in itself empower them to do anything without your permission. If a company does respond and asks to stage the play, make sure you are content with their terms.

Unsolicited submissions used to be a common opportunity, the standard way that companies dredged for talent. Feedback was, if not universal, relatively common. Many playwrights who are now household names first learned through this system, and all literary managers dreamed of uncovering a masterpiece in a brown envelope. It was still rare that an unsolicited submission would make it to the stage, but it was a way to form relationships that could eventually lead to new projects or commissions.

Again, however, cuts to funding mean that provision to read unsolicited scripts is becoming a luxury. It hasn't disappeared completely, but many companies now only accept unsolicited submissions in certain windows, so they can handle the volume. The Bush Theatre, for instance, only opens to unsolicited submissions twice per year. Other organisations channel submissions into awards or competitions with set deadlines. You should investigate thoroughly the submissions process of a company before applying; respect the requirements.

You should also manage your expectations. Few companies are able to make a personal response unless they wish to take the script forward. Even those that do deliver this courtesy seldom provide feedback. Papatango, perhaps quixotically, continue to feed back on everything, and can attest how much of a challenge it is. Writers who send off an unsolicited submission, joyfully expecting an extended correspondence as a result, will be disappointed. Thousands of submissions are made each year, and teams are stretched merely to read them, let alone respond. Most literary teams go by a simple rule when approaching an unsolicited script: if they aren't gripped by the first ten pages then they won't read on. This doesn't mean that you have to fill the opening pages with all-out action, but do build your world quickly and tightly.

Nonetheless, an unsolicited submission is likely to be the main way you share your first script. It can be worthwhile provided you moderate your expectations and research the company. If you get that right, you can land your play where it will be received most sympathetically and attract some attention. It would still be a massive long-shot that it would lead to a production, but earning any response gives you something to build on. You can then position yourself on the company's radar with further scripts or showcases.

Important to bear in mind is that programming takes time; bigger venues may not have slots available for a year or longer. Even smaller, more agile companies programme months ahead. Writers need to be inhumanly patient.

Playwriting prizes

The principles of submitting a script to a prize or competition are akin to making an unsolicited submission. While prizes are open call-outs for scripts, with a commitment to consider every entry, you will be one of many entering. You should therefore approach a submission with care.

Consider the guidelines thoroughly and respect all eligibility requirements. Do not send a script in that does not conform to a prize's stated requirements simply because it is all you have available; readers will not appreciate it and you will not gain by it. If you have nothing suitable this time, then no matter: there will always be another chance to submit.

One point of difference between entering a prize and making an unsolicited submission is that the reason you are submitting is self-evident, so do not worry about personalising an explanation as to why you are reaching out. Equally, do not look to exploit any personal contacts; adhere to the rules very strictly.

It is best not to augur artistic preferences from the history of the prize; without a season to programme, and with a commitment to reward at least one script, prize judges are more likely to respond to quality than subject matter. They are reactive, and can only pick the best play(s). Most prizes therefore have a varied history of winners, and it is seldom possible to discern any underlying pattern. Papatango Prize winners range from futuristic dystopias to realistic dramas to gentle comedies. One of the greatest pleasures for us is not knowing what our next production will be; we relish being surprised by a new voice and a new story.

Do not, therefore, decide not to submit because you suspect a prize's judges of certain inclinations; if you have a script you believe in that meets their guidelines, it can only be worthwhile sharing it. Every writer who has won a prize or been shortlisted probably never expected it; where would they be if they hadn't chanced their arm?

Prizes are increasingly prominent, and have begun to replace unsolicited submissions as the way that new plays are uncovered. As such, if you have a script ready to share, it is important not to overlook prizes or be put off by the competition – it's no more steep than any other unsolicited submission process.

Showcases

Plays are meant to be seen not read; sometimes readers can't make the imaginative leap to envisage your inky words as living speech. If you have the resources and know-how to get your play performed by actors, even if they are just sitting down reading, it may come alive and impress in a way it doesn't on the page.

Famously, Tom Stoppard's *Rosencrantz and Guildenstern Are Dead* made its triumphant professional premiere only because it caught the eye of a critic in a student performance at the Edinburgh Festival. Less prominently, but no less romantically, many shows have an initial airing in a theatre's backroom or above a pub before being snapped up for a full production. Katori Hall's *The Mountaintop* was originally developed at the Bay Area Playwrights Festival but struggled to find a home, eventually making an unostentatious premiere at the tiny Theatre503 in London before taking both the West End and Broadway by storm, and winning an Olivier Award.

Showcases are not simply about getting a script programmed. They also play a pivotal role in its development. Seeing and/or hearing the work in action reveals what works and what doesn't. Often this is exciting for producers; we relish the prospect of getting stuck into something with rich potential yet to be tapped.

Don't bank on a showcase leading to a production deal; it may result in nothing more than an enthusiastic conversation, but that's still a sign you've caught the eye and may accelerate consideration of your next draft.

Showcases tend to take one of the following forms:

Rehearsed reading

The script is given rehearsal time, anywhere between a few hours to several days, and then performed. The longer the rehearsal, the more opportunity there is to explore the script and make edits or rewrites.

Actors are seated and the director's focus will be on how the cast speak the lines, rather than their physical performance. It is almost always 'script-in-hand', meaning no one has learned the lines perfectly, but the better rehearsed and prepared the cast, the more effective the reading.

Provided you have given a good-quality cast sufficient preparation time, a rehearsed reading is an excellent way to showcase the virtues of the script. A reading that prioritises clarity, without the clutter of staging, means that the plot and dialogue receive full attention and can be assessed on their own merits. Be aware, however, that a botched reading or poor casting can undermine your work unfairly.

That it is seated is no disadvantage; producers looking for new projects often appreciate a script that comes without a director's staging already imposed, as they prefer to assemble their own creative teams.

Staged reading

This is more ambitious; the cast endeavour to perform the play on its feet, although with minimal or no set, props, costume or other design. It is usually still script-in-hand.

Staged as opposed to rehearsed readings tend to happen as public, sometimes even paid-entry, performances. This is often because venues or producers have a play they like but are unable to programme as a full production, or because they have run a playwriting programme which they wish to have wider public impact.

Staged readings are thus about giving a little more to an audience; they are unnecessary for a specialist industry showcase. Assuming you are offering the script alone, and are not wedded to working with the director or cast, then there's little to be gained from adding the pressure of staging. It may even detract from the actors' delivery. A rehearsed reading is sufficient for a producer to weigh up whether they like the script.

Without-decor performance

This is another step up. It's a proper performance, sans script, usually after several rehearsals. It isn't yet a full production, because there are no sets or costumes and limited if any props, lighting or sound.

These are often the mid-point of a script's journey; sufficiently strong to earn a slot at a venue and to merit proper rehearsal time, yet not developed enough to have a full creative team or funds for a production. They can be a mark of validation for a script. The King's Head Theatre in London, for instance, hosts a festival of plays without-decor, and there is intense competition for a slot. Equally, there is appeal in watching a more complete performance.

The caveat is that all the potential downfalls of a staged reading apply in an escalated fashion; a weak cast or clunky direction can become inseparable from the script, tarnishing both in the mind of a programmer.

It's usually worth pursuing a without-decor slot if you are confident in the all-round qualities of the project and hope to find a producer willing to take it on fully formed. Some producers do like ready-made shows they can pick up. So if you have someone in mind and know there is a gap in their programme, this could be a great way to pitch. Short of this, though, be wary of without-decor opportunities; they may expose you to financial risk or put undue pressure on your script. A less high-risk reading could work better.

Excerpts performed at a scratch night or short-play festival

Showcasing an entire play can be daunting, and often logistically or financially impossible. In this case, finding opportunities to present extracts may appeal. This tends to be more useful as part of a development process rather than as a showcase. For a writer, seeing part of the draft in front of an audience can be hugely useful, but seeing only a fraction of a ninety-minute piece isn't particularly revelatory for a producer (though it may be enough for them to commit to reading the full script).

If you choose this route, select the extract carefully. It should work without needing the context of the whole script, and should take characters and audience on a journey, demonstrating your ability to shape a scene as well as to generate drama and/or comedy.

It's obviously more of an investment, and more of a risk, to share your script in a showcase than to send it as an unsolicited submission, but one which may pay dividends.

Insider's View: Stewart Pringle

One way or another, either from unsolicited submissions, colleagues' recommendations or solicitous agents, in my time at the Bush Theatre we looked at over 1,800 plays a year. I tried to read at least one or two, in full, every day. And every year we produced about six. Not six of the 1,800 we read – we might produce one of those, if we were lucky. The rest were commissions, or transfers, or international plays. We had the resources to engage meaningfully with only a few dozen writers every year.

I'm not saying all of that to discourage you, just to put what comes next into some kind of context. To show you what you're up against. To make it clear what it is that readers might be looking for. It's not necessarily a watertight structure. It's nice if you've got one, but if you haven't, that can be worked on. Readers don't look for a play that says everything about life in Trump's America or Brexit Britain. But they might be interested in what *you* have to say about it.

We have to know why it's *you* who's writing this play. We need to know why it's *this* play you're writing. It's a horrible cliché, but there are plenty of playwrights out there, and they're plenty good enough to go on, but there's only one you. And you might have something very special.

Stewart won the 2017 Papatango New Writing Prize and Papatango's production of Trestle saw him nominated for an OffWestEnd Award for Most Promising Playwright. He was previously Artistic Director at the Old Red Lion Theatre, for which he won the OffWestEnd Award for Best Artistic Director, before joining the Bush Theatre as Associate Dramaturg. He recently became Dramaturg at the National Theatre.

Which Route(s) Should I Follow?

These programming pathways all have their pitfalls. It's likely that you'll have little choice which you follow; barring an offer of a commission, you will have to pursue a mixture of unsolicited submissions and showcases. We've discussed the rudiments, but as showcases are a more complex undertaking, let's go into detail on how to mount one effectively.

How to organise showcases

If you decide that the best option for your script is a public sharing, then usually we would suggest that situating your showcase within a structured event organised by others, like the scratch and short-play festivals mentioned already, is best. It should mean you avoid financial outlay or risk, have the validation of your work being selected by others, and attract industry attention through the wider brand of the event.

If this is not viable or does not offer the right platform for your particular piece, then you will probably take the step of organising your own showcase, which will require you to step into territory usually inhabited by a producer. Don't fear, there are no monsters here. Producing revolves around common sense and hard work; there are no financial dark arts up the sleeve or poisoned blades in the spats.

If organising your own showcase, these are the matters to tick off:

- Decide what form of showcase is appropriate. Should it be a rehearsed reading, a staged reading, a without-decor performance or a staged excerpt? Knowing what you want to achieve will be crucial to obtaining maximum benefit.

Equally, having grounded expectations will help you target feasible, beneficial outcomes. Know who you want to attend and why, and what successful next steps would look like. Setting your heart on Sonia Friedman arriving and declaring her intention to produce a West End run is probably doomed to disappointment.

• Be canny with finances and draw up a budget. In other words, know how much you are willing to lose. Sadly, the chances of attracting funding for a showcase of a new play by an emerging writer are small (though see the tips on making funding applications in the chapter 'Moving On'). Your best chance will probably be a crowdfunding campaign that taps into the kindness of friends and family.

Regardless of where the money comes from, you'll need to cover hire of a venue for rehearsals and performance, printing of scripts and programmes, hospitality for guests, and fees, or at very least expenses, for director and actors. After all, a showcase will usually be to promote a writer; while an actor may appreciate some exposure, they're less likely to gain significantly and should not be left out of pocket.

Obtaining costings for most of these can be done by ringing around different suppliers (haggle once you have some comparative figures), while the rates of remuneration for creatives can be accessed on the ITC's (Independent Theatre Council) excellent website. If the first total you calculate makes you blanch, then locate areas that can be trimmed down, starting with the hospitality (contrary to popular opinion, theatre-makers will assess your writing the same whether they have wine or tap water in hand). Protect creative fees as long as you can. Ultimately, do not commit to losing a penny more than you can afford, because there will be no guaranteed gains from this venture.

- Organise a venue for both rehearsals and showcase, staying within budget. Usually it's best to hold a showcase at a recognisable venue. It's vital that this be easily accessible, with good transport links. Resist the temptation to book a grand, large venue; the cost will be exorbitant and showcases will seldom draw enormous crowds. Studio spaces are ample and affordable.

- Selecting a venue will depend upon which are available at the best dates and times. We'd suggest seeking a slot on a weekday afternoon at least eight weeks away. The latter allows time to make invitations and dodge clashes in busy diaries; the former maximises the appeal.

  Often people assume that hosting evening or weekend events will give the best impression, as these tally with the schedule of professional productions, but this is misguided. Theatre professionals already have to sacrifice enough evenings and weekends to attend shows and rehearsals. Slate your showcase for a weekday afternoon. The appeal of popping out after lunch, justified in checking out some new work after a productive morning, is stronger than abandoning one's loved ones on a Saturday to take a punt on a random reading.

- Confirm cast and creatives. You may choose to direct it yourself, but usually an outside eye is helpful and allows the writer just to focus on the script. (See the chapters on 'Working with Collaborators' and 'Going into Production' for tips on how to recruit these people.)

  Be clear from the outset what the engagement dates and financial terms are; never elide or obscure the fact it is only a showcase, and don't speculate about potential outcomes beyond your control. Stick to the known facts and no one can be disappointed or resentful.

  If you are handling recruitment, you could try using Spotlight, the online casting resource used by professionals. It has a hefty subscription charge, however, so you could save money by using Casting Call Pro instead – though the calibre of actors isn't necessarily as high.

The benefit of a relatively small commitment (most showcases only rehearse for a day or two) is that in-demand actors may sign up if they're free between bigger jobs and like the play. Many brilliant actors relish developing new plays; it can't hurt to ask.

Send the script alongside an offer. If you are auditioning, then make clear what 'sides' of the script the actor should prepare. Deciding whether or not an actor can reasonably be asked to audition for a short engagement is a sensitive matter; calling in a recent drama-school graduate with no credits is fine, but trying to get Idris Elba to audition for a one-day gig in a pub theatre would almost certainly be futile. Offering him the part, with a careful explanation why you think he's perfect for it, might just work…

- Issue personalised invitations, preferably four weeks in advance. It may be time-consuming, but writing individually leads to a far better result. Pestering busy people by phone is seldom welcome; emails are always best. If impossible to uncover on a company website, then make contact on Twitter and request an email address to which an invitation can be sent.

Keep the invitation itself concise and informative; include an image, if relevant, otherwise just give the date, time, venue, anticipated running time, one hundred words of blurb about the play (mentioning any recognisable cast or creatives) and perhaps sixty words about yourself. Resist any bold claims and use clear and honest language. Provide a nice explanation about why you'd like this person to attend. If you mention their work, be specific. It is always easy to see when somebody has picked a random title from your back catalogue, claiming they enjoyed it while just regurgitating the show copy. Don't attach a CV or script.

If uncertain how to devise your ideal guest list, research key personnel with artistic or literary responsibilities at new-writing companies (some of which are listed in the appendices). You could also approach freelance producers and agents; to navigate this field, look up those who produced or represent writers whose work you admire.

Keep your list updated as responses come. Don't be disheartened if you don't get many; it's the norm. Send a follow-up email a week or so before the showcase to anyone who hasn't replied, and a reminder to those who have. If someone can't make it, offer to send them the script or a recording instead.

- Showcases tend to work better in more intimate venues; there's little point booking a four-hundred-seat venue when only fifty guests are expected. Have friends and family primed to step in if the house is looking thin. There are few things more stressful than performing to a handful of VIPs and rows of empty seats. If it's bench seating, then aim to be around 75 per cent full, leaving space for guests to feel comfortable, not crammed. If it's individual seating, then aiming for capacity is fine.

- Keep an eye on rehearsals to iron out any confusions and provide any rewrites; one of the key purposes of rehearsals and a reading is to learn what works and what doesn't. In organising the showcase, never lose sight of the fact that the performance needs to be as strong as possible. Don't let producing duties distract you.

- Sometimes people record a reading so that video or audio footage can be shared afterwards, but only do this if you can guarantee the quality, or if the show must be seen rather than merely read (e.g. a musical or spoken word poetry). Generally sharing a well-presented script will be preferable to grainy film on a wobbly video recorder; recording live shows is a real art! If you must do so, review your set-up carefully and check the equipment and positioning are optimum.

- Be relaxed and unobtrusive at the showcase. If industry guests have attended, you've done your job. By all means welcome them with warm appreciation, but don't feel like you need to shepherd them around or launch into detailed reflections on the play. Don't panic if they rush off afterwards to another appointment; this is usual.

- Consolidate. Follow up with those who attended with a short, appreciative email and a request for feedback; they should certainly provide some notes and these may serve as the basis of an ongoing relationship. For those who couldn't make it but at least replied, do ask if they would like to read the script. The showcase is a real investment of time and money, so exploit it to the hilt.

These steps should help deliver a successful showcase. Managing your own expectations and being clear to collaborators and guests are at the heart of everything. Really, it's no more than common sense and common courtesy!

Things to Bear in Mind

Whatever route you follow, here are answers to some of the most pressing questions facing writers as they attempt to share their scripts.

Who is on a reading team?

Relatively few readers work for a company in a full-time capacity. There may be a designated literary manager overseeing the department, which in practice means an obnoxiously large amount of admin and spreadsheets. Most readers, however, are freelancers, dabbling in reading while building careers as directors, producers or writers. Do not assume that your script has been laid on a gleaming silver tray and presented to an ascetic, meditative reader by a smartly uniformed and astonishingly coiffured porter. It will have been emailed over as part of a barrage of scripts, clicked through and skimmed at offensive hours of the day and night. You cannot expect a swift response, or detailed notes, from an unsought submission, because the infrastructure of a reading team is simply not able to provide this.

What you can hope for is a response, and that the reading team is sufficiently trained and diverse to respond to a wide range of scripts. If this is not so, then the company needs to improve. Papatango's reading team – twenty at the time of going to press – are all theatre professionals and complete an intensive reading assessment (with a hundred applications for every place, it's almost as competitive as bagging a production!). 50 per cent identify as female and 25 per cent are people of colour. Most companies seek similar stats. A range of perspectives are needed to recognise a range of voices.

Theatre has often failed to achieve this, hence the relative scarcity of female, ethnic minority, working-class or regional artists on our stages. Your script may be vulnerable to being misunderstood by a reader from a different background. But reading teams are growing more diverse, and provided they are sufficiently trained, should assess good writing purely as good writing. Of course, anyone has the right to ask, politely, what process and safeguards a company has in place to ensure this.

How persistent should I be?

Literary departments that still accept unsolicited submissions are under huge strain – so don't demand a response immediately. Hassling overworked people juggling multiple responsibilities – because no one simply gets paid to read scripts; literary managers often have to chip in with administration and sometimes fundraising and producing – is not a recipe for success. It can be frustrating to wait, but imagine how vexing it can be to a stressed reader to be bombarded with emails demanding a swift response to a script at the bottom of a teetering, gigantic pile. Do you want to provoke that kind of annoyance in the people assessing your plays?

Respect cuts both ways. Playwrights absolutely deserve honest and polite acknowledgements from those to whom they entrust their hard work; in exchange, they need to recognise that the sheer demand and strain on people who still accept unsolicited submissions is intense, and there is always a backlog to work through.

We'd suggest that if there has been no acknowledgement at all after four weeks, it's reasonable to follow up to ask if the script was received safely. For a proper response or feedback, you may need to wait up to six months (although some companies will respond more quickly; at Papatango we tend to do so within three months). If you do need to follow up, be polite. Certainly don't start cracking your whip after a fortnight.

How should I react to rejection?

Let's be clear. Every single artist will experience rejection at some stage. This is especially true of theatre, as there will be endless variables, many outside a writer's control, determining whether their script lands favourably: other programming commitments; the long-term vision of a company; the effect of cuts to artist-development programmes; the list goes on. Understand this, and you'll realise that it is virtually inevitable that even the best writers will sometimes be rejected. It isn't necessarily a comment on your writing.

Knowing this doesn't make it any easier to live with rejection, but being prepared in advance will help you to carry on, to keep sending that script out. Ultimately, it only needs to land with one person, and everything can flip from despair to joy.

Generally, if you are sent a rejection message, you don't need to reply. If you do, then content yourself with a polite acknowledgement. The temptation may be to respond defensively, or take up the cudgels, but what good will that do? Souring any future relationship for the sake of wounded pride is not smart. Most especially, accusing the company of some kind of bias or other flaw in their selection process without solid evidence is at best injudicious and at worst smacks of prejudice. The most egregious instance, which is becoming wearily common, is when white male writers complain of 'positive discrimination' affecting their chances. The implicit assumption is that if a person of colour earns a programming slot or commission, it is not entirely on merit. This is a grotesque insult, and also profoundly misguided, as there is hardly a dearth of white men having plays produced. Do not mistake a dilution of long-standing privilege for active oppression. That said, if you have cause to feel hard done by for any genuine reason, do make contact with the company; just take care to express it in a way that doesn't malign other artists.

Rejections are not always dead-ends. If there is an invitation to further correspondence, then that is a huge positive! There is a world of difference between the rejection that flatly dismisses the play, and the rejection that expresses an interest in other work or invites further discussion. This indeed is barely a rejection at all; getting a foot in the door is a big achievement. So, always look for the positives, and don't burn any bridges, however hurt you may feel.

Believe in yourself. Sometimes others won't, which is all the more reason that you must.

One script or ten?

Writers often ask whether they should have a stash of plays ready to share. There seems to be a common perception that the more scripts in circulation, the greater the chances of success. Numerically, perhaps; artistically, perhaps not.

The simple fact is that quality not quantity counts. If you are in a position to perfect more than one play to your complete satisfaction, then by all means put the work out there, but do not impose this pressure of output upon yourself; if you only have the time or resources to work on one play to a high level, that's not a limitation. It's far better to hone one script rigorously than it is to flood inboxes with multiple, half-formed plays. Readers will remember your name. If they associate it with botched jobs, you may find that reputation hard to shake.

The notion of needing lots of 'product' ready to hand probably derives from the very sensible understanding that if a script is noticed, it's likely to lead to a request to see more of the writer's work. In that sense, having a flurry of plays with which to follow up on any spark of interest might be handy, keeping you firmly at the front of the reader's mind and establishing your commitment and range of ideas. Equally, however, if someone liked your script enough to enquire about reading more, they will wait. After all, an expression of interest is not a commission, so they can make no demands – and they will assuredly be focused on other projects in the meantime. Taking a while to follow up is no bad thing. Indeed, you could even ask for a quick chat about your proposed next project, to build on their interest and involve them in your creative process. Asking for meetings is never unreasonable.

If you do have more than one play in good enough shape to share, then it may still be advisable not to bombard the same company with them all at once. Readers will be able to get a sense of whether your writing is of interest from one play; asking them to trawl through several plays may give the impression of desperation, and certainly be a drain on their time. Instead, send a particular play to the company it suits best. If you have a story with a very specific setting, it may land well with a local theatre; if you have a story that plays with form and theatricality, somewhere like the Royal Court would seem a good fit. Use your range of scripts to target companies strategically.

The key principles are to submit with sensitivity and to focus on quality.

Do I need an agent?

This is a question that often preoccupies emerging playwrights. It's understandable. Attaining an agent is a clear validation of writing talent and by its very nature puts the act of playwriting on to a professional basis. But this does not mean that you *need* an agent; indeed, it doesn't even mean that you *should* have an agent.

Accepting representation is a major creative step; it is a collaboration that ought to shape a career profoundly, and should therefore not be rushed. Equally, an agent will not improve your chances of having a script produced; not even the most silver-tongued can persuade a producer to invest in a play if they are wavering (and nor should they; if you end up with an hesitant producer the play will suffer). An agent is there to help refine a script during development, provide moral and artistic support, and protect a writer's interests when productions or commissions are negotiated. They will usually drum up interest or share your script directly with decision-makers, and receiving a script from a respected agent will encourage a response. Their connections might get you meetings and a foot in the door, but ultimately the onus will always be on you and your work. An agent is helpful but not vital.

Writers usually only land representation after they have shared their scripts with some success, using the techniques and advice of this chapter. Good agents won't risk producers' respect for their judgement by bombarding them with rough scripts from unknowns, and they won't sign writers on a whim; they wait to see industry figures taking note first. Simon Stephens has shared his rejection letter from Mel Kenyon, a renowned literary agent, to prove that a writer–agent relationship only gets ratified once both parties are satisfied (it ends happily, as he did eventually sign with Mel). So, in a word: you do not need an agent to share your script. In fact, you are unlikely to bag an agent until you have already earned some industry credits under your own steam. Therefore, prioritise approaches to companies and focus on sharing your script rather than agonising over finding an agent to do it for you. (The role of agents is discussed further in the chapters on 'Working with Collaborators', 'Making Deals' and 'Going into Production'.)

What am I pushing?

Finally, understand what ask you are making of a venue or producer. Do you want them to read your script as an introduction to your work and with an eye on future collaborations? Or is this an invitation to develop and produce the play? Is this a potential world premiere, or are you hoping for a professional production of a play that's previously run the gamut of amateur or fringe productions? In short, what kind of proposal are you making and how should you frame this to give yourself the best chance of success?

The classic model is simply whizzing a script in as an unsolicited submission and letting the play speak for itself. This is what we'd recommend in nine out of ten cases. Whatever extraneous information you add, be it information on its history at scratch nights or the development process, is only likely to complicate matters. These may even be used as reasons for a decision-maker to say no. Of course, if some big names are attached, or if there has been a previous showcase or run that earned some nice reviews, you may include these as a marker of quality (see the chapter on 'Reflecting'). Just consider how much, if any, information is needed to supplement the script – and make sure that this fits with your ask.

Sometimes writers accompany a script submission with a description of the director/designer/cast they've assembled. This is natural; often scripts have been tried out in scratch nights or workshops, other artists have become enthused, and the playwright naturally sees this as a step forward. A degree of loyalty to those who have been part of the journey thus far is also creditable.

Certainly, in some cases the accrual of other artists is like the grit that nurtures a pearl. It may well be appropriate to pitch a script with a director or cast attached to a fringe festival with lots of slots to fill, or a receiving house that hires out its space, keen to be assured that whatever they programme will be delivered. Larger producing organisations, however, will seldom be drawn to scripts that are already halfway to production. As we noted in the section on organising showcases, most producers prefer to lessen the risk on a new play by assembling a crack creative team they can trust. Learning that the playwright has already made job offers on the producer's behalf doesn't inspire confidence; for every untried or unfamiliar artist involved, the risk factor leaps exponentially. Of course, if you have a name artist attached it's a different matter – nonetheless, the pleasure for most producers is in shaping a play creatively. Few of us welcome being asked to pay for someone else's show.

So, be aware of what you are asking for. Someone to develop you as an artist, or someone to come on board a project you've already begun? The nature of the ask will affect whom you approach and how you make the approach – if you have got several creatives on board, a showcase is almost certainly better than an unsolicited submission, as you are pitching more than just a script.

If reading this has suddenly clicked a switch in your brain, and you've realised that you haven't been asking venues to produce a new script but to host a ready-formed production, then you have two pathways. You can explain to the other artists that you need to put the script forward on its own for now, and revert to the model of an unsolicited submission that's completely open to development. Or you can change how you're pitching it, to convince a producer why you are working with these people and what they offer to the project.

If neither of these are working, then there is a third option. Just go the whole hog and produce the thing yourself…

Self-Producing

Just as you shouldn't depend upon an agent, you may decide to go it alone as a producer in order to get your script noticed, or because you know the artists and collaborators you want to work with (see the chapter on 'Working with Collaborators').

As a consequence of the dearth of programming of emerging playwrights, artists are increasingly producing their own work, donning hats that more conventionally belong to directors, producers or publicists (see the next chapter for these roles and their relationship to a playwright). Often this is done to kick-start a project, attract attention, and ultimately hand over to a professional producer down the line. But not always. Sometimes writers self-produce throughout and achieve a project that works brilliantly in its own right.

It's worth reaching out to specialist producers before going down this route; combining the roles of playwright and producer (and perhaps more) is a big undertaking, bringing all manner of extra challenges. If, however, no producers are responding or willing to take a risk on a new artist, or you don't feel that they adequately understand the play, or you need to do more to prove the project has legs before they come on board, then self-producing is a completely respectable option.

Self-producing is a spectrum: at one extreme, it means running the entire project, from fundraising to recruitment to negotiating with venues to handling publicity; at the other, it may mean leaving traditional, day-to-day producing tasks to a designated producer, having been the initial driver in finding a venue, raising money, and making the project possible.

Be very careful in considering what kind of role you want in self-producing. Producing is a specialist and hugely wide-ranging job. It makes or breaks a play. We'd suggest that the less full-on end of the spectrum is probably a wiser place to situate yourself, allowing more time to focus on writing once the project is safely launched, whilst retaining a degree of control. Operating as sole producer with multiple responsibilities entails the risk of botching artistic and production tasks, simply from being overstretched.

Finding enthusiastic producers willing to take on some of the responsibilities of a project is not as hard as it once was. Producing courses are springing up – Birkbeck, the Royal Central School of Speech & Drama and Mountview all run formal accreditations, while organisations like Stage One support aspiring producers. These provide useful databases.

The manifold elements of producing are too substantial to tackle here. A good place to start is James Seabright's *So You Want To Be A Theatre Producer?*

Case Study: Nina Raine

A highly successful writer, having been commissioned by the National Theatre, Hampstead Theatre, Out of Joint and the Bridge Theatre, as well as several TV companies, Nina Raine made her breakthrough with a production of her first play *Rabbit* at the Old Red Lion Theatre, a sixty-seat room above a dingy pub. The reviews were strong and a transfer to New York followed.

This fairytale success was, to an extent, self-made: Nina wrote and directed the piece, and although she had a producer, she instigated many elements of the project herself. The lesson seems clear: if others won't take on a new play, then don't fear to make it yourself.

Yet there is more to this success story than sheer guts and talent. Nina already had a reputation as a director behind her, and a name that audiences and reviewers recognised; she knew the industry and the roles of a director and producer; she had planned to devote herself to this project and was fortunate to have some money to put towards it. These attributes were major factors in enabling her success.

So, understand the significant demands and risks of self-producing, and seriously consider whether or not you can meet them.

One cautious note to sound is that if you do self-produce, build your own fee for both writing and producing into the project.

Everyone should be paid – the instigator as well as the cast. (There are some opportunities that exist purely to support writers; see the chapter 'Moving On'.) Nonetheless, in an ideal world, a playwright self-produces as a means to an end, as part of a wider strategy to gain traction in the industry. Long-term self-producing occludes the writer's role and risks detracting from the artistic focus.

Plunging into self-producing as both an emerging writer and a producer is doubling the risk. Before starting the journey, do all you can to prepare and give yourself the best possible shot. Be inspired by the success of others, but don't dismiss the horror stories of bankruptcy or heartbreak; producing, after all, is about weighing the risks.

ACT TWO:
MAKING THE SHOW

Once you've learned the skills of playwriting, polished and shared the resulting script, and been programmed, it may seem like the hard yards are over. In a sense, yes: only one in a thousand scripts will come to fruition, so getting to this stage, hopefully *the* stage, is a remarkable achievement.

In another sense, however, only now can the really vital work begin: as long as a script is contained within the relatively safe circuit of submissions and scratches, there is always the reassurance that it is not yet necessary to perfect a rehearsal draft or face the glare of public scrutiny. Once someone has programmed the script, that changes. A playwright must switch to production mode, requiring a different set of skills. That means working as hard as ever.

This act discusses the various processes that prepare a script for production: how to collaborate with theatre-makers and understand different roles; what to expect from and how to negotiate deals and rights; R&D and how to get the most from it; finally, what to do once a show is in rehearsals, previews and production. Making your script into a play – that's what this act in a playwright's career is all about.

WORKING WITH COLLABORATORS

Even once on the path to a production, a new script is seldom if ever 'finished'; playwrights should expect to be part of the process throughout, tinkering with lines that actors find troublesome, discussing production aesthetics with a director, letting designers know what references they had in mind at key moments, and debating promotion strategies with producers. You must conduct all these relationships with sensitivity, to give collaborators the space and trust to flourish and bring your script from page to stage.

This requirement, to be available, engaged and alert, yet open-minded and unobtrusive, is hard. Playwrights spend so much of their time working in solitary conditions, even those who rely on devising or co-writing processes, that relinquishing sole control over a script is inevitably challenging. No one gets collaboration right all the time, but the playwrights who get it right most of the time enjoy the most success.

'Working with Collaborators' is trotted out as a buzzword in lots of discussions about making art. It doesn't, it can't, mean anything precise; the collaborative process will differ each time. There are nonetheless certain basic expectations and responsibilities underpinning each relationship; appreciating these will allow you to build tailored, effective collaborations on an individual basis.

Who Collaborates with a Playwright?

The most important relationships that you will experience in making a play are with a producer, director, actor and designer. This is not a comprehensive list of everyone with whom you will have dealings, but most other roles – such as casting directors, stage managers or publicists – will report to one of these people, rather than engage directly with the playwright. It is the people in these four roles with whom you will chiefly work; they in turn will represent your ideas to the rest of the production team.

Producer

This is a crucial relationship. Producers are the head honcho of any production – unless the artistic director of a venue or company is also involved, in which case the buck will ultimately stop with them. Even in this case, the designated producer usually runs the show on a day-to-day basis.

The producer helps develop the script and shape the creative vision of the project. They raise the funds, organise the venue, recruit the team to turn the script from abstract idea to concrete show, pay everyone's fees, oversee press and marketing, and keep an eye on a host of other matters. At least, if they're any good they do. A producer will do more than anyone else to determine whether your script becomes a successful play. They will also influence future opportunities; a single producer may well commission one playwright again and again, because a high-quality writer who can be trusted to deliver is a real find.

Lest such influence seem daunting and hierarchical, remember that producers of new writing are invariably passionate. Producers with a purely pragmatic bent tend not to dabble in new plays; with a few honourable exceptions, commercial theatre-makers stick to musicals and revivals. The days of world premieres opening straight into the West End are long gone. That means the producers you meet will seldom if ever be looking to make a profit; instead, they will probably rely on subsidy from grant-makers or donors to make a new play possible. They undertake this for their own creative satisfaction (and to earn a living, hopefully). They are motivated by the same passion as any artist, will expect a respectful and creative collaboration, and don't regard playwrights as simply providers of lucrative scripts.

A playwright's relationship with a producer will normally begin early in the process; it may even be the first collaboration. Producers tend to inaugurate productions, and often spend time developing a play before bringing others on board to take it to the stage. They give notes, discuss options for the creative team or appropriate venues, and set deadlines for drafts. It is in your interest to respect these contributions. Otherwise, how can they understand the project well enough to recruit the right team, allocate funding, and effectively promote it?

So, understand the producer as a creative figure, don't be afraid to be open about creative or personal issues, and above all do not buy into the cliché that they are at heart a cynical moneybags. A producer of a new play takes an enormous risk, and has to work hard to pull it off; if you don't collaborate effectively, you may compromise their ability to pull a show together.

Respecting the producer and meeting your responsibilities is therefore a given. In return, you have the right to expect that a producer be respectful, committed and receptive. If you aren't keen on a note, or are struggling on a draft, a producer should provide constructive advice and be willing to talk it through.

A producer should also be transparent. Before any collaboration begins, they should draw up a fair commissioning/production agreement (see the chapter on 'Making Deals') to outline responsibilities, rights and expectations. They should thereafter keep you informed of the progress being made towards production. Don't be backward in enquiring about this, but don't be frustrated or sceptical if there's little to report. While a few producers relish keeping their cards close to their chest, most are open. It's just that sometimes a producer can do no more than wait on a response from a funder or venue.

Once a script has moved from development into rehearsals, a producer will probably fade into the background, now focused on marketing and project management, while you work more closely with director, designers and actors. Don't be disheartened at this shift; if anything crops up that requires the producer's attention, they should be involved immediately. Usually there will be regular chances to discuss progress, and you have the right to ask a producer for help inviting industry figures and for advice on how to exploit any success (see the chapters 'Going into Production' and 'Moving On'). A producer should never seem out of reach; if they do, it's a sign the relationship needs more work.

A collaboration with a producer is perhaps the trickiest that a playwright has to manage. Unlike other collaborators, who tend to be engaged for precise periods with clear remits, a producer–playwright collaboration can stretch for years, abruptly change dynamic as the producer's role turns from development to production, and then potentially revert back if new commissions or a transfer become likely. Navigating this long-term, shifting collaboration, especially as money is an element, is not easy. Operate with respect and care, and expect positive and creative contributions from the producer in return.

Director

This relationship is equally important. The director will give life to your script. They will have ultimate responsibility for casting, design aesthetics and, of course, the action on stage. Beyond shaping the play definitively, this relationship has wider ramifications for a writer's future. Directors pitch to venues and producers, and a strong director–playwright association often generates new productions.

A good director can elevate a script; a bad director can sink it. It is vital that this relationship is built on trust, which can only be earned if there is mutual understanding. Sometimes an ostensibly excellent director simply fails to click with a script; whatever their technical virtues, this is usually fatal. Finding the right director is essential.

Do so in conjunction with the producer, who may have a director in mind from the off. Even if this is so, keep an eye on directors you admire and advocate for anyone you deem a good fit. Think about the directors whose work you have admired, or who have staged successful productions by writers with whom you feel an affinity; give your thoughts to the producer, who can make contact to check availability. Once you have, together, drawn up a shortlist, send the candidates the script and information and see if they will meet to discuss it.

You should have some say in appointing the director, although ultimately this rests with the producer. When making this joint decision, look for somebody who suits the piece, not necessarily the candidate with the most impressive credits. It doesn't matter if someone has directed at the National Theatre if they can't convincingly discuss your script.

A good director should serve the play, not impose any ego, and yet also have original ideas that open it up beyond the words on the page. This is quite an ask! It can be hard to discern at an interview, but useful things to consider include:

- What do they think your play is about and are they sufficiently enthused and clear-sighted?

- How do they see it working in production, and are their proposed aesthetic and casting choices appropriate?

- How do they envisage the relationship with the writer?

Once appointed, a director's collaboration with a playwright becomes paramount across several stages: pre-production preparation; casting; rehearsals and previews; finally throughout the production run.

During preparation, a good director will probably have notes on developing the script. It is important you are open and receptive. That doesn't mean jumping on their command – you should always feel able to stand your ground – but remember that ultimately you want the same outcome. If you appointed the director carefully, you should have good reason to trust them. Try not to be defensive if they keep proposing changes. Remember: if they didn't like the play they wouldn't have accepted the project. It's just that as a script heads towards the practicalities of staging, new discoveries are inevitable. An open conversation about notes will enhance the director's understanding and ability to direct it in the room.

Once these conversations are completed, plans will turn to casting. This is the preserve of the director and producer. The script and notes should have given them plenty of insight into how you conceive the characters, and should be all the influence on casting that a playwright needs. Nonetheless, writers often join auditions at the recall stage to help make a final verdict. You are also entitled to ask about progress and proffer opinions throughout.

The same goes for rehearsals. That does not mean you should expect to be ever-present, but you should be involved on key days – the initial read-through, the first full run, dress rehearsal and previews (see the chapter 'Going into Production' for an explanation of these). There is no question of the importance of the writer's input on these occasions. Outside these, the degree to which a playwright will be present varies, according to the director's preference and the writer's availability and inclination. Sometimes playwrights are in constant attendance, sometimes not.

Don't be downhearted if the director doesn't want you in the room every day; each director will have a different approach and there is no definitive process. Sometimes a playwright's presence can inhibit the cast from asking questions of the script or detract from the director's authority; sometimes the playwright is vital to explain technicalities or support directorial choices.

Whatever the process, a director should keep you regularly updated and involved. Equally, if you feel something is important to the play, then make it known. All your notes on the production, whether they relate to acting or design or staging, should be made to the director; do not undermine them by going straight to a member of their creative team or cast.

The key to the director–playwright relationship is to remember that you are both of equal worth to the production. It is important not to feel intimidated by your director, and equally as important not to make them feel that your script is sacrosanct. You are each specialists, with particular authority over discrete realms. Should there be an insuperable difference of creative opinion, then the producer should intervene to affect a resolution. Nonetheless, ultimate responsibility for the script always resides with the playwright, and this should be built into any contract or licence (see the chapter on 'Making Deals').

A thought-provoking example can be found in the playwright Simon Gray's diaries detailing his time working with his long-term director Harold Pinter, honestly capturing the frustrations and tensions of making new plays, but also the productive and nourishing nature of a strong collaboration. It's a model from which we can all learn.

Dramaturg

Not every production will have a dramaturg but it is becoming more common, influenced by theatre traditions from elsewhere in Europe and America. Dramaturgy covers a wide range of practices (see the 'Writing for Theatre' chapter). Generally, in Britain it tends to mean someone who provides notes on a play and is not necessarily retained beyond this, whereas in other countries a dramaturg is often continually involved in every stage of the production as a research and aesthetics specialist.

A dramaturg may well be involved in a play under the guise of a literary manager, who brings a writer into a company and develops the play as a commission. Or they may be a specialist hired specifically by the producer to lead the development process. Whatever the situation, their job is to help the playwright and the script to flourish.

In many ways, a dramaturg will be your closest ally, as it is their job to understand your intention and to convey that to collaborators and ultimately the audience. They act as a go-between for the playwright and the rehearsal room, ensuring the script's vision is upheld in the production. A dramaturg should know the play better than anyone, perhaps even the writer.

A good dramaturg will act as a friendly critic, questioning the decisions in the script and challenging you to make the play stronger. They will also contribute research and shape the script with an eye on the needs of a production. At Papatango, George acts as dramaturg. He will take all of the notes from Chris, the director, and anybody else involved in the project, and filter them into something actionable for the playwright, to prevent the writer being assailed by different voices. He will fight the playwright's corner if a note isn't right, and accompany the playwright throughout development, rehearsals and production.

It is important that you are able to trust your dramaturg implicitly. The challenge is that, unlike a director, a playwright often will not have a say in appointing their dramaturg. If, say, a script is picked up by a new-writing company, the likelihood is that the in-house literary manager will be the de facto dramaturg. A playwright therefore needs to work hard from the first to establish a fruitful relationship with a dramaturg.

It is permissible to refuse the services of a dramaturg if they are offered to you, especially if the nominated dramaturg is attached to the company rather than an individual hired for your specific project – but bear in mind that many companies may then be uneasy at staking a production on a script that hasn't followed their preferred process. A good approach is not to reject a dramaturg outright, but to ask to meet to discuss the development and production methodology; once you understand this, you will be able to explain why you don't require a dramaturg or outline what it is that your script needs instead – or even decide that actually, it may be worthwhile.

Designer

A playwright won't necessarily be directly involved with set, costume, lighting or sound designers, but these people may ask you for reference points. It is a designer's job to realise the world of the play, so picking the writer's brains for specific details is often helpful. They will want to serve the script but also have to make it work on stage (and within budget), which may lead to imaginative rather than literal representations. It is important to trust designers, as more often than not the results will be beyond your greatest expectations.

Set and costume designers tend to produce sketches and models of their proposed designs, which evolve as the process grows. A 'white card' model is an initial representation, open to amendments, before a final model box is made and sent to the builders. If you have specific thoughts integral to the staging or the world of the play, raise these with the director early. Equally, if something seems off in the costume sketches or white-card model of the set, then mention these before the designs are signed off. If you loathe the proposed design, it's no good waiting to speak up until it's been built. Any such notes should be channelled through the director.

Actor

A playwright's relationship with an actor can be one of the most rewarding parts of a production. These characters have floated around your head for a long time; now you meet the people who will embody them. Equally, however, it can be frustrating to see an actor interpret a character differently from your conception. It is vital to understand when to intervene in an actor's process – which should always be via the director – and when to allow space to explore.

Actors love to ask playwrights questions. The writer is a fount of knowledge, providing insights into character beyond the words on the page. When giving backstory to an actor, make sure it is relevant; telling them an obscure fact from a previous draft that is no longer part of that character's arc might muddy the waters! This should also be a symbiotic exchange; you should take the opportunity to question the actor on their character(s). A playwright has to focus on so many elements of the story that sometimes palpable gaps in a character's journey, or implausible lines or actions, are somehow overlooked. It is an actor's job to plug these holes. Their notes can be incredibly valuable.

That said, if you are in the rehearsal room, be patient with your actors. Remember that the purpose of rehearsals is to allow them to explore their characters. If they aren't quite getting a line immediately, give them time. Don't start cutting or changing lines unless certain that the writing is the problem.

Tread carefully at every stage, because a playwright's interactions with an actor should never undermine the actor's relationship with the director. If you have particular notes on their performance, or if some aspect of their work has made you reassess the script, approach the director first. After all, the actor might have been directed to perform it a certain way, so it is best not to cause divisions by leaping in. Defer to the director's authority in rehearsals, and prioritise that relationship.

These collaborations are at the heart of a playwright's experience of development and production. Always consider notes before responding, think carefully before suggesting anything to collaborators, and respect the appropriate channels. It is inevitable that at points there will be miscommunication, even confrontation, but always focus on being constructive. If a relationship becomes tense, do not despair, repair – your play depends upon it.

Case Study: Collaborating on a Papatango Prize-winner

Every year we select a new play, from 1,300 to 1,500 submissions, to win the Papatango New Writing Prize. Within eight months it is developed, produced, published, and the winner launched on a stellar new career. Prize productions have chalked up OffWestEnd, Critics' Circle and Royal National Theatre Foundation awards and the scripts have gone on to new productions in over twenty countries as well as the West End. Clarity of collaboration is at the heart of this success.

Our process is simple – and, crucially, communicated to the playwright from the first. Initially, we spend two months working, one-to-one, with the writer. George, as dramaturg, steers all notes and condenses feedback from a range of advisors into consistent, practical points.

Once we have taken the play through as many redrafts as necessary, we go into an R&D workshop. Here, George leads a team of carefully cast actors, chosen for enthusiasm and intelligence, as well as appropriate characteristics, interrogating choices and identifying holes. The writer makes notes, asks questions, and has time to rewrite or try out new ideas.

Then a fresh draft is undertaken. At this point, when we understand the script perfectly, we recruit a director, taking care with multiple interviews to find the right person. The writer is generally relieved to have fresh eyes look at the latest draft, and bring a pure production-perspective to bear, after several months of running the gauntlet of our questions. The director then takes charge of signing off the rehearsal draft, and going into casting and preparation. We, as producers, slip into production mode, recruiting the remaining creative team – with the director's approval – and getting the show ready.

Every stage works to clear timelines, and everyone's role is determined in advance. Crucially, everyone knows what happens when, and where responsibility resides. Really, that's all effective collaboration means.

But consider all the stages of this process that are vulnerable to confusion or tension. Say multiple people took advantage of access to the playwright to voice their personal opinions; the script could end up being torn in different directions. Or what if the workshop process were not led adequately, and the actors cavalierly rewrote sections or undermined the playwright? A range of nightmare scenarios are easily envisaged. The more you imagine, the easier it is to circumvent them.

How to Find Collaborators

Thus far we have discussed the collaborators you are likely to encounter if a script is picked up by a company or producer. But how does a writer find collaborators before or without this? After all, early input from another artist may make a huge difference to the script's eventual chances of being programmed.

Firstly, know what kind of collaborator you seek. Do you need a dramaturg to help with research and execution? Or is a director's eye required, to tease out possibilities of staging and visuals? Understanding this will make initiating fruitful collaborations easier.

To meet people who might bring these requisite skills to the party, identify practitioners whose work you appreciate – and be realistic. Rufus Norris is unlikely to take time out from running the National Theatre to help note a work-in-progress from a stranger.

You should also ask for recommendations from any other theatremakers you know. Informed matchmaking can lead to great connections.

Once you have a list of people who may be sympathetic, reach out. Most artists have an online presence that will enable you to obtain an email address or send a tweet. As a general rule of thumb, emails and Twitter are professional platforms on which it is permissible to initiate a conversation; Facebook and Instagram and the like are a little more personal and intimate, with more private information buried within their account, so it's best to avoid reaching out through these. Keep any messages friendly and concise, and don't attach anything other than a CV; leave it up to the recipient to request more. Be clear about the offer: is there any money involved, what kind of relationship is being proposed, and what is the state of the project? Do not exaggerate the opportunities. Be honest.

It's best not to message more than one or two people. For one thing, your list should be targeted; several names suggest too loose a search. For another, many artists know one another, discuss potential projects, and could be unimpressed if the approach seems blanket.

If you can't find anyone to approach, then attend theatre events. Some venues run networking events, while scratch nights can be a great way to talent-spot, and workshops connect budding theatremakers (see the 'Training' chapter). Start growing your network.

You can also put the word out on social-media platforms; groups like Playwriting UK on Facebook facilitate introductions, while many companies will retweet any pitch. This approach comes with the risk of being deluged by responses. Nonetheless, social media makes a game-changing difference to how creative networks form, and with the usual warnings about safety, it's too great a resource to ignore. Theatre is at heart a collaborative enterprise, so don't shy away, however daunting, from connecting with collaborators.

Working with Agents

A playwright's relationship with an agent is a peculiar thing. It is different from any other collaboration, and no two playwright–agent relationships are alike. Technically, an agent will be employed by you, as they earn a living by taking a cut of between

10 and 20 per cent of a writer's income, but it can often feel the other way around. A playwright has to pitch to an agent in most cases; persuading an agent to represent you can be a formidable task. Usually you will need not only impressive writing samples but proven successes, such as earning a residency or having had a fringe production. This is not to discourage novice writers from sending scripts to agents, but the likelihood is that this will at first lead to no more than a meeting, at best. Even if they like your work, most agents will wait to see concrete proof of your ability to attract industry attention before committing to representation.

Playwrights often regard representation as a vital step early in their career. It's understandable, as such validation is a huge confidence boost and a marker of professionalism. Frankly, however, it's usually not very helpful until an artist is at a later stage of their career. Agents seldom get clients work; it is the quality of the client's writing that does that. Your script will have just as good a chance of success coming from you as from an agent – although it may take longer and be a lonelier experience.

This is why seeking an agent is not something that should dominate your agenda. Better to put your energies into attaining opportunities and demonstrating your talent. In purely practical terms, an emerging playwright is unlikely to need an agent anyway. Agents tend to be most beneficial when an artist is ready for bigger opportunities with more resources at stake, as they can hustle for gigs and negotiate contracts.

That said, some rare agents do shape a playwright's practice. Many agents don't have the time, skills or inclination to provide dramaturgy, but some play a significant part in realising a writer's talent. These agents are infinitely valuable for a developing playwright – but they are even less likely to have space on their lists for an unproven artist.

As a general guideline, therefore, feel free to approach agents as soon as you have a script, but don't set your heart on representation. This is an introduction. As further opportunities materialise and you build a profile, these conversations will develop. The best agents will not rush to sign a playwright. Be prepared for a series of meetings, and to send several pieces of work, before any formal relationship is agreed.

This prolonged mating dance may seem elaborate, but it's a sensible process. An agent needs to understand their potential client and decide whether they want to invest time in their career, with no certainty of a return. Equally, you should remember that an agent is there to work for your interests, and assess any prospective agent carefully. You both want to ensure that you embark upon an enriching, mutually beneficial collaboration. After all, it may last for a professional lifetime. Far better to weigh up all options methodically than rush into an unsuitable partnership from which extrication will be painful and prolonged.

What is it, then, that a 'good' agent does? It can be anything, really, from critiquing scripts to sharing them with industry figures to negotiating contracts to setting up meetings with professionals and pitching for commissions. A playwright's rapport with an agent will develop over time, and the dynamic will be different according to need. Some writers want their agents to give copious notes, some only want moral support, some will simply ask that agents can negotiate a killer financial package; equally, some agents have no interest in nurturing the creative output of clients but focus only on commercial matters, while others insist on helping with scripts. This is why getting to know an agent first, to understand what kind of collaboration is proposed and what you actually need, is so crucial.

Here are some questions to ponder before signing with an agent:

• What other playwrights do they represent?

An agent with big names on the books may benefit you by association. That's no small thing – but it may also mean that you are a lower priority for them. It's a tricky balance to strike. Being signed by a hugely respected agent will unquestionably earn you more attention, but will they have the time to invest in you and build on that attention? An agent with a lower profile may be able to devote more time – and have more motivation – to win better chances for you. See how much time an agent seems willing to spare for a meeting, and what proposals they make about how to grow your career, rather than being dazzled by the famous names on their list.

- What kind of work, and how much, do their clients make?

  If an agent's writers are not very active, or commissions do not seem to be flowing in, that may raise doubts about the agent's efficacy. Even if an agent presides over busy writers, check that is relevant to you. If they represent writers predominantly working in a different field, this may suggest their knowledge or contacts are not entirely appropriate. You want to make sure your agent has the connections and nous to drive your particular interests forward.

- What offer are they making?

  An agent should be able to comment astutely on your work, and have clearly considered it with care. Agents should make concrete suggestions informed by their client as an individual. If an agent seems too ready to take you with minimal attention to your writing, or doesn't have to be wooed with good work, chances are that they aren't the right choice to look after your career. Equally, if an agent makes clear that they would focus on developing your creative skills, while you want someone to look after the financial aspects, or vice versa, then it may not be a good fit.

It goes without saying that you are well advised to approach several agents. Don't be indiscriminate – only contact agents who offer something appropriate – but as with sharing scripts, do not be tentative about opening multiple conversations at once. Only by meeting several agents will you be able to judge whom you prefer. (See the appendices for some suggestions.)

Once represented by an agent, you will need to establish a working collaboration. It's helpful to set targets, which might range from setting up meetings with producers to organising a showcase to promoting a script. In return, agents should set you deadlines for new projects, and chew possible ideas over, to make sure work is continually generated.

Growing to understand the rhythm of these mutual expectations takes time. A playwright should expect to meet their agent every few months to discuss progress and reflect on what is working and what isn't. Don't be afraid to explore new models. One writer we know agreed with his longstanding agent that she would no longer take a cut from his theatre commissions, as he earned all of these directly and was not satisfied with her handling of negotiations; she therefore refocused entirely on his screenwriting projects. As a playwright's collaboration with an agent is ongoing, unrestricted to any single project and any single outcome, such revisions are important. A playwright and an agent should continually stretch each other.

Insider's View: Kirsten Foster

There are almost as many different types of agent as there are types of writer. It's up to you to find out which agent is the best fit for you, depending on what you want and need to thrive. What your agent does for you will therefore vary, but it generally includes: advocating for your work, i.e. telling artistic directors and producers how fantastic your plays are; sending your scripts out; putting you up for jobs; arranging meetings and making introductions, not only with theatres but also from within their own client lists. If your play could benefit from a movement director, or you're looking for a composer, they will often be well placed to match you with one they already represent and think would be a perfect fit.

Agents also offer advice, both long- and short-term, listen to you, read your work, and give notes and feedback. They deal with contracts and make them the strongest they can be to protect your rights, and raise invoices to process your monies. If any tricky issues arise, they are there to mediate, trouble-shoot, negotiate. As well as being there to support you along the way, agents are also there to celebrate your successes: to be at your side during press nights and generally be your biggest fan.

I know it's the golden ticket, but unfortunately there isn't an algorithm to break down what it is that makes an agent decide to sign a writer. Being a self-starter, already having developed good relationships in the industry with directors/venues/producers, and being personable are all positive attributes. However, for me, it's all about the writing. It's essential that you and your agent have the same taste: when I take on a writer, it's because I love their writing. It's this that needs to be special: my heart rate must quicken while reading their play. I can admire a highly competent, savvy writer who has their finger on the zeitgeisty pulse, who may become hugely successful and earn bags of money – but I couldn't be their agent if their writing didn't excite me. It's got to be beautiful and – even in a gentle way – original.

You know that feeling of first catching sight of someone across a room, someone who becomes important in your life, with whom you might fall in love? It's the agenting equivalent of that. For me, taking on a writer is a long-term relationship. I hope in my sixties still to be working with the same wonderful writers I look after today.

Kirsten is an agent at Casarotto Ramsay & Associates Ltd.

MAKING DEALS

As the process of making a play begins, a playwright will encounter questions about financial remuneration, licensing, casting and creative team, and authority over changes to the script in rehearsals. Some of these were referenced in the previous chapter's analysis of the different collaborations you will manage. These are all sensitive matters, and it's imperative to have a formal written agreement that ensures clarity and mutual understanding, so that all involved are protected and nourished.

As with entering into any working relationship, establish a framework of rights and responsibilities. Whether it defines who has the moral right to claim authorship in a collaboration between a playwright and a dramaturg, or how royalties are divvied up, laying out a clear and transparent deal from the first can save much heartache and legal wrangling later.

It's surprising how often even relatively large professional organisations operate on somewhat lax terms. It's seldom because of any consciously shady practice; it's probably more because a lot of people working in the creative industries fear that imposing legalistic documents at the start of a process can stifle or intimidate an artist. Moreover, creative relationships often evolve gradually, which can be hard to enshrine in the precise language of a contract. These are mere niceties, however; the simple fact is that no one should enter into a working relationship without a mutually agreed, written arrangement. In a cynical light, it protects all parties and inhibits counter-claims or accusations; in a more positive light, it makes all parties feel secure and sets out a clear path of responsibilities that makes final success all the more likely. A good agreement should empower not just protect.

It is not your job to draft any contracts, unless you are also the producer (see the chapter on 'Getting Noticed'), but familiarity with some of the recurring points in any formal agreement will always be advantageous. This chapter therefore discusses what a typical agreement for a playwright might cover, how to arrange and negotiate it, the different commissioning and rights models available, and what an agent's role might be. It also covers deals with publishers.

What to Expect in an Agreement

It seems fitting to open this section with a disclaimer: we are not lawyers and we speak only from experience and observation in discussing some common details found in playwriting agreements. If there is ever any doubt as to a contract's terms then professional legal advice should be sought. Contact details for the Writers' Guild of Great Britain, the Independent Theatre Council and Equity are available in the appendices. All provide a fantastic service for arts professionals.

So, with that caveat, this section discusses the main points that it is useful to consider in an agreement. This is by no means exhaustive, but should provide helpful food for thought in setting out key terms for any proposed relationship. Be aware that not all of these will be relevant to every agreement.

Rights, licences, options and exclusivity

The nature of an agreement – and the remuneration deemed appropriate – will depend on whether it is providing a licence for performance or the option of acquiring such a licence, and whether or not it is a commission. Sound complicated? Don't worry, it's actually fairly simple.

If the agreement is purchasing the **rights** to an extant play, this is because a producer intends to produce it. The agreement will define the period in which this can be done, and acts as a **licence** for performance, specifying how long the producer's right to produce the play lasts and how many performances, and on what scale, they are entitled to mount. So, an agreement may state that a producer has the right to produce the play for X number of performances in the West End/regional tour/throughout the world by X date, after which all rights in the play revert to the playwright.

If a producer is interested in a script but not convinced a production will be feasible, an **option** is usually agreed instead of an outright licence. This means that the producer has the right to acquire a full licence for performance in exchange for further payment by a certain date, and in the meantime no one else can take on the licence; it functions like a deposit, reserving the property for a certain period.

A full **commission** usually includes a licence for production, should the producer deem the final script production-ready. Having paid a proper fee for a playwright to write a script, the producer should have the right to take this through to a show and potentially recoup on their investment. A smaller or **seed commission** is unlikely to include a full licence for production, as the remuneration paid is not sufficient; these occur when a producer is interested in a playwright, but not sufficiently confident that the script will be feasible for production to pay a full commission. In light of the smaller fee, the contract may instead stipulate the producer has the exclusive option to acquire a licence should they wish once the script has been completed, upon payment of a further sum (see the 'Remuneration' section below for guidance on rates).

Remember that neither a licence nor an option oblige a producer to stage the show; they simply now have the right to do so if they wish. Sometimes, at a commercial level, a producer may acquire the rights to a play in order to prevent a business rival capitalising on it, even if they themselves have no intention of staging it. In the subsidised or fringe sector, this is almost unknown; money is too tight, and goodwill and collaboration too important, to squander licensing fees so negatively. So, if a commercial producer acquires the rights, it may still be a long journey to production, if it happens at all; if a subsidised producer acquires them, the intention of production can be assumed, although it may not transpire.

Sometimes a commissioning budget has to be spent within the financial year, with no guarantee that a production budget will be available to produce any of the plays. So a licence or option, especially if paired with a full or seed commission, should be welcome signs of faith in your work and provide blessed cash, but a production may not necessarily follow.

Therefore, it is a fundamental rule that no writer should ever sign an agreement that gives a producer the rights or option to their play in perpetuity. The licence or option period is usually for only twelve, eighteen or twenty-four months, after which the producer will need to re-purchase the rights if they still intend to produce. At this point a playwright can reflect on whether they want the rights to their play to remain tied up, or whether it would benefit from wider availability.

The degree of exclusivity offered by the licence or option varies. Sometimes they apply worldwide, in effect guaranteeing the producer is the only person who can possibly produce the play; more usually, they apply only to one nation or region, meaning that productions outside this territory remain open. The different regions tend to be defined as: UK and Eire (excluding the West End); UK and Eire (including London's West End); Australia and New Zealand; Europe; USA and Canada; the rest of the world (glorious disdain there for most of the planet…).

The level of remuneration paid will reflect the extent of the licence or option; if a producer wants the exclusive rights to mount one thousand performances anywhere in the world for the next five years, a much greater fee would be appropriate than if the proposal were to mount five performances at a fringe venue in one region next month.

This assumes that it is a professional company seeking to acquire the licence or option; these tend to apply only to professional productions. Amateur rights are usually separate (and are either looked after by the agent, a rights licensor or the publisher). In the event that an amateur company are keen, such groups usually request a licence, as they know they want to stage the show, and as there will be little money involved, they tend to pay a fee for each proposed performance, depending on the size of the venue. They won't expect exclusivity or any of the privileges attendant upon a lucrative professional deal, so it may be possible to grant multiple amateur groups the performance rights simultaneously. This is not something to be scoffed at; several amateur productions running at once can comprise serious revenue, as well as deliver meaningful and moving new productions of your script.

Further options

Often included in professional deals is a clause that, should the producer mount the play for the minimum number of performances specified in the licence, they then have the automatic option to acquire the further rights to other regions. This is because if a play is a success, it's fair that the originating producer should be able to capitalise on this. Moreover, that producer is the likeliest person to realise a transfer or new production. This option tends to be relatively short, and will require the producer to pay a further sum to obtain the rights, but it means that the producer's interests and investment in any production are protected.

Remuneration

A playwright, like any other member of a production, should be paid. It's amazing and somewhat galling how often creative teams and cast are considered surplus to budgets. No matter how small the show and how stretched the fees, every contributor should be included in the financial calculation.

A playwright's remuneration takes two forms. The first is either a commission for the play, an amount determined by its length and the commissioning organisation's funding status (a new full-length play for the RSC would be due a much larger sum than a short play for an independent fringe theatre), or if the play already exists, a fee for the rights to produce it. For instance, if the play already exists (has been commissioned by another organisation whose rights have now expired, or was written by the playwright on their own initiative), then the producer will pay to obtain the rights, rather than offer a commission. A commission is only appropriate if the play is to be created at the producer's behest.

The second form is in addition to the commission/fee, and consists of a royalty from the box office, either calculated gross (this means before credit-card fees, VAT, taxes or any other charges are applied) or net (after such charges are applied). Again, the exact percentage of this royalty varies according to the scale of the show. Royalties are usually due within twenty-eight days of the last performance, although in practice it will depend how long it takes the venue to provide a box-office settlement. Current rates for both commissions and royalties can be checked on the WGGB or ITC websites.

Not all companies can afford to provide the full rates of both commission/fee and royalties, especially for a new play from an emerging playwright. New plays rarely sell as well as popular classics by a 'name' artist. Unless a company is subsidised, it's hard to pay an emerging writer the going rate for a new play with limited box-office potential. If a company were to invest that much money, chances are they would pick an artist who sells; less well-known writers usually have to negotiate a smaller deal. This is problematic, and has distressing consequences in terms of the demographics who can afford to pursue playwriting, but it is the truth.

Companies in receipt of subsidy should pay decent rates. That goes without saying – though alas, not all do. If you are in a position to be working with a large company, especially an NPO (National Portfolio Organisation, meaning they get a tranche of public funding guaranteed every year), then insist on proper pay.

Companies who are not in that position should start from the ideal rates and work out how close to these they can get; you should ask to review their financial model and see the figures, so that you and they together can agree a fee that is fair without unduly compromising the success of any production. Remember, a degree of risk is inherent to all theatre, and a company should have budgeted to pay the writer as well as possible, accepting the risk this brings – so don't be delicate about expecting decent remuneration. Equally, a writer ought to respect that taking on a new play is probably more of a financial stretch than churning out a play from Oscar Wilde's back catalogue, so be aware of the limitations that may be an inevitable reality. The key is transparency and an effort to find a balance from both sides – this is where an agent can be useful.

Schedule of payments

Does what it says on the tin – it is important to know what money is owed to whom, when. It helps the producer figure out cash-flow, means there can be no room for disgruntlement or resentment about paydays, and enables you to budget your life.

Moral rights and copyright

Regardless of whether an agreement offers a commission or a fee, issues a licence or an option, a clause that makes clear the named writer's moral right to claim authorship of the play is vital. Usually this will also stipulate that in the event of additions to the script being made in development or rehearsals, any such additions must be subject to your approval and any so agreed will accrue to your moral rights.

This is important, because new scripts go through so many changes and tweaks that credit could otherwise become a free-for-all, scrapping over who suggested what line. Equally, all copyright in the play should reside with the playwright; assigning a licence or an option in no way vests that copyright with the producer. Never sign any agreement that does not protect your moral rights and copyright.

The converse is that to assert moral rights, you need to pledge that you have the sole right to assign licences for production, that you have no other obligations that prevent you from fulfilling the terms of the agreement, and that the work is your own. It should be obvious that any instance of plagiarism is a breach of etiquette, ethics, and probably legality.

Music and PRS

The exception to this is the use of any music specified in the script. It is the producer's responsibility to obtain the rights for this, corresponding with the Performing Rights Society over fees and credits. This is usually specified in an agreement, for the avoidance of doubt, helping you cite whatever soundtrack will bring your script alive.

Credit

You should take top billing on promotional materials, from posters to flyers to playtexts. An agreement should stipulate the exact title of the credit and its size and location relative to other creatives. Commonly, a playwright's credit is no less than 30 per cent of the size of the play's title and either adjacent to or immediately underneath it, on its own line. Usually only the title, and the names of the venue/company, are allowed to be bigger than that of the playwright.

Approval of director and cast

It's commonplace for production agreements to stipulate that writers have the right to approve the director and actors (note that this does not mean recruit them, simply that a producer ought to check any candidate with you before making a formal offer). Be chary of exercising this too enthusiastically – if a producer is suggesting someone, they probably have good reason, so raise any concerns in a conversation not an outright veto! If this clause is not included, be tactful in pushing for it. Do so in a way that emphasises your desire to be part of the process, rather than implying a lack of trust in your producer or director.

Rehearsal allowance

It's helpful to specify a writer's access to rehearsals. These are usually at the discretion of the producer, whose authority over rehearsals is final, but it's standard practice for the writer to be able to request attendance, any such request not to be unreasonably refused. Usually you can expect to be present for the first few days, for the table work, and then visit to see key scenes or run-throughs later on (see the 'Going into Production' chapter). Sometimes a playwright is present throughout, provided this won't undermine the director's authority. It all depends on the relationship and process.

There is sometimes an agreed daily rate for a writer's attendance at rehearsals or for any rewrites requested, but this will depend upon the show's budget and scale. A play at a subsidised venue ought to pay you a fee for your time in rehearsals, but a fringe venue may not have the resources. Don't be afraid to ask, but be realistic about the financial situation.

Comps

You should be provided with a certain number of complimentary seats ('comps') at previews and press night. The exact number will depend on the capacity of the venue. It's also customary for the playwright to have the right to a seat for their personal use only at each performance, subject to availability.

Participation in future productions/earnings

In recognition of the investment made and risk taken by a producer in presenting a new play, it is common for that producer to be entitled to a small share of any royalties/fees the writer receives from future productions. It reflects that a good premiere, which may cost tens or even hundreds of thousands of pounds, will shape the play's long-term success, and some part of your future earnings from it may therefore be due to the original producer.

Say a producer mounts a new play, investing significant sums. If that play is later picked up for a West End run, which makes vast riches, the original producer would be due a small percentage of those earnings above a pre-agreed threshold. This reflects that they launched the play and made this new life possible.

Clearly any participation in future earnings can only apply if the producer actually staged the play – merely acquiring the licence or the option gives no right to claim a cut of your future earnings from it. The producer has to have contributed by staging the play. Then, once you have earned a sum above a certain threshold from exploiting the rights of that particular play, the producer should be due a small cut of subsequent income deriving from this, within a limited number of years. The WGGB suggest standard thresholds, participation percentages, and period of entitlement to participation.

These are important areas to cover in an agreement, but there can never be a universal contract to adhere to; each project will have its own needs and concerns. There will inevitably be other factors to broach, so these are just some of the important principles that it is helpful for a working playwright to be aware of. If you have an agent, then expect them to take care of this; if you don't, then review any contract carefully – and take legal advice if necessary.

What Constitutes an Agreement?

Any written exchange can constitute an agreement – whether you are formally aware of it or not. An email thread or even a text message can be adduced as evidence of a binding commitment.

The point is not simply to be wary of what you commit to written record, but that drawing up an agreement is more straightforward than generally supposed. Of course, a properly calibrated contract is infinitely preferable to relying on WhatsApp messages rife with emojis, but you don't need to shell out a fortune to a solicitor, unless it is a particularly finicky arrangement.

Templates for agreements are available on the ITC website – we heartily recommend that all producers of new writing become members of the ITC. However you draw an agreement up, it is usual to specify when completing a formal contract that this replaces any previous arrangements, to preclude those pesky WhatsApp messages from fouling the pitch.

If your agreement contains clauses that address the subjects outlined above, you will be on the right track. The most important thing is to ensure the language is clear, and the formatting legible and consistent. These are things that the producer should have responsibility for, but any signatory to an agreement should check these aspects.

Remember that any legal contract needs to evidence the principle of mutuality. This means that all parties obtain a benefit. If an agreement specifies that one party provides everything and the other party nothing, its validity can be challenged. It needs to demonstrate symbiotic benefits. Of course, the easiest way to do this is for one party to provide a service (like a play) and the other party to pay money in return. If for any reason this isn't the model of your agreement, make explicit on what the principle of mutuality rests.

The Agent's Role

Reaching an agreement can be an energy-sapping, stressful process. It's especially challenging for a playwright and a producer, who have to foster a supportive and creative relationship, to be simultaneously locked into a discussion over the sensitive issues of rights and money, however much goodwill may exist. This is where having a mediator who understands industry standards and models of good practice, and knows the situation for both parties, can prove invaluable – an agent (see the chapter on 'Working with Collaborators').

An agent should act as a buffer between their client and a company, to ensure that any tension in negotiations does not adversely filter into the creative process. If you do not have an agent, it's not inevitably a limitation – but it means that certain conversations about money or rights may be a little more uncomfortable.

Agents have a good understanding of how agreements should be structured and worded, and what industry guidelines stipulate. This means they are in a position to negotiate and to insist on key points. Remember, however, that an agent is just another person involved in the arts, not a super-being able to conjure up radically improved offers, so be realistic about what you expect them to accomplish in any negotiation. Ultimately, no decision should be made by an agent without their client's approval, so if your agent is being obstreperous or unreasonable this will be traced back to you. As ever, behaving with decorum and maintaining a discussion about best practice and what is realistically achievable are important for all parties.

Agents will also be available to advise on other parts of the process. An agent can support a producer with issuing industry invitations or possibly recruiting creative teams, as many agents look after artists in multiple disciplines. Agents are often regarded with suspicion by producers, and it's true that sometimes there will be a squaring-off, but it's best for all concerned if the agent is able to bring their expertise and connections to the process. You should feel able to run ideas by your agent and seek their opinion (while always respecting the producer), and the agent should definitely be at readings, showcases, or press nights, to note attendees and plan next steps. Again, these contributions are easier if the negotiation stage was handled courteously.

Publishing Deals

Having a play published is wonderful. It means the script becomes widely available – with good publishers, this may even mean internationally – and hugely improves the chances of further productions, including amateur performances. The royalties from sales can be a lovely extra revenue stream, and seeing the play on sale at places like the National Theatre Bookshop is a guaranteed thrill.

We won't discuss self-publishing options, because anyone can instigate that, it brings very limited channels of distribution and publicity, and it's meaningless in industry terms. Any aspiring playwright should look for professional publication.

Only a few publishers specialise in scripts: Faber & Faber; Methuen Drama (an imprint of Bloomsbury); Nick Hern Books; Oberon Books; Samuel French. There are smaller outfits, like Playdead Press and LazyBee Scripts, but most professional playwrights are signed to one of these five houses.

Each has its particular emphasis: Samuel French tends to print a wide variety of plays from classics to recent productions, with the latter mainly picked up from shows that have been staged without finding a publisher; Methuen Drama produce editions of established writers as well as some new plays; Faber & Faber predominantly rely on their enviable catalogue of famous writers but do, occasionally, add a new playwright to the stable; Nick Hern Books and Oberon Books unquestionably lead the market in new writing.

None of these publishers will consider printing a script unless it is heading into production, usually for a minimum of three weeks.

The financial reality is that a publishing business cannot possibly recoup on the costs of designing, editing, printing and distributing a script unless there will be a show – partly because the producer will place a large order of copies to sell at the venue, partly because a production raises the profile of a script and builds a potential market. There's thus little point bothering a publisher with a script unless a production is planned.

As such, the vast majority of new plays that are published are done as 'programme-texts'. This means that as well as the script itself, the production details such as creative team and cast biographies and production company information are included; they're a combination of a script and a programme. Again, this increases the chances of sales at performances, as audiences will be doubly attracted to shelling out a few pounds for all this material. Plays published as scripts alone are generally reissues of classics, or acting editions.

If you have a script that is heading into a production, you, or your producer or agent, should definitely approach one of these specialist publishers. Send an email with the latest draft as well as the information about the production, its dates and venue, and any casting or creative information. You should approach a publisher with as much notice as possible; they will need several months to assess the proposal and turn the script into a book.

The publisher will want to see the script before making a decision, not just to determine its quality but also to ascertain commercial potential. Do not necessarily take rejection as a comment on your writing; it may be that the subject matter or roles do not fit with the publisher's target demographic, or that the circumstances of the production (the venue or the length of run) are not sufficient to guarantee sales that will make publication feasible.

If a publisher does accept the script for publication, they will provide a formal contract. Most contracts are standard templates, but as with any legal document all clauses should be checked carefully. The contract will specify key dates for delivery of the final script (or at least, a rehearsal draft; it's widely understood that a new play may change between going to print and the first performance), as well as the advance paid by the publisher to the writer. An advance is the sum of money the publisher is willing to pay before publication. Once the book is published, the number of sales will be tracked and you will be due a royalty from each copy sold. However, no royalties will be paid out until they exceed the figure of the advance; the publisher in effect pays the advance as a loan from your expected royalties. Of course, if the royalties never add up to more than the advance, that's the publisher's loss. Usually advances are fairly small to minimise this risk, often just a few hundred pounds. Publishers issue royalty statements twice a year; don't base your mortgage on them as sales can vary widely from one period to the next!

If your script is published as a playtext, it will be the producer's responsibility to provide the information on cast and creatives for the programme section. You should concern yourself only with the script. The publisher will then collate these and provide proofs; the image and blurb will usually be based on those used for the production. Check these over carefully before signing off – it's unlikely there will be a second chance to make any corrections, unless it is to an ebook version or there will be another print run in future years. Nonetheless, this will be the version of the script that future productions may regard as absolute.

Publishers take responsibility for distributing the script, so all you need to do is frenziedly share the link on social media. You should anticipate with relish seeing the book on sale; at any one time half the people hovering by the shelves will be proud writers keeping an eye on their literary progeny. Shuffling your script to the front of the shelves is not unknown but scarcely acceptable, unless masking a piece of Quentin Letts piffle.

Once a publisher has committed to a playwright, that writer is normally under their wing; future plays are likely to be published by the same house. This is therefore a relationship that may last for decades, so as with finding an agent, take care to join a publisher you trust on a deal that works for you.

Theatre thrives on being live and ephemeral; here one moment, gone the next. That shared experience – actors telling a story to an audience in the same room – is one of its unique qualities. So no playwright should think about the written script as the final product – it's a blueprint for something more. That said, words on a page is where, more often than not, your play will start out.

It's these words that publishers of plays are committing to paper and ink (and digital devices these days) – any published text will act as a permanent record of that evanescent moment. Having a book with your name on the spine is undoubtedly a thrill, but the publication is also an invitation and a provocation for a future life. It enshrines a play as a literary work that can be read, taught and studied – or revived, by professional and amateur companies, in future productions around the world.

In choosing what to publish, our attention is grabbed by bold, distinctive and original voices, the ones telling daring stories that get our hearts pounding when we read them, just as they will when an audience sees them on stage. But before we can even consider a play for publication, the first and foremost criterion is that it shall be getting a full-scale, full-length professional production.

There are lots of advantages in waiting for that moment: firstly, the play will really be 'edited' at that point, as you hone and finesse your initial drafts through the collaboration of rehearsals, taking in and blending your words with the input and expertise of the director, cast and creative team. Secondly, and perhaps more prosaically, publishing alongside a production guarantees a certain level of sales that makes a publication financially viable. Many theatres and companies will take copies of a playtext to sell as the programme for the production, with company biographies, venue information, introductory material and so on in the front pages of the book. This is a great boon to playwright, publisher and reader alike: immediately getting the play into the hands of the first and most interested market – the live theatre audience – at a cheaper price than would otherwise be possible. Many audience members buy these programme-texts because they want to take a piece of the play away with them, to read, digest or consider as a text for teaching or future performance. Or even just to act out on the bus home.

In order for us to publish the script contemporaneously with the first production, your play will need to go to print before the end of rehearsals, even as it may still be evolving, with changes being made. Most publishers can now work to tight deadlines and will incorporate as many of these last-minute alterations as possible. Even when it's not achievable, we are happily in a position to do so later, at the click of a button for ebook editions, which we then use as the basis for future reprints of the 'definitive' text.

We receive many proposals for plays to publish from multiple sources: direct from theatres, from agents, as winners of various playwriting awards (including the Papatango, Bruntwood and Theatre503 Prizes), and from our own 'scouting' – but if you have a play that's being performed, then there's no harm in sending it to publishers yourself. Scour the various publishers' websites and see if you can get a sense of the work they like to publish – and if there are other writers on their lists whose work and careers you admire and aspire to follow. Submissions guidelines will appear on each website.

It's worth considering this choice carefully at the outset – the relationship between playwright and publisher tends to be lifelong, not unlike the relationship you might have or develop with your agent. Just as we are continually reading and assessing playwrights to see whether we think they'd be a good fit for our list, so too will you want to check and see how much you feel at home working with your publisher.

Matt is Managing Director of Nick Hern Books, a specialist theatre publisher.

RESEARCHING AND DEVELOPING (R&D)

Research and development, to use its full title, is a designated period to explore a script without the pressure of a looming performance. It's an opportunity to test out the ideas of the play and, potentially, hear it read aloud by actors in a safe environment. Exactly how this process works, when it occurs, and what the aims are will be particular to each project.

R&D is a phrase bandied around a lot in new writing. Perhaps once regarded as a luxury, it's now common, if by no means universal, for producers to build an element of R&D into commissioning or production plans. This is on the whole a good thing, provided that the abbreviation does not mask a notional sense of obligation to interfere with a script, but is instead a carefully conceived and properly executed stage in the life of a play.

Papatango tend to go into a designated period of R&D after a few drafts have been completed, as we like to know the story and characters before trying to make the play as tight as possible. For others, however, R&D occurs earlier in a play's journey, as a formative trial of concepts or characters before they are fully committed to the page. There's no predetermined 'correct' time to undertake R&D; it will depend on your process and the nature of the play. No two Papatango R&D sessions have been the same because each of our writers has particular needs, but all have been instrumental in shaping the final draft.

R&D will undoubtedly require collaboration, for it is fundamental to any R&D process to open a play to outside input. This is often key to unlocking a script's potential.

In this chapter we consider the aims of R&D, list who is likely to be involved, outline the different ways to capitalise on the opportunity it presents, and discuss techniques and practices.

What are the Aims?

Quite simply, the main aim of R&D is to make the play better, by finding out what works and, just as importantly, what doesn't. The exact aims will, in practice, be dependent on what stage the play is at and what needs the most work.

It is therefore important to enter into R&D with clear aims and objectives. It could be that you want, before undertaking a first draft, to explore characters and themes by using actors in a workshop environment to help shape initial ideas into something that can then be written up. Or maybe you have a full draft but can't quite figure out some elements and want to improvise different options. Or perhaps it is time to hear the current draft read aloud to test dialogue or map out individual character arcs. It may be that the team needs to research and experiment with the subject matter more intently, to find ways of making it dramatic and understand how a full production would work.

Understanding exactly what you need from R&D will determine when it happens, how it is structured, and who contributes. There is sometimes a tendency for R&D to be assumed to be a given in a creative process, as if it speaks for itself. In fact, not all playwrights understand when and for what they need R&D. To identify your aims, consider these questions:

- Is the plot clear?

- Does each character have a role and journey?

- Is the timeline consistent?

- Are the team confident in handling the subject matter and themes?

- Do other creatives, such as director or producer, need to try out the script to ascertain the viability of a full production?

If you answered yes to most or all of these, then you will probably find that writing some scenes, even a whole draft, before R&D will crystallise your creative vision. R&D can then interrogate any specific issues that arose in the drafting. If you predominantly answered no, it may be that some R&D before attempting a full draft will generate clearer ideas.

Whether or not you have a draft already, go into the R&D process with material to explore. Actors are not magicians and cannot conjure up characters or plotlines from thin air; the more you provide in terms of character breakdowns, references, settings and research material, the more useful the R&D will be.

Do not assume that simply entering a room with other theatre-makers will accomplish all your ambitions. Having other creative minds around can be incredibly useful, but in order to stimulate ideas and keep the play on track, you will need to know what it is you are ultimately looking for and have a clear plan of how to achieve it.

Forms of R&D

Workshops

A workshop is a development activity that enables collaborators to contribute to and test out material. The main purpose is either to interrogate the text, if it exists, or to improvise around the premise if it does not. The duration of a workshop will be dependent on the aims of the creative team and how much they want to achieve; it typically lasts for a few days, but can encompass anything from half a day to multiple weeks.

A workshop usually takes place in a rehearsal space. Indeed, it often resembles elements of the rehearsal process itself, as the actors will take responsibility for creative choices and discuss themes and motivations (see the chapter on 'Going into Production'). The main difference is that, unlike rehearsals, a workshop doesn't end in a performance. This can be freeing, as it allows everybody to focus on process rather than outcome.

The creatives will usually consist of a director and cast. Recruitment is the producer's responsibility but you should have some involvement in, or approval over, those appointed (see the chapter on 'Working with Collaborators').

The flexibility of a workshop, in that you can try ideas out as and when they materialise, means they can be very productive. The important thing to remember is that there are no fixed rules to run a successful workshop. Whatever exercises you might find helpful should be attempted. Anything goes in a pressure-free environment.

The form of a workshop will depend on whether there is a script or not. If there is, then the director and cast will probably read it through at least once, to see how the whole story holds together, and raise any issues that this uncovers. Bearing these in mind, you can then examine it scene by scene, either with table work – which means discussing lines, annotating decisions and motivations, and unpacking wider ideas – or by getting the actors on their feet and acting out what has hitherto been confined to the page. A workshop thus breaks the script down in detail.

You might take a specific character and follow their journey through the play, only reading the scenes in which they appear. In effect, treat that individual as if they are the main protagonist, no matter how small the part. This allows you to see if the character is well-written or if they are merely used as a plot device. It also helps to imagine what might have happened to the character between scenes, further shaping their journey. You can also do this for character relationships. Again, read only the scenes between specific characters. It reveals if their relationship progresses or merely repeats. These things can often be hard to see when reading the play as a whole – a fast-moving main plot can conceal a sluggish subplot. Actors are especially attuned to these things, as they take responsibility for one character and see the play through that lens, rather than holistically.

If there is no script, just stimulus material, then you will probably talk through the ideas in depth, before asking actors to improvise or role-play certain key situations. Indeed, even if there is a script, it can still be valuable to look beyond the text and do some exploratory work around character and theme. Improvisation is a useful tool, a great way to test ideas quickly. It puts the onus on the actors to be creative and allows you to observe and cherry-pick from the results.

If it seems that something is missing in a particular scene, then you might ask the actors to read the scene until a certain point and then improvise from there, to test out options for improvements. If you feel the script is missing some story, then you might want to give the actors a few basic plot points and ask them to work from these. If a character's decision at a key moment seems contrived, then initiate an improvisation as to alternatives. The more precisely you can pinpoint the weaknesses that need solving, the better chance that actors have of providing solutions by playing out different choices. Always listen to your cast.

You could also improvise scenes outside the play itself, exploring significant moments that might have happened before the play begins or that fall between scenes. This can build more detailed character backstories and enrich their underlying situation. Even if none of this makes its way explicitly into the next draft, this work is never wasted; it can generate a lot of useful knowledge that may shape future rewrites and rehearsals.

When setting up an improvisation, it is important to give the actors clear plot points to hit. You don't want to be prescriptive, but nor do you want the improvisation to ramble. Sometimes it can be useful to tell each actor the beats you want them to hit privately, so that each actor follows only their character's arc, without feeling obliged to prime a moment for another actor. This allows the interactions more naturalism and authenticity, and can often engender dramatic tension.

Another tip is to let any improvisation run on for longer than strictly necessary; often it is only once an actor stops thinking and relaxes into the part that the best work is created. Most of an improvisation won't be useful, but you can discover some wonderful moments simply by letting interactions stretch. It is therefore worth recording all improvisations for future reflection.

In essence, then, a workshop is a chance to test out not only the actual script, whatever shape it is in, but to explore wider themes and alternatives that the writer alone may not have grasped. The more willing and adventurous everyone in the room is, the more productive the workshop can be, for the script, for rehearsals, and for production.

R&D

Readings

If R&D is intended to fix small issues with a script that has already been carefully formed, then it is often a good idea to opt for a reading as well as, or instead of, a workshop. While a workshop may include a read-through, a formal reading has a slightly different focus.

A reading looks purely at what is contained within the script, and attempts to realise this as successfully as possible, rather than pursuing alternative choices or improvisations. As such, a reading is usually most helpful later in the process, when the play is refined and heading towards production. There is relatively little benefit in reading a script that is still an early work-in-progress, as it will probably just reveal the gaps or weaknesses you already recognise.

A reading is relatively straightforward, compared to a workshop, and follows a more conventional structure. Usually one or two days' rehearsal precedes a formal reading. This can be staged or seated, but usually the latter is more beneficial. It means the actors can focus on the lines, makes limited rehearsal time more efficient, and enables the creative team to consider the script alone rather than worry about niceties of staging.

It is hearing the play aloud that is invaluable. The words, after all, are ultimately meant to be spoken, and this can really help to illuminate key areas in need of work. Moreover, like a workshop, good actors should be able to pinpoint any confusion or holes in their character's arc, raise issues of deliverability with lines, or unpick ambiguity around intentions, as well as reflect on the quality of the play in its entirety.

It may be that a reading reveals that sections considered weak actually flow well in performance, while areas that seemed strong on the page fall flat in actuality (especially true of jokes!). A reading can therefore reveal important final notes before a script is signed off. Don't be disheartened, however, if sections of the play don't emerge as you had envisaged; certainly do not panic. The actors are most likely reading the script fairly cold. To give them the best chance of doing proper justice to the play, it is helpful to talk them through it, explain your intentions, and provide some background information. It goes without saying that the more preparation time a director and cast have, the stronger a reading will be. Nonetheless, they will never perform the script as well as it will be done after weeks of rehearsal in a full production, so adjust your expectations accordingly. Try to filter any flaws in the script from the limitations imposed by the reading.

The level of scrutiny that accompanies a reading varies. It is always worth inviting a few trusted confidantes, but do not scatter invitations like confetti unless you are confident in the play's ability to bear up under many eyes. Having varied feedback and opinions can only help the development and will provide greater insight into your play and where it needs to go, but it's unwise to ask serious decision-makers from companies, unless you know them personally, to attend a reading of a script still in embryonic form. Only invite these people if the reading is intended as a public showcase (see the chapter on 'Getting Noticed'); if it is R&D activity, then better to bring in people whose notes can be trusted and on whose good opinion of the script you are not staking everything.

Discuss and debate

R&D does not perforce have to mean the intensity of a workshop or a reading. Sometimes writers benefit simply from discussion of research, themes and material. Part of an R&D process may include reaching out to experts in relevant subjects, to help give background and context to the work. It is important to have a high level of detail and knowledge, especially if you are touching upon sensitive issues, and R&D may focus on attaining this. It's heartening how open and welcoming people are to approaches from theatre-makers; most are genuinely flattered by anyone who has an interest in telling stories based on their work. Nonetheless, be aware that such experts will probably have limited time and/or knowledge of theatre, so it is best to involve them in R&D in a manner sensitive to their commitments and timetable.

Case Study: Developing *Unscorched*

Unscorched, winner of the 2013 Papatango Prize, is a hard-hitting play about the people who police the internet, investigating and eradicating the darkest, most unforgivable content. It asks what the personal cost is to those who spend their nine-to-five confronting humanity at its worst. The subject is obviously sensitive, so a truthful representation was paramount. The script therefore underwent multiple forms of R&D after winning the Prize, to make sure it was grounded in reality and told not only the most affecting but also the most genuine story.

We firstly arranged a meeting for playwright Luke Owen with a representative of the Internet Watch Foundation. Luke was able to ask specific questions about the working environment, methods of protecting employees from burnout, and the processes governing the working day. Lots of the material related by these specialists reappeared in the final draft. These were not necessarily about the explicit subject; a joke about workplace tension over car-parking spaces struck Luke as beautifully normal, casting a humanising light on a heavy, visceral world. R&D can throw up little gems of insight as well as 'big picture' knowledge; you never know what will be uncovered until you start asking the questions.

R&D can be very simple, and utilise personal connections. Chris drew on the expertise of his sisters-in-law, who work in child protection, to discuss the legal processes in the play. As a result of an informal chat over a home-cooked dinner, the script fundamentally changed.

As well as these components of specialist research, we also explored the play's storytelling qualities and structure. A week-long workshop at the Bristol Old Vic involved theatrical improvisations, performing new scenes or alternative sketches, and discussions with actors, before culminating in a reading before an invited audience. During this week the script evolved; a romance subplot became much more central, and the notes from the audience at the reading inspired Luke to alter the ending.

The R&D process thus incorporated a range of techniques involving very different people, some theatre-makers, some not; each contributed to the script in profound ways.

If reaching out to specialists is not practical, or simply not relevant, then discussion and debate can be built into R&D in other ways. This could include setting aside a period of intensive research with a dramaturg or director. Equally, R&D that incorporates a read-through or a workshop is a perfect opportunity to have an open discussion, with everybody in the room invited to chip in.

Question your cast on their characters and the play as a whole. Actors focus on their character and often bring insights into specific moments or details that someone focused on the whole play may overlook. Ask what made sense and what didn't. Are there glaring errors in the character's arc? Do any specific lines or actions fail to ring true? You have brought each actor on board specifically for their thoughts, so use them. That said, don't feel that you have to change anything just because of something said in the room. Better to take notes or record conversations and reflect afterwards than rush into a hasty decision – after all, actors in R&D feel obliged to contribute, but can walk out at 6 p.m. without worrying about actioning their notes.

The same applies to audiences or participants at readings. As well as a discussion, it may be worth handing out feedback forms, so that they can share thoughts anonymously. People can sometimes withhold opinions when speaking face to face, or may not want to contravene the consensus for fear of sounding stupid. Enabling honest feedback will produce better results.

Insider's View: Sharon Clark

I know quite a few writers who push back against the idea of structured R&D in their writing process. I can understand this. For some time R&D has been a way a theatre can work with a writer without having to produce the play at the end. Writers often talk about being trapped in 'development hell'. However, as a writer, R&D has been a necessary and vital part of my development, and this is because it can take so many forms. We talk about R&D as if it is a fixed concept, as if it takes X route and produces Y result, which is, of course, far from the truth. My own development processes have involved a wide range of activities from the all too vital reading of an early draft, to workshopping with actors and director to really iron out dramaturgical creases. This early exploration of a play, hearing it for the first time, ascertaining what feels heavy-handed, where the narrative starts to limp, where a character feels untruthful, can save pain later down the line. I find these development activities help deliver and cultivate ideas, speeding up the writing process as discoveries are made, as drafts are built and as other opinions are involved (but listen only to those voices that make sense to you).

When starting a new script, I build my own R&D structure into the first draft with conversations with other writers, readings done by friends over a glass of wine, or investigations with directors or designers. Writers don't always have to wait for a company to offer development opportunities, they can invest in them themselves by taking time out to explore their creative idea, their play, with other people.

Sharon was formerly Literary Producer at Bristol Old Vic, and previously worked at the National Theatre, Watford Palace and Theatre503, before becoming a full-time playwright, dramaturg, and creative director of immersive theatre company Raucous. She was runner-up in the 2017 Papatango New Writing Prize and won a Judges Award in the 2017 Bruntwood Prize.

Who Will Be Involved?

If the R&D includes a workshop or reading with actors, then it is likely that this will be led by a director or dramaturg; it may even have both. It is important that whoever leads the activity knows the play well. Do not bring someone in who is not fully versed in the material.

You could run such a workshop or reading yourself, but in general it is useful to designate someone else to take the lead, in order to be free to observe and absorb. A director or dramaturg will use different exercises to provoke and stimulate ideas from the playwright, challenging you to see the play in new ways.

It is likely actors will be present, whether to read the script aloud, or to be creatively and actively involved through improvisation or discussion. When casting for a workshop it is important to remember that you aren't casting the production. The type of actor who best fits a workshop is somebody positive, good at improvisation and willing to challenge the script in a constructive manner. It doesn't particularly matter if they are not perfect casting, as long as they are close enough not to distract from the role and provided they can bring energy and insight into the room.

It is possible that the producer will be present for parts of the R&D, to keep track of progress. Beyond this, it is unusual for other members of a creative team to be involved, unless the script is inextricably interwoven with their particular discipline. Remember, R&D is not a production in microcosm; the team required will probably not be as extensive.

Outside the creative team, it may also be that experts or relevant theatre-makers are invited, in order to provide feedback. Be precise in arranging this. Only open the R&D to those who will understand the nature of a work-in-progress phase and provide constructive insights. This again comes down to understanding the needs and aims of your R&D process. Only once you know what the R&D should accomplish can you plan its form and contributors.

Must I?

R&D is a process, or a range of processes, to help make the script as good as it can be. If delivered effectively it can transform a play. If you are fortunate enough to have access to some form of R&D, then with careful planning and the right collaborators it could make all the difference to readying your script for production.

That is not to say, however, that all projects or artists will benefit from R&D. Sometimes good scripts get bogged down in endless cycles of behind-closed-doors exercises, and the confidence to take a play into production is eroded by the temptation to try just one more workshop. Sometimes R&D is a placebo rather than a medicine – and it is important to call this out.

Moreover, plenty of writers do not have access to R&D resources, yet still produce brilliant plays! You should, therefore, have complete flexibility over whether or not you want to take part in R&D, what form it takes, and at what stage in the writing journey it occurs. It may well be that you do not think a workshop or reading or debate will be helpful – and this is completely valid. R&D should make playwriting easier, not be a burden or distraction, and your collaborators should respect that.

GOING INTO PRODUCTION

This is it. The reason you endure all the drafting, pitching, show-cases, development and headaches. That moment the script becomes a proper play, when the lights go up, the actors step out and the story unfurls, is magical for anyone and utterly spellbind-ing for the writer. It is the culmination of years of work, not just on the script but in building the relationships and collaborations that underpin a production. And it determines whether or not it was worth it.

A production can be a tough, stressful experience; the stakes have never been higher and yet you are no longer the sole, even the lead, authority. This chapter therefore discusses the stages of a pro-duction and the playwright's role in each of these. Knowing how to exercise influence without overstepping the mark can make all the difference to whether the script soars or flops, while knowing how to capitalise on a production will be vital to your career.

What Counts as a Production?

A production may be a one-night-only performance above a pub, a prolonged triumph in the West End, or anything in between. The difference between a production and a showcase is that a produc-tion is a fully formed realisation of the script on stage, not a pitch for further contributions or development. If it's open to paying members of the public, and thus fair game for reviewers, it counts. If a script is being mounted purely to attract notice, then it may be better to present this as a showcase or work-in-progress rather than a full production (see the chapter on 'Getting Noticed').

Of course, it may be that a production is intended to attract potential co-producers for a transfer or tour, but that intention is not relevant to the audiences shelling out hard-earned cash for a seat. They will expect and be entitled to a production that works in its own right; naturally, delivering to this standard will make any further opportunities all the more likely.

As soon as a venue and performance dates are confirmed, the play will enter production territory. This does not mean that R&D will necessarily wind down forthwith – Papatango tend to have our production dates booked months in advance, and will generally still be developing the script until the start of rehearsals – but it does mean that all aspects of making the play will now be done with an eye on the final outcome.

This can energise or intimidate. As a rule, savvy producers will not book a production without good reason to trust the play will be ready, so any development work still to be done should not buckle under this pressure. Beware, however, of those producers who are desperate to find a product to fill a pre-existing slot, because that can mean a play is rushed untimely into being. This happens more often than one might imagine; even reputable venues have to fill their programme and, frankly, there aren't enough production-ready new plays to satisfy all the venues that crowd British cities. Having a play produced before it is ready can adversely affect a writer's career, so only consent to a production, however tempting, if the time is right for your script and if any remaining development is achievable.

Once the development is formally signed off, a new mode will be entered. There will be pre-production planning and casting (the most important elements of which we have covered in the chapters on 'Working with Collaborators', 'Making Deals' and 'R&D'). We will begin this chapter, therefore, by considering the playwright's contribution once the production proper is underway.

Lucy Prebble has written in the *Guardian* that 'there are three acts of writing: before rehearsal, during rehearsal and during previews'. Each of these acts will take a different form and require something different of you. We will start with rehearsals and any final changes to the script before moving on to previews, press night, and the run itself, with an eye on how to make the production as impactful as possible, and thereby sustain a playwriting future.

Rehearsals

In an ideal world, all of the script development will have been completed before rehearsals, so that the creative process can now be focused entirely on the show. That being so, the responsibility will chiefly fall to the director and the cast. That is not to say that a playwright's work is now done or that the script is sacrosanct; you should remain an integral part of the process and be available for notes, but these should be subsidiary to the all-important affair of actually staging the play. If there is still a substantial amount of work to be done on the script, then your role in rehearsals is likely to be the same – only more intense!

As mentioned in the chapter on 'Working with Collaborators', a playwright's attendance in rehearsals will depend on their relationship with the director (and on how much work remains to be done on the script). However often you may or may not be in the room, it is a given that you should attend at least the first day of rehearsals. Everybody, no matter how experienced, is nervous on this day, and the initial meeting before stepping into the unknown is often a little strained, so a smile goes a long way.

It will usually begin with an introduction to the cast and design team prior to a showing of the model box. This is a scale model of the design of the show. It is an incredibly exciting moment, a first glimpse of how the world of this production will look. The director and designer will talk through the design and discuss how the various elements will work. After the model box, you will probably be invited to discuss the play, so prepare notes beforehand. Remember that these activities are intended to help a cast relax, but it is also an overload of information for them. Share the things that inspired you to write the script to inspire the actors in turn, sustaining them for the slog ahead.

Most directors like to hold a read-through after this. When listening to a first read-through bear in mind that it is just that – the first time this group have ever attempted the play together. Don't expect the finished article. Actors take different approaches to a first read-through; some attempt a performance, while others prefer to hold back and give a neutral reading. It will undoubtedly feel disjointed, and dramatic moments will be missed, but it is important not to feel disheartened or that this is a doom-laden indication of the end production. The cast and director have a long journey ahead. Trust in the process.

Often, directors and cast can be resistant to changes to the script mooted at this point. In the best case, that's because they want to see how the script develops after a little work; in the worst case, it's because they are rigidly set on their interpretation. Philip Ridley, after the first reading of *Ghost from a Perfect Place*, suggested a few changes, to which the veteran actor John Wood responded that there was no need, for the play was superb – and besides, he had learned the lines already! In any case, withhold rushing to judgement at this early stage; if you are certain that changes are needed, then be sensitive to how the team will respond. It's best to wait until the script has undergone some fairer tests before proposing tweaks, if you can.

After the read-through, there is usually a discussion, to see what points emerge and to identify any points that require clarification. If a director opts not to hold a read-through this early, it's usually because they want to prime the cast with more ideas and more material before putting them on the spot. In this case, the director will probably proceed to table work straight away, in which you will probably take an active part.

Table work is that rare pleasure in theatre: a technical term named simply. It is script work done around a table. The purpose is for everyone on the team to understand the play from a united viewpoint, so that when they get the play up on its feet the performances cohere.

Each director will have a different way of conducting table work, but most often it revolves around sharing research, delving into characters, and identifying the dramatic structure that needs to be played. A common technique with which it is useful to be familiar is 'uniting' the play. This is about rendering the play in manageable, coherent sections. Uniting is a Stanislavskian technique in which scenes are broken down into sections based on dramatic beats, the principle being that every time a line or action shifts the momentum of the scene, a new unit begins. The outcome is to bring layers of detail into the show, by understanding the rhythm of the script.

Table work may also include 'actioning'. This involves breaking each line down into its constituent thoughts, then ascribing an 'action verb' to each thought, to pinpoint the exact motivation of each character in each line, moment by moment. These verbs are transitive, that is, they focus on affecting another character rather than on introspective reflection. Thus, actioning is about specifying layers of intention and detail within the dialogue that can drive the relationships on stage. Under these intense microscopes, it is inevitable that questions will surface, so having the playwright present for table work is invaluable.

After the table work is finished, which may take several days, the director will probably begin to block the play, at which point you will generally no longer be needed in the room. Blocking means physically staging the play scene by scene. Having the writer sit in can be a distraction, and even lead to actors referring to them instead of the director. Don't be insulted if the director doesn't require your attendance – if they need you, they know where you are.

Some work on the script is almost inevitable as rehearsals progress, as a sustained exploration with actors will reveal things that no amount of dramaturgy or R&D alone can turn up. More often than not, they will only be line tweaks or cuts that won't require much effort, but on occasion it may be necessary for you to watch rehearsals and make changes in the room. Sometimes rewrites are suggested by the director or cast, but all should be approved by you, so don't switch off.

You shouldn't feel pressured to make any alterations with which you disagree – provided you can explain why you disagree and answer whatever concern a collaborator has. That being said, rehearsals can uncover structural problems or character inconsistencies, so you should always be open to work on the script. This will usually need to be done quickly in order for the director to implement it. Resist the temptation to pen swathes of new material; the script as it is has got this far on its merits, so lavish alterations, conducted hastily in the crucible of rehearsals, are probably not called for, and may crack under pressure! It is also an added burden for the cast, so tread lightly.

You are very likely to be invited into rehearsals for a run-through. Runs generally take place in the penultimate and last weeks of rehearsals, and the quality will depend on what stage the rehearsals are at. For example, an early run-through ('stagger-through' as it is called, with grim wit) often forsakes costumes or props. It is about actors piecing together scenes for the first time, discovering the journey of their characters and the arc of the story as a whole, rather than delivering all the fine detail covered during table work and blocking. A later run, once the cast are confident with the structure and timing of scenes, might involve props and costume. This will be far closer to how the finished show will look, but will still undoubtedly be rough around the edges.

A run is part of the rehearsal process, not a pale imitation of the ultimate performance; the actors are still trying out ideas and discovering new things. There is time to make changes so your input at this stage is completely valid; indeed, a director and cast will be keen to hear the writer's opinion and may become despondent if no feedback is forthcoming from you. It is, however, worth remembering that the director and cast have been working on the play intensely for weeks, so notes should be given with respect and discretion. Be constructive, and focus on the clarity of the narrative and the characters. Don't tell the director that one of the actors is rubbish (unless it's truly devastating the play and a replacement must be found); instead, identify the beats that are being missed or places where the story isn't clear, as these are actionable, helpful pointers.

Each run should get tighter and stronger. Changes and cuts may assist with this, and some playwrights like to see as many runs as possible with this in mind. Others prefer to see only one or two, in order to experience the show as an audience member or reviewer would, without being too jaded. It should be up to you, although perhaps discuss the mood of the cast and when they are most likely to welcome the writer's scrutiny with the director!

Ultimately, rehearsals are the only true test of a new play, so you should be able to request the access you need to assess the script, in conjunction with the director's need to retain overall control of the process.

Technical Rehearsals

Invariably referred to as 'tech', technical rehearsals take place in the venue or performance site and are the point at which rehearsals meet the design. It is here that the full production takes shape. There is usually a gap of a few days between the final rehearsal and the start of the tech, during which time the fit-up occurs: set is constructed, lights are rigged and focused, sound is installed, and costumes and props are prepared.

The tech begins only once these disparate elements are in place, and its aim is to blend them seamlessly, checking every moment of the play against lighting and sound cues, scene changes, and stage directions. It's not a smooth, continuous run of the whole play; instead, each moment is worked until the design and stage-management teams have confirmed their work is integrated with the actors' performances, and only then does the tech move on to the next scene.

Tech is slow and laborious. Each section will be worked again and again until the team are happy. It is called rehearsal for a reason; it is unlikely that all technical aspects will be perfected during this time, and lighting, sound, set and costume are likely to be tweaked during the dress rehearsal and throughout previews. If you decide to attend the tech (most playwrights don't; avoiding the frustrations and setbacks of tech is one of the great boons of being a writer!) and have notes, it's often best to refrain until you have seen how the dress run goes, unless the director specifically asks your opinion.

The amount of tech time a production has depends on various factors such as the schedule, the budget, and the technical complexities of the show; usually techs are pushed for time and there is little opportunity to provide acting or script notes. Indeed, the tech is very much the domain of the director and the design team and there isn't any particular reason for you to attend. Any writer who is present is advised to keep a low profile; technical rehearsals are invariably stressful, there are always more things to do than hours in which to do them, and everyone comes to loathe the ratbag who airily wrote the stage direction that a unicorn should spontaneously combust.

Dress Rehearsals

Once tech is complete, the final hurdle before a production opens to the public is a dress rehearsal. These are a run of the show under full performance conditions – often the venue's administrators or ushers will attend to form an impromptu audience.

You should definitely witness every dress rehearsal and take notes. This isn't strictly the end of the rehearsal process, as there is still time to make adjustments during previews, but it is probably one of the most important moments in the life of a new play, the final chance to give notes prior to facing the public. It assuredly isn't time to sit back and marvel at your creation being brought to life – although perhaps treat yourself for a second or two.

Don't expect that everything will go smoothly. Actors will drop lines, cues will be missed and props will disappear. The team will be tetchy after a long tech. Dress rehearsals are not intended to recreate the ideal performance, but to find out what is working and what needs polishing before the show is unleashed on a paying audience. The more weaknesses that are revealed, the more that can inform the opening show. Indeed, theatre lore dictates that a bad dress means a good first night – and vice versa!

The notes that accrue from a dress are therefore crucial, and may encompass performances, design, stagecraft or the script, coming from any member of the team. At this point, changes to the script are unlikely, but it may be that certain sections of the play which seemed fine in the rehearsal room haven't quite translated to the stage, meaning you may contemplate last-minute cuts. In this case, the timing is important. Small line tweaks could possibly be achieved between the dress rehearsal and the first preview, but any substantial changes are better left to any extra rehearsals during the preview period.

Always remember to be encouraging during and after a dress rehearsal. If flaws are apparent, you will not be alone in noticing – and the cast have to do it for real soon! Your support, and constructive comments, will be vital in helping them give a successful preview – even if work remains to be done.

Previews

Assuming the production runs for several days or weeks, there will probably be a preview period. Previews comprise a certain number of shows before the official opening. Everyone holds their breath: will the play work in front of an audience? Previews are a litmus test of audience reactions (but remember that no audience is definitive; some nights will see different responses to the same show! This is why more than one preview is a good idea).

It is likely that some tweaks will be undertaken after each preview. After all, until the curtain call you can never be sure what works and what doesn't. A play thus should, ideally, run the gauntlet of different audiences several times before it faces the press.

Preview prices should be lower to reflect the fact that audiences are not guaranteed to see a perfect, finished production (when one high-profile show charged full price at previews, several critics broke the embargo on reviews and wrote about the first night, justifying this breach of etiquette on the grounds that if the audience were being charged full whack it should have been of commensurate quality). Designating and pricing some performances as previews encourages punters to appreciate the work may not yet be fully formed. Indeed, many preview audiences relish seeing something raw and fresh and rendering their verdict. It's not a good idea, however, to schedule a formal discussion or talkback after a preview; while audiences may welcome the chance to proffer input, the creative team will be exhausted and quite sensitive after a gruelling production week, and being hauled before public inquisitors may be too much. Better simply to listen to the audience as they congregate in the bar and queue for the toilets. That should communicate all you need to know. Resist the temptation either to bask too much in warm applause, as there will always be areas to improve upon, or to despair at muted clapping, as there is much that can change before the official opening.

A preview is not a chance to crack open the bubbly; it's a working night, even if friends are in the house. Position yourself somewhere unobtrusive – because there's no need to stress the cast unduly by making your reactions prominent – and have a notebook to hand to jot down any thoughts. This can be about the script itself, or the staging or performances or design; the playwright is a bona fide member of the creative team and making notes on all aspects of the production is perfectly legitimate.

It is important not to tread on any toes, however; respect the chain of command that puts the director in charge of actors and designers, so that only one authoritative voice is issuing notes. All of your suggestions should be discussed with the director privately, which includes any you may have for the script. These should be broached privately, not broadcast in public, because until a decision is made, it's best not to air concerns widely as that can cause despondency to spread. Of course, it may be that the preview is a triumph, but even if not, the atmosphere should be as positive as possible, especially for the actors who have to summon the energy to repeat the performance and incorporate any changes.

Once the dust has settled from the preview and the notes have been assimilated, the director will oversee any re-rehearsal necessary. You may or may not be present – it will depend on the nature of any changes. It is only if the script is under examination that the playwright will be the central agent. Making cuts is fairly straightforward, but verify them with the actor(s) concerned, as it can be a sensitive matter to avoid casting any aspersions on their performance. Rewrites are more challenging; the creatives and cast will need them as soon as humanly possible, in order to incorporate new staging or learn new lines, so the likelihood is that the writer will have to work through the night. Rewrites should only be undertaken if absolutely vital, and kept as minimal as possible. No one benefits from waking up to a new play!

This process of taking notes, having discussions and initiating clear action points should be repeated for each preview. Hopefully, each time there will be fewer notes. For most productions, there will be only a handful of previews, as new plays seldom run for more than four weeks, and there is a premium on garnering early reviews (and limiting the number of cheaper preview tickets). New plays at subsidised theatres, or by known playwrights, may enjoy longer runs and extra previews, but even these tend to have no more than a week of previews, unless there is a complex technical or musical element (musicals always enjoy longer preview periods). Regardless of the number of previews, the principle remains the same.

It may be that the preview period flows really nicely. Papatango seldom if ever make any rewrites during this period, as we prefer to undertake extensive R&D in advance. It is mainly small-scale work on design or performances that occur here, matters of detail only. You should not feel guilty if you have no work to do – you will have been working far longer than anyone else by this stage and are fully entitled to leave it to others. Just don't clock off until the first rapturous thunder of applause has played out... After all, Mozart only finished his overture to *Don Giovanni* the morning of its first performance, allegedly leaving no time for the musicians to rehearse it. While we wouldn't recommend this as a model, it attests to the fact that sometimes getting it right takes until the very final moment.

Press Night

Previews yield to the official opening night, known as press night. This is when reviewers are invited to judge the work, deemed ready after its preview period. It is the producer's responsibility to organise the press night; really you should be free to enjoy a well-earned drink. It is nonetheless helpful to understand how press nights work.

The date selected will be affected by several factors. Most important will be the length of the run, the number of previews the producer can afford and how quickly the reviews are needed. A short run will inevitably see the press night scheduled earlier. The competing press nights should also be taken into consideration (the producer will check the Society of London Theatre – SOLT – diary); it's best not to go head-to-head with a big opening. This is somewhat out of a producer's control; sometimes major companies shift their press nights, or there are a deluge of large shows opening. Understand the context of your press night and set expectations accordingly.

A press release issued months in advance will make the reviewers aware of the date. They are unlikely to book in until a week or a few days beforehand, however, as schedules and review space – especially for print publications – are decided late by editors (not by the reviewers). Do not despair, therefore, if no one has booked in; hold your nerve and let the producer or press agent push for confirmations.

Moreover, reviewers will not necessarily attend the formal press night. Other commitments may take precedence. This does not mean that reviewer will not come at all; an opening night is only the declaration that it is now open season, and often critics will book for another performance. Sometimes they will ask to attend the final preview if they can't make press night, which makes everyone grit their teeth but is usually worth acceding to; most reviewers will bear in mind that it is a preview and be forgiving if it is a little raw, and the coverage can be invaluable. Certainly there would have to be very solid reasons to turn a reviewer away.

A majority of seats are usually set aside for reviewers, but a producer should not fill the house exclusively with critics as that can result in a deathly silent, intense audience that unsettles even veteran performers. Some seats should go to guests, and ideally also paying members of the public. These people simply relax, unburdened by the tension of a press night. Prime some friends to come whom you can rely upon to carry a nice energy.

It is a convention that, on opening night, cards and gifts are exchanged. It's much appreciated and can be a welcome fillip. It's also a nice way to bolster a relationship, with an eye on future collaborations.

If you watch the show – although your attention may be fixed resolutely on critics rather than the performance – the same principle applies as with previews: stay out of the cast's eyeline. After the performance, there will be a post-show party; you will be expected to line up for congratulations, interviews and publicity photos. Be positive – reviewers may be lingering.

Once the witching hour of midnight has struck, people will start surreptitiously fidgeting with phones to look for the first reviews. These usually trickle in from the small hours, from critics filing online; it may take days for print publications to release them. Try to resist the urge to check obsessively – you'll hear quickly once the reviews appear. Instead, take some time to enjoy your opening night!

Your experience in the rehearsal room will be dictated by who the director and actors are, so these two decisions prior to rehearsal are paramount. Hopefully you've landed a cast you love and a director you trust. It's important to remember to take your lead from the director. It's their rehearsal room and they're in charge. Try not to contradict them or undermine their authority. I generally sit by the director, so I can whisper notes. This way they can filter what is helpful and what's not. As much as possible, let them be the mouthpiece to the actors. If you feel something isn't going the way you'd envisaged, or it's a larger point, then wait for a conversation with the director alone. You must say if you have a problem; it's your play and you need to stand up for it. All being well, you should find a compromise.

Rehearsals are anything from three to six weeks. They break down something like this:

First week: Cast read-through. You can't help but notice you're the only person bravely tittering. You play some trust exercises or some ball exercises. The actors might do some improvisations. One of the actors makes a bloody strange choice of accent that doesn't fit their part.

Second week: More script work. The play should start to be on its feet. You discover Quavers sprinkled with Cup-a-Soup powder is an excellent snack. Only downside is the carpety dryness of your tongue post-binge, and the industrial, almost instantaneous migraines.

Third week: One of the actors is a nightmare. He/she/they takes zero direction. They're probably the person who made the strange choice of accent in the first week. Historically, at some point there is a honking great argument. It will not involve you; your job has always been to look awkward.

Fourth week: The actors are finally as scared as you were in the first week – but attempting to mask it by being incredibly jolly and singing. Everyone should be off book but they never are. You're going into the theatre soon and for an unknown reason one of the actors has (i) grown a moustache or (ii) bleached their hair.

Tech/previews: You've stopped drinking coffee or *really* started drinking it. Either way time has started bending and contracting. There are headachey longueurs when nothing seems to happen and others when there's no time at all. You seem to be endlessly walking down carpeted corridors, through swing doors, up narrow staircases... All your meals are from Pret. Mistakenly you thought treating yourself would magic the nerves away.

Press night: No one enjoys press night, but try to be positive. Your instinct is to lurk in a dark corner. You imagine everybody must recognise you as the writer. Don't worry, they haven't got a clue who you are. You are about to watch a play you wrote with a real audience and real critics. This is an amazing achievement. How many people can say they wrote a play? The satisfaction of hearing an audience respond to what you wrote is electric. With the shows that follow the pressure subsides and you can enjoy each performance incrementally.

Moses's first play, Shrieks of Laughter, *premiered at Soho Theatre, and his second,* Donkey Heart, *premiered at the Old Red Lion Theatre and transferred to the West End.*

Handling Reviews

'Asking a working writer what he thinks about critics is like asking a lamp post what it feels about dogs.'
John Osborne

In recent years, the critical landscape has drastically changed. Shrinking budgets at print publications have meant fewer column inches for the arts, leaving competition for reviews fiercer than ever. Increasingly, newspapers focus on high-profile shows and established artists, often celebrities. It's relatively rare for a new play from an emerging writer to land a coveted slot in a paper, so don't be downcast if no broadsheets flock to your world premiere.

Fortunately, there are alternatives, as the diminution in traditional media's coverage of theatre is in inverse proportion (and invites some to infer a causal link) to the explosion in online theatre blogs, some well-established with large teams of reviewers, others the domain of lone enthusiasts. Where once productions would seek the judgement of Fleet Street's discerning few, now the net stretches further and the sources of expertise are far more varied (relative to the newspaper industry's continuing prevalence for journalists to be middle-class white men). This offers vital opportunities for new writing; greater diversity in reviewers supports greater diversity in artists and plays. Moreover, blogs arguably reach a more theatre-focused crowd than a newspaper. Consequently, a series of good reviews online can prove as influential as a cluster of stars in print. Savvy producers will invite a wide field of reviewers across both traditional and new media.

Nonetheless, degrees of influence across the blogosphere vary. Many sites liberally toss out five-star reviews in the hope of drawing traffic to their own platform; the online publications with more stringent editorial oversight, like Exeunt or WhatsOnStage, carry greater weight. Celebrate every good review, but be canny about which truly have significance.

We all love to pretend that we are not affected by the opinions of reviewers, but inevitably any praise or criticism will leave its mark. While Osborne's line undoubtedly holds a grain of truth, spurning all who dare to criticise is misguided. A critic has a role in theatre's ecosystem. Like a parasitical tick that cleans the skin of the lion it feeds on, they help refine and purify the industry. And they are also audience members; it's a reasonable bet that any review will tally with the perspective of at least some of the public. It is therefore as important to learn from a one-star slating as to furiously retweet a five-star rave.

So, what are the best ways of responding to reviews?

Give it time

Reviews hit at the end of an arduous process, when the entire team is at its most vulnerable. You will not be in the best position to see things objectively. Some writers have reacted and become embroiled in public spats with critics, which is at the very least demeaning. Try to absorb a review, positive or negative, slowly and carefully. It is the producer's job to scrutinise reviews for immediate marketing; you can enjoy a little more distance, and reflect once the dust has settled for a more enlightening experience.

Don't read too much into it – or don't read it at all

Reviews are only an incidental part of theatre-making, and their importance is perhaps overstated. A few positive reviews will not in themselves attract a new commission; equally, a few negative lines will not be remembered for long. This is as true of the production as it is the writer's career. If the play is a critical success across the board, there might be a noticeable difference at the box office or more interest from the industry, but this isn't guaranteed. Likewise, if you've been given a bloody nose, all is not lost. The power of word-of-mouth reviews, especially with the rise of social media, matches the opinions of professional critics in getting bums on seats or impressing industry decision-makers.

Remember, reviewers are obliged to profess an opinion, often formulated, expressed and published in a short time. They are not always reliable. The true test of a show is how audiences respond. Famously, *We Will Rock You* was panned by reviewers yet ran for a decade in the West End, pleasing tens of thousands of people and giving Ben Elton a career after the glories of *Blackadder*. So treat reviews as a useful barometer of opinion, but recognise the flaws and limitations. Don't overreact.

Indeed, many writers profess not to read reviews at all. We would say this is a perfectly wise idea during a run, but it would be a shame to dismiss all critical discourse around your play in the longer term. Good criticism contains ideas from which artists can learn (see the next chapter, 'Reflecting').

Understand the context

Reviewing is not a standardised system. Context matters. Many critics take account of the parameters and resources that are available, as well as the experience of the artists involved, when passing judgement. A show that earns an enthusiastic five stars at a festival might have got an encouraging three stars at an established venue. Lyn Gardner has helpfully acknowledged that she assesses shows at the Edinburgh Fringe, with its pressures of time and money and appeal for emerging artists, differently from shows on subsidised stages. So bear this in mind. Assess the reviews you receive with an eye on how other shows in this context are faring.

It is also wise to realise that new writing is scrutinised in a very different way from a revival. Reviewers are primed to critique the script in a way they do not with, say, Shakespeare; some reviewers of new work virtually ignore the production itself and deliver what amounts to a literary rather than a theatrical assessment. It's definitely harder for a new play to earn four stars than it is for a revival of an established 'classic'. But a critic can be both an admirer of a new play and still see room for improvement. A warm but reserved review of a new play may in fact be equal to a more gushing celebration of *Rutherford and Son*. It's all about the context.

Don't obsess over stars

Social media can be an incredibly powerful marketing tool but it has led to an obsession with simplistic or clickbait judgements. While three stars may not look as exciting as five, the body of the review might contain some fantastic remarks. Go beyond the headline and really weigh up what is being said. It is also worth remembering that stars are often awarded by sub-editors rather than reviewers, and are not necessarily a reliable indicator of the review itself. Infuriating, lamentable, but true.

It's only an opinion

A writer has relatively little control over the audience's reactions – in rudimentary literary theory terms, each person's 'horizon of expectations' differs and how they construct their experience varies. Some will chime with your feelings, others will see things that you weren't even aware were there, due to each individual's background, perspectives and personality. A reviewer's opinion will thus be affected by many factors beyond what is happening in the theatre. It can be wonderful to discover the different ways that people receive your play, but it means that a review can only ever be subjective.

Find a balance

It is important to find a balance when handling reviews. Remember that you are the same writer you were yesterday! A one-star rating hasn't suddenly made you terrible, while five stars haven't made you a genius. Try not to be too affected either way; learn from the rationale behind the rating. What has the reviewer singled out for praise or contumely? Is it within your control? If it is, how should it be acted upon?

In assessing reviews, it's vital to temper any extreme verdict. One person's reaction should not necessarily influence your process. Obtain a wide a range of opinions before drawing any conclusions, which we will discuss in the next chapter.

Making the Most of It:
Invitations, Transfers, Adaptations, Translations

Once the critical and audience reactions are known, the hard-headed business of being a playwright – that is, the self-promotion and strategic pitching for new opportunities – kicks in. While some producers may assist, the onus is mainly on you, or your agent, to capitalise on the production during its run. Invite important theatre-makers or funders to see it, keep an eye on possible transfers or adaptations, and hustle for fresh opportunities.

Invitations

Weeks before the production opens it is advisable to have drawn up a list of the theatre-makers, funders, commissioners or agents whom you would like to introduce to your work. It is sensible to collate this list with other members of the team, or with your agent if you have one; they may have personal connections that you can tap in to or be able to issue an invitation more effectively.

Plan the invitation strategy carefully. Regardless of the angle and the person making the approach, the more notice that can be given the better. Send invitations well in advance, concisely provide all key information, and if you get no response, wait until some good reviews have been harvested and then re-invite with some juicy press quotations.

The same principles of issuing invitations discussed in the 'Getting Noticed' chapter apply here. The only element that is perhaps different when issuing invitations to a production is that it is customary to offer complimentary tickets. After all, the people on your list probably receive dozens of invitations each week, and cannot possibly afford to pay for all of these. Offering a comp will make their attendance more likely, and renders the invitation more gracious – otherwise, it is just direct hard-sell marketing!

Bear in mind that a production will have a break-even target at the box office. A producer will not provide endless comps for industry guests. The number of comps to which the writer is entitled should have been stipulated in the agreement (see the chapter on 'Making Deals'); any further tickets will have to be paid for, unless the producer is exceptionally generous or unless the guest is directly relevant to the production's future life. This tends not to be too financially onerous, since the vast majority of invitees will not attend, but nonetheless be aware of the potential for a bill to accumulate in your name!

The positive consequence of this is that, if someone accepts a comp, they should be open to a conversation afterwards. They are quite literally in your debt. Don't hassle them too quickly, but if you've heard nothing after a few days, then do follow up.

Don't be despondent if not many industry figures attend. Most are perpetually busy. That does not mean they are oblivious of the production; good reviews or social-media buzz travel a long way. The production, simply by being on, will build your profile and reputation in ways you aren't always aware of. Just because invitations don't conjure up impressive theatre-makers bearing even more impressive commissions, doesn't mean they haven't drawn attention to the play and to the writer. As ever, building new relationships is a matter of attrition, not easy breakthroughs, so send those invitations and strive hard!

Extensions and transfers

A successful new play is a thing of wonder. If in possession of such a property, do your utmost to keep it alive. Never let a hit fade away if there is any way to squeeze more impact from it. If it enjoys further life, you can expect copious acclaim and, just maybe, some extra dosh. Authoring a play that not only thrives in its premiere but soars to new homes or fresh performances commands the industry, marking a playwright to watch. But be canny about how you approach further life; make sure it is the right thing for the play and for you.

Most new plays from emerging playwrights debut in a fringe context, meaning small houses and smaller budgets. Even new plays from established writers often premiere in studio spaces, as producers warily test audience appetite. Consequently, there is a trend for theatre-makers and critics to regard a premiere partly as a test-ground for further life. Too often, the measure seems to be: do we expect this to achieve validation by going elsewhere? This attitude is sometimes thrown around in rehearsals. Actors especially fixate on prospects for further life, at least if they don't have another project lined up. Sometimes it can feel like a show is only taking place now because of some vague hope that it will go somewhere else. All this means that writers can become overly invested in the hope of a transfer or extension.

It goes without saying that you should not be swept up in this fervour. Concentrate on making the show as strong as possible; productions should justify themselves, not yearn for some imaginary future. It's counterintuitive to envisage transfers or extensions; any further life will stem from the quality of the show as it is, not as some might dream of it being. Any premature eyeing of other options is a distraction, although by all means do open conversations if you have a strong connection with an appropriate company or producer who may be interested and appreciate the approach. Otherwise, focus on the production – for now.

If a play has been in development for years, the prospect of settling for a relatively short run, often in a small venue, may be unpalatable, but settle a writer should: merely getting to production is a phenomenal achievement, and the measure of a play's success is not whether or not it transfers, but how audiences respond. Getting that right makes all the difference to future prospects. For if further life does materialise, it will be due to exceptional reviews of the show in its original form. A clutch of respectable three stars will not be sufficient to justify a transfer; a deluge of rapturous four and five stars may make it feasible. Such reviews make finding investors or co-producers, or pitching for subsidy, possible, upon which any further life will depend. Get it right in the first instance, then ponder fresh options or pick up the conversations with other contacts.

Most hit plays consider either a transfer or an extension. A transfer can be to a different (more prestigious) venue in the same locale and/or to a new region. Alternatively, a successful play may not transfer at all but extend its initial run, or return for a second run, at the same venue. These categories of further life are distinct. Each offers something different.

Transferring to a larger venue signals that the play's quality and ambition deserve a bigger platform, in turn implying you are ready for bigger opportunities. Extending has the advantage of keeping the play in an environment in which it is clearly thriving, minimises costs in comparison to relocation, and exploits existing audience demand. It is less eye-catching but also less risky.

Touring the show into a new region may combine the best of both these options. It shows that the play stands up to new environments and wider exposure, without necessarily forcing it onto too big a platform; you can target similar-scale venues.

Each of these approaches has merits as well as drawbacks. Assess potential benefits as well as possible challenges. What message do you want to send about your writing?

It will probably be the producer's decision (see the 'Making Deals' chapter), but you can exert influence by canny invitations, strategic suggestions, and ultimately by providing or withholding final approval. You should know better than anyone what scale and stages will suit the script. (The same principles apply in seeking further life as in originally pitching; see the 'Getting Noticed' chapter.)

Transfers should not be rushed for their own sake; the word has a wonderful ring to it but belies how easy it is for a show that shone in a smaller venue to fall flat on a bigger stage with higher expectations. Every year, plays that were roaringly successful in an Edinburgh pub's backroom march triumphantly into 'proper' theatres, and every year a huge proportion of these slink away with a whimper.

The play must fit its new home. It may be preferable to seek transfers that extend the reach rather than the scale (like a tour of similar-size venues rather than a transfer to a huge auditorium). Think strategically about what will be of most benefit not only for this show but your future. Cashing in on the chance to move an intimate, delicate two-hander to a towering proscenium arch may be good for the bank balance, but a failure could do long-term harm to your other prospects.

This sounds remarkably sceptical, doesn't it? Further life will nearly always be a positive. Most producers are too sharp to propose anything that will damage a play, so in nine out of ten instances it's an easy and pleasurable decision to transfer or extend. We just sound the warning bell because of the one case in ten that burns a writer; we have met a few playwrights who innocently assumed that transfers could only be a good thing and thereby stumbled into a situation that tarnished the original production's success. Be positive about further life, be hugely proud if it comes to pass, but consider it from all angles first.

Adaptations

Another form of further life after a successful production is adaptation for a new medium. Papatango plays have been developed for television and radio; these sectors increasingly recruit writers from theatre. Arguably, many writers now treat theatre as an extension of these media (hence why the 'Writing for Theatre' chapter bemoans the dearth of writers with theatrical skills independent of the pervasive rhythms of TV). When drawing up an invitation list it is definitely worth thinking of television and radio commissioners. An agent can make a significant difference in this regard.

Whether the play will be deemed eligible for adaptation is largely outside your control. You should develop the script for theatre and trust that, if a TV or radio executive encounters it, they will be drawn to the story. These people are accustomed to taking new scripts through intensive development, and do not need ready-made scripts to lift straight from stage to screen or microphone. Don't try to smuggle a cinematic or radio story on to the stage; the chances are it will be rejected, and if it does enter production, it may flop in live performance. Better to impress producers in other media with the quality of your theatre writing. Leave it to them to invite you to pitch for an adaptation (or a new commission/project); that is the time to prove you have what it takes to flourish in their medium too.

If invited to adapt a play for screen or radio, think carefully about how the story would work. How long would it need to be? Would it be a stand-alone episode or a series? Would the story narrow in focus, or need supplementing with new plotlines? Immerse yourself in some of the recent work made by the producers and imagine fitting your story to that canvas. Remember that adaptation is a creative endeavour, not just an imitation of an existing work; don't be afraid to tell the story in different ways. The more convincingly you can address the different opportunities of a new medium, the more likely a commission is.

A great example is Douglas Adams's rambling, anarchic, hilarious *The Hitchhiker's Guide to the Galaxy*. This behemoth of a story morphed from radio to novel to TV to film, shapeshifting like one of its bizarre alien creatures. Each felt fresh because the plot was conceived anew for each medium.

If an adaptation is offered, there is no question: leap at it. Getting a foot in the door of the TV or radio sectors can be lucrative, as well as creatively stimulating. Many playwrights supplement their theatre income and hone their skills by working in these fields. Keep your expectations in check, however; a radio adaptation is likely to be broadcast – because the commission fee is one of the major expenses and, once it is incurred, producers are incentivised to use the resulting script – but TV commissions have a notoriously low rate of conversion to productions, because of the formidable cost of filming. Even if the adaptation does not end up being broadcast, earning the opportunity and establishing the relationship is a major accomplishment. (See the chapter 'Moving On' for more on working in these sectors.)

Translations and foreign transfers

Revivals, translations and adaptations provide booming business for many a playwright. British theatre is globally renowned as a writer's theatre (whereas auteur directors stalk the playhouses of Europe). The world really does watch what happens in British theatres – even the tiny ones – and a well-reviewed new play above a pub in Birmingham could find itself plucked across the seas and re-imagined in Berlin, Beirut or Brisbane. This can lead to new opportunities or creative relationships overseas, as well as generate revenue from a writer's back catalogue.

Case Study: Going International

Foxfinder by Dawn King, which won the 2011 Papatango New Writing Prize, made its world premiere in a forty-eight-seat theatre in Earl's Court, a quiet London suburb. By the year's end it had scooped up a spot on the *Independent*'s top-five plays of 2011 and won OffWestEnd, Royal National Theatre Foundation and Critics' Circle awards. It made its West End premiere in 2018.

And you might think that would be that, but companies in America, Scandinavia, Germany, Spain, Iceland, Greece, Australia and many other countries have taken note, obtained the script, and mounted new productions. The beautiful thing is that Dawn did not have to do much to solicit this; the mere fact of the play's production, and its success, advertised itself, and generated a near continuous income stream for the writer for several years.

Of course, *Foxfinder* was a standout; few plays can expect that level of success. But the international circuit doesn't just court the biggest hits. There is a market overseas for all sorts of new British writing, and it isn't just fed by one or two cherry-picked shows. A very talented young writer, and former Papatango Prize reader, called David K. Barnes had his play *Birthday Suit* run at the Old Red Lion Theatre, above a pub in Islington. It gleaned positive reviews but hardly, one would have thought, universal attention – yet within a few months it was playing in Malta.

Publication often helps attract international interest, and makes the script more widely available and high-profile, but is not a prerequisite. Reviews, comments on social media or industry recommendations can spread globally – and it's always worth a writer or their agent sharing any especially good reviews as far as possible. You never know where it might land.

Lest it sound like an international transfer is the fate of all new plays, it remains the exception, not the rule. Not as exceptional as one might think, however, so it is worth being aware of how it works.

Usually, foreign companies keen to land new British plays will scout reviews and social media (oh, brave new world!). Agents can also recommend international contacts who may be beyond your ken. If you don't yet have an agent and your play is a hit, you may procure an agent off the back of it, but if representing yourself, then research foreign companies that produce English-language plays (see the appendices). Send any who might be interested a reviews round-up (see the chapter on 'Reflecting') as an opening salvo. Any bites will then want to see the script; hardly ever will they consider transferring the original production, as the costs are prohibitive.

If interested, they will enquire about the rights; they will only (usually) want them for their specific country, so be wary of agreeing to any territory-wide rights as this may preclude other countries from hosting the play. If it is an English-speaking territory, the producer may simply purchase the rights to the script as it is (though you could take the chance to make new tweaks). Otherwise, they will probably commission a translation – but you should still be due a full fee for the rights, and also have approval over the translator and their version. Either way, negotiate the fee; if in doubt, aim high, for they are after all interested enough to reach out over the ocean. You may also swing free flights and accommodation! (Most of these negotiations will follow the course laid out in the chapter on 'Making Deals'.)

The only other thing to think about is that different countries have different theatrical traditions. Things that work in your play within a UK tradition may not translate; don't be overprotective of the original script, as the director or translator will have good reason for any changes. When *The Fear of Breathing* was translated into Japanese and mounted in a new production in Tokyo, the editor/director Zoe Lafferty and Chris, the original producer, were perturbed by the utter silence of the audience and the heightened mannerisms of the performances – until they saw other Japanese theatre and realised this was customary. Trust the local artists!

International productions or translations can be a vital income stream for playwrights. While they are not to be counted upon, the prestige of new British writing means they should never be overlooked as prospects.

This completes this act of the book. The show has been made. The last act discusses how to consolidate this and grow a writing career further; seeking transfers, translations or adaptations is only the beginning.

ACT THREE: TAKING THE NEXT STEPS

This is the third and final act – though in many ways it takes you to just the start of a professional career. It covers what to do once that production is in the bag and your thoughts turn towards even bigger and better things.

Most writers find it such a task to attain a production that they naturally assume that things can only be easier thereafter. In fact, the gradient remains as sharp, possibly even steeper. British theatre is very small, geographically and often financially, and there is a fetish for new writers. Funders prefer to plough money into a discovery, audiences are drawn to something new, and companies often emphasise debut talent in any programming that ventures away from established artists. Odd as it sounds, opportunities for emerging or even mid-stage writers are perhaps scarcer than for brand-new writers.

To land more productions, it's often a case of returning to the drawing board and repeating many of the initial steps outlined in the first acts of this book – only, hopefully, these become a little easier with familiarity, and you will be armed with extra know-how, reputation and track record.

This act, therefore, tackles how to transition from being a writer with one or two full productions under your belt, to being a professional playwright able to earn a living.

REFLECTING

It's important to learn from a production so that you become not only a better writer but better at managing your career. Factor the experience into your next steps. However successful the play was, there will be matters to improve. Reflect on your writing process and lay the foundations for the next project. This chapter suggests some strategies by which to achieve this, making it easier to bring a new production to fruition (with luck) and from there to build an entire career.

How to Assess a Show

In the weeks following the final curtain, when the hangover from closing night has faded, it is time to take stock. A playwright should learn and grow with every play if they are to make a career.

Playwriting is an undeniably personal art form; while sometimes difficult to detach yourself emotionally, it is important when assessing a show to be objective. Your first productions are only the beginning of a journey and mistakes will inevitably have been made, even in a five-star sell-out smash. The aim is to nurture the good and learn from the bad. Having watched many performances and seen audiences react to the world and characters you created, you should know more about your writing than ever before. How you use this to develop your work will have a huge bearing on your progression as a playwright. Ask the following questions as a starting point for reflection.

Were you satisfied?

The answer to this should go beyond whether the show was deemed a success or a failure. As the curtain descends, and before the audience show their opinion, there is a tiny, almost imperceptible window in which a writer knows whether or not the production delivered what they wanted, whether or not the script was as good as they hoped. That moment is rapidly swept aside by the ensuing audience and press opinions, but try to recapture it. That was when you, as a writer, had the purest response to your work, which matters more than anyone else's proclamations.

Analyse these feelings rigorously. Generalisation won't help you grow; really think about the specifics of the process the play underwent, and what worked and what didn't. Work through this list of provocations:

- Was any development work useful, or, if there wasn't any, would it have been?

- Did the production match your vision?

- Was the show a good representation of your writing, or were you forced to make compromises?

- Was the play suited to this particular space?

- How were your relationships with the director and producer? Would you work with them again?

- Did the people you wanted to watch it, watch it?

- Might the play have a further life, and if so, how would you help this to happen and would the script need changes?

- Has your career been moved on or set back?

Write down well-formulated answers, to stimulate clear reflection. Once you've weighed up the production, you'll be in a better position to think about what to work on for your next projects. Be sure to prioritise your truthful feelings as an artist; if it is tricky to answer some of these, get friends to discuss them with you. A sympathetic sounding board helps.

Were others satisfied?

From early notes from your collaborators, through rehearsals and performances with creatives, to audience feedback, it will by now seem that everybody has shared an opinion on your work. This is perhaps exhausting but it is all valuable knowledge. Draw on it to figure out:

- Did the play land with its audience?

- Were there notes you should have resisted, or did you rush any changes?

- What feedback have you received from the director? The actors? The producer? The audience?

- How did the critics react to the show, and the writing in particular?

Combine your answers to this section and the last section. They will help trace which elements of the show succeeded and which failed, and whether the responsibility for this lies with the script. They will also reveal whether you agree with collaborators or critics – and what to take from these relationships.

When making this assessment, try to keep a balance. Some elements of the writing will have worked better than others. While tackling any weaknesses in your process or craft will be a priority for future projects, it is just as important to build upon the things that went well.

Start by looking at the areas in which you had less success and explore why this was the case. What practical steps can you take to improve upon these and avoid the same mistakes? (It may be wise to refer back to the 'Writing for Theatre' and 'R&D' chapters to see if any of the techniques discussed there are relevant.)

It is undoubtedly important to push yourself to improve, but remember that focusing too much on a perceived area of weakness in a new script could, paradoxically, compromise your talents. If you know that your dialogue is strong but you struggle with structure, do not focus solely on one and neglect the other.

Lessons can be learnt as much from success as failure. If you have received positive feedback about one element, figure out why it worked well and replicate or sharpen this in the next play. Above all, don't obsess over a flaw; keep an eye on your strengths, as they were enough to get this far, and play(wright) to those.

Maintaining Records

To avoid slipping into the trap of self-doubt, which is all too easy with a remorseless introspection of craft and process, it's often useful to consider the impact and quality of your writing more widely. You can learn all sorts of useful, often inspiring, things from the people who were drawn to the show. To do this, examine not just your own writing, but keep records of all the other information you can lay your hands on. Hunches and half-remembered snatches of audience chatter are not really the evidence on which rigorous development of craft or winning a new commission can be founded. Collect material that will help to inform reflections and shape future planning. Much of this will have been compiled by the producer or box office, and all you have to do is ask for it; some you may record yourself.

Press archive

A press book is usually maintained by a production's PR or producer. It should consist of every reference to the show, both online and in print. As most, if not all, reviews or features now have a virtual as well as a physical incarnation, it's easy to keep tabs on them by setting up a Google alert.

Make sure that all press coverage is included. You may cherry-pick the best quotations and stars, and highlight these in a separate document, but you also need a comprehensive record. It allows you to assess all points of view, good and bad, and see the full range of responses to your writing. Whether or not you agree with the reviews is, perhaps, irrelevant: what's more useful is what it indicates about the public perception of your work.

Is there a consensus about strengths or weaknesses? Are you regarded in a certain light (for instance, as a 'political' writer)? These may be provocative jumping-off points for deciding on what projects to explore next. If several journalists have labelled you in a way that you are not entirely comfortable with, you may find it refreshing to challenge that assumption, or you may decide to plumb that well deeper and build your reputation further. Of course, never set out simply to confound or confirm critics – no one should dictate your work except you. It may be that you are inspired by what you find others have seen in your writing.

Even if you prefer not to be creatively influenced by reviewers, being aware of their verdicts can be useful. As well as harvesting bitesize praise as concrete evidence to support future commissions or funding applications (see the 'Moving On' chapter), you can get a sense of how the industry as a whole is perceiving your work. Knowing what has been written equips you to understand how venues or producers may respond to any approach; what notes should you hit or which associations should be emphasised.

Creative notes

As beneficial as it is to log the ponderings of critics, you should also keep notes on the feedback of the creative team throughout the process. Do these reveal anything that could be improved? If lots of rewriting was mooted after the initial read-through, then perhaps a more rigorous development or dramaturgical process needs to be considered. If some stage directions were ignored or changed by the design team, it may be worth thinking about how to better incorporate a sense of the visual and physical world in the next script. Scribble down anything that strikes you as reveal-ing something about your writing; often comments made in passing are the most insightful, and almost certainly the most truthful, and it is generally a writer's collaborators who understand the work best.

Industry guests

Ask the producer or box office to record all industry attendees. Knowing who has seen your work personally is hugely important in being able to target future commissions or applications, or in pursuing new collaborations. Did a TV executive drop in? That may lead to an option for a screen treatment. Is a friend of a cast member a big player in a venue? Check to see if they have seed commissions or attachment schemes. Even if nothing direct is likely, any nice words from an industry insider can fertilise other applications.

Your planning and next career moves can thus be heavily influenced by who saw your show. It doesn't need to be someone who was formally invited by you; whether or not a big agent only came because they are mates with the lighting designer, they still saw the show and now have a view of your work. Unabashedly reference the production when making contact; hopefully it will at least earn a coffee and some useful feedback, perhaps more.

Playwriting careers really are shaped by the connections you make, so tracking those and building relationships should be a central part of your focus during and after any production.

Audience data

This may sound like the preserve of audience development specialists, but any glimpses into the profile of those who watch your work are useful. Increasingly, writers now make independent Arts Council or local authority applications (sometimes but not always supported by a venue or company), so arm yourself with facts and figures that tick the boxes beloved by some funders. (There is more detailed advice on making funding applications in the next chapter.)

After all, why should companies use this material to accrue untold riches but not the writer behind the story that drew a particular audience? If you can demonstrate that your work appeals to individuals who may not be traditional theatregoers, or who may not be well represented among certain audiences, then make use of that. Even if not directly applying for subsidy, mentioning matters like this can sway a wavering producer or venue looking to bolster their audience-development offer.

Useful insights about your audience can be gleaned from tracking things such as:

- Age range (preferably broken down into the weightings of different age groups, e.g. what percentage were under twenty-five or over sixty?).

- Gender identities (e.g. what percentage identified as male, female, trans or other?).

- Ethnicities or cultural heritages (preferably self-identified rather than ticked from a prescribed list).

- Mental and/or physical disabilities or divergences.

- Home postcodes or regions (usually only collected from online bookers or those paying by card – which is most people!).

- Employment status (this may not be directly collected, but can be inferred if concessions for those on Jobseeker's Allowance or benefits are recorded for bookings).

These kind of demographic measures can prove extremely revealing about the reach, appeal and impact of a play. What community did your script foster? Be sensitive about gathering this information – leave it to the box office, as they will be aware of the proper processes, terminology and legalities.

Of course, data-protection laws limit a writer's access to personal information, but broad statistics should be available. Things like age or ethnicity can be recorded without necessarily compromising an individual's privacy, and are easily tracked in most modern box-office software systems, so don't be afraid to ask.

Moreover, learning about your audience, the people who are interested in your stories, can only be a creative spur. What would you like to share with them next – or what stories could broaden your following?

Last Reflections

Triangulating all the opinions and noise that surround a show is a challenge; making mature and constructive decisions based on these is even harder.

It's important therefore not to lose sight of that initial writerly impression; hold true to your reaction as an artist. The questions suggested here, and the records and material you might scrutinise, are intended to cut through the opinions of others and get to the heart of what worked in the script and what didn't. This is vital if your next play is to be even stronger, and you are to be empowered to pitch even more ambitious projects.

MOVING ON

Despite the cliché, a playwright is not only as good as their last play – they are only as good as their next. Collaborators and critics alike will expect a second, third, fourth or tenth play to be a step up; it may not be fair, but the pressure is always on a writer to show progression and exceed, not just satisfy, expectations. This is why the last chapter outlined ways to reflect on those expectations.

Moreover, with so many new plays hitting fringe stages, playwrights feel the burden of sustaining any initial success with relatively quick follow-up shows, with the adage 'out of sight, out of mind' a natural fear. Speaking practically, personal finances may also compel a productive rate. This combination – a financial and/or public obligation of prolific output with ever increasing expectations – is hardly conducive to good art.

The writers who sustain long careers are those who understand how to remain productive and satisfy critical and public expectation without compromising what allowed them to succeed in the first place. This chapter discusses how to do this, focusing mainly on writing for theatre, but with some advice on branching into film or TV commissions. (For further tips see the section closing the 'Going into Production' chapter.)

The process mapped out in Acts One and Two remains applicable at every stage of a writer's career, so these thoughts should supplement and extend how you practise that, not replace it. Move on by widening your connections, sharpening your skills, and perfecting your process.

A Portfolio Life

Let's start with an indisputable fact: few playwrights, no matter how artistically successful and respected, earn a living purely from theatre; almost every writer will dabble in teaching, TV or tele-marketing to live. It can feel like an admission of failure, once you have been produced, to confess to still having a 'day job'; banish that thought and undertake whatever other work will help pay the bills. Don't hand in your notice and dedicate yourself to writing only after one production; good plays are not – repeat *not* – writ-ten when starving or facing eviction, and there is no shame in having work besides writing. It's the norm.

Learn to balance professional demands

As your playwriting career develops, more will be asked of you in terms of deadlines and drafts. The transition from writing for yourself to writing for others will bring new pressure. Be careful not to overcommit yourself, and don't compromise whatever earns you a living – at least, not until you've racked up several success-ful shows and have the writing chops to cope with increased risks. You may want to look at the questions posed later in this chapter to determine your writing capacity and the number of commit-ments you can realistically handle.

Choose a complementary profession

Assuming that at some point non-writing work will feature in the schedule, you may want to consider how it relates to playwriting. Some writers like to situate it as close as possible to their primary professional identity, perhaps teaching creative writing (think of Winsome Pinnock at Kingston University or Steve Waters at UEA), or working as script editors or copywriters. This keeps the writing muscles sharp, may help continual development, and pos-sibly fosters new industry connections. Conversely, it may also dull the pleasure of writing or dispel the energy needed to snatch moments for your own writing.

Others prefer to preserve their playwriting resources, and earn a living in unrelated roles. This has the undoubted benefit of providing material from a wider field, but may not sit as easily with the other side of your professional life; employers may be less sympathetic to taking writing sabbaticals or disappearing for rehearsals.

It's important you settle on a work/writing balance which suits you. Remember, it's no failure to balance playwriting with other work – it's only a handful of writers who are lucky, not just talented, enough to live from theatre alone. This should inform all the decisions you make in building a career; don't overcommit or risk your health or bank balance. On which note:

Funding Your Writing

If it's a blow to be told that one shall not live by plays alone, don't despair. Writers don't have to resort to waiting tables in dimly lit dives. There are opportunities to be funded to write which, once you have landed a full production, you should be in a position to apply for, independent of any producer's sponsorship.

You will need to use the materials and evidence so assiduously collected following the guidance in the previous chapter, and you'll need to think a little bit like a producer – but your writing skills should stand you in good stead to pen successful applications.

Applying for grants

Some trusts and foundations, like the Peggy Ramsay Foundation, provide pots of money to support artists to write. Usually these are given to writers of proven pedigree but not yet in a position to command regular commissions. Approaching a funder having notched up one or two productions would be perfect timing; it's enough for them to trust your ability but not so much that they'll regard you as having passed beyond the need of support.

You will need to have a clear project and demonstrate a genuine case for funding. This tends to boil down to answering these key questions: what is the work and why is it important; why is support needed now; how exactly have you calculated the finances and can you justify your ask; how would a grant advance your career in a meaningful way?

We suggest some potential funding sources in the appendices. We especially want to emphasise that, contrary to popular belief, the Arts Council and the British Council will fund individual artists and R&D phases, not just concrete productions. You should definitely consider these resources.

Arts Council England exists to fund work in England, Creative Scotland serves this function north of the border, Arts Council Wales does so in Wales, and so on, while the British Council supports work by UK artists abroad. In its 2018 restructuring, Arts Council England introduced a new funding strand, catchily entitled Developing Your Creative Practice, which enables individual artists to apply for between £2,000 and £10,000 to support their work.

Competition, whether to private trusts or public funding bodies like the Arts Council, is undeniably fierce, and it is often necessary not just to prove artistic merit but a wider public benefit. That's not as intimidating as it seems, however; simply having a rehearsed reading or conducting a platform event (as discussed in the 'R&D' chapter), can be considered giving members of the public access to art, and these benefit playwrights in their own right anyway.

Our top tip on approaching a funding application is to complete this table:

Input	e.g. A £1,000 grant and in-kind support of a rehearsal space.	e.g. A £5,000 grant.
Activity	Funds a week's R&D with actors.	Funds three months of writing and buys a new work laptop.
Output	A new draft honed through R&D; a rehearsed reading for an invited audience.	A new script.
Impact	Develops artist's process; connects artist with other theatre-makers and professional resources; public showcase.	Reaches out to producers and companies, grows the writer's profile, increases chance of a production.
Beneficiaries	Playwright; the cast and collaborators; audience at reading includes invited industry figures and young people at risk of social exclusion.	Playwright.

This helps you refine your pitch and clarify what exactly a funder would be supporting and why. The headings should be self-explanatory; they map out the stages of the project and demonstrate how any support will translate into the activity, what will result from that, and what the impact of this will be and for whom. A good funding application tells a story.

There are two examples in the table above. Neither is 'better' than the other or inherently more likely to succeed. Different funders will be interested in different things. So a funder who values developing new artists may be drawn to the second application, whereas a funder who prioritises experimentation or public engagement may prefer the first. If you understand the ask you are making, you can identify appropriate funders to approach.

Research a potential funder thoroughly – check their latest accounts and report on either Companies House or the Charity Commission – to get a sense of what they like to fund and how much they generally grant. Then use this table to figure out whether your project would be a likely fit.

As well as referring to our appendices, hunt out other relevant grant-giving bodies – look up funders name-checked in published plays or in a venue's publicity – and don't be bashful about making an approach. Often philanthropists or funding officers are thrilled by the prospect of developing a personal relationship with an artist and helping to shape their career.

While it may seem rather too much like producing, if it's going to earn you time to focus solely on playwriting it may be the best investment you've ever made. These grants can make a massive difference to completing a project or experimenting with new processes. And they can be vital in sustaining artists outside the small slice of privilege that, regrettably, so often produces our plays.

Insider's View: Alex James

A key reason Arts Council England exists is to support artists to make work that responds to, and asks questions of, the contemporary world they inhabit. Traditionally in England's cultural history, playwrights have been at the heart of this process of reflection.

One of the most responsive grant programmes Arts Council England administers is Arts Council National Lottery Project Grants, our open-access fund. Perhaps crucially for playwrights, you don't need to be an organisation to apply. In 2016/17, we offered to fund 184 applications for new work from individual applicants across England. Many of these were proposals from independent playwrights seeking support for time to write, and hoping to develop or present original plays. In theatre, we still invest more in 'new writing' than any other category of work.

So, what are the key characteristics of a good application?

Having a finished draft ready for production is not a prerequisite, but a successful application to Arts Council National

Lottery Project Grants will almost always start with a clear, concise synopsis of the work. You may not know where the piece will end up in terms of form and content, but you should know where you are starting from. When you begin to write, do you envisage a studio piece with two actors, or a large-scale epic with a chorus and a six-strong cast? What are the key themes you will explore and why are they relevant?

You don't need to be a commissioned or published playwright to apply, but you should be able to articulate your track record, however brief. Have you taken any writing courses? Is this your first full-length piece? Who has seen or read your work?

When writing your application you should also think about how you detail the process you are asking us to fund. How well-evolved is the work at the point you submit your application, and where do you want it to be once the process is completed? Every application includes a project plan – be specific. What will your day look like? Are you developing a one-page story outline or redrafting for the fifth time? A successful applicant will often be open to subjecting their work to criticism as it progresses; who might be your 'outside eye'?

It is likely to strengthen your application if you have a keen sense of which companies or venues may be a good fit for your work – and all the better if you have been able to open a dialogue with them. In this regard, in particular, the Papatango New Writing Prize is vital. It sits in a cohort of respected schemes and initiatives open to both new and established writers. Knowing the scope of these opportunities is crucial – diarise the submission window for open-access competitions; read up on the criteria for writers' response events; familiarise yourself with the application process for the various writers' groups.

Addressing these points can't guarantee funding – the programme remains highly competitive – but it will hopefully help you to make your application as compelling as your play.

Alex is a Theatre Relationship Manager at Arts Council England.

MOVING ON

The ethics of funding and the patron–playwright bond

Sometimes artists worry that taking someone else's shilling could compromise their work. The concern tends to be that some malign influence or pressure will be exerted over the play being written. This may, perhaps, very occasionally be true of a grant from some soulless corporate monolith looking for propaganda, although we've never encountered it. For the most part, funders are motivated by a desire to help someone to create; the reward is in facilitating a vision rather than posturing as a patron. They'll naturally want to share in the work, or have glimpses into the process, but don't distrust that. It's only natural to build a relationship with someone who has committed to you and who cares about your work – and often funders are very insightful, and can help in all sorts of ways besides just stumping up cash. Respect them as people, not as moneybags.

That said, the ethics of funding are an increasingly sensitive subject. In recent years, for instance, protestors have – rightly, in our view – challenged arts organisations for taking BP's coin without regard to that company's record of appalling environmental damage. Reputational risk is a concern for anyone in receipt of funding; while there will certainly be less scrutiny on an individual artist taking relatively small sums, that doesn't mean the ethical position is any different. How would you feel about taking a donation from a glossy-suited, sophisticated arts fan who just so happens to be an arms dealer? Or from a foundation built on the profits of the tobacco industry?

Don't panic – these are extreme examples. Happily, most of the funders interested in supporting emerging talent are not shady outfits who tend to support relatively high-profile institutions as part of an effort to repair their toxic public image. Anyone funding the small-scale, less-visible work of emerging artists almost certainly does it from genuine passion. Nonetheless, make sure you're comfortable with the basis of their fortune before you bank the cheque.

Take opportunities wherever they may be

As we mentioned in the 'Getting Noticed' chapter, commissions and funded residencies or attachments within theatres are fiercely competitive. You should definitely start to apply for them once you've a production under your belt and the reviews and evidence collated to support an application, following the advice in the last chapter. These are absolutely vital to any emerging playwright's career.

But don't just assume the only paid gigs are industry-specific. As we also noted, many universities, libraries and other arts or education organisations fund writing positions of some sort, sometimes in conjunction with a theatre and sometimes not. These non-theatre schemes can be an equally vital resource. We cited some examples in the 'Getting Noticed' chapter, but new opportunities arise frequently, so do some digging. The London Playwrights' Blog does a superlative weekly round-up of opportunities nationwide (despite the name); get on the mailing list.

Becoming a writer-in-residence or playwright-on-attachment to these kinds of institutions is often as well or better funded than seed commissions from theatres, and you usually have much more control over the work and the rights. They also validate your talent and make pitching to theatres a little easier. So moving on from a production need not be to a theatre; it can be within a broader and richer sector.

Wherever you seek new opportunities, and however you fund yourself, it is important that you think strategically. Understand how each decision or commitment will build your career or develop your writing. Therefore:

Know the Next Level: Keeping a Career On the Up

There's no absolute hierarchy in theatre that dictates which productions, commissions or positions are 'better' than others. Dodging the horror of corporate rankings is one of the pleasures of working in the arts – and also one of the challenges in ensuring that one's career continues to soar. Playwriting is such a tough, competitive slog that many writers leap at any opportunity that crops up. They're often right to do so. But if it is possible, be selective about where, how and with whom you work. Never be precious or ungrateful, but due care and strategy may prove invaluable in making your work sought-after and high-value. There are a few different elements to factor into this decision-making.

Size and scale

There is a brutal economy in theatre: the number of seats dictates the finances – and often but not always the prestige – of a production. It's not just the box-office potential but also investment or subsidy that are influenced by the numbers who can experience a show; if only a few hundred people can witness it, persuading funders to make up box-office shortfall will be harder. Equally, persuading professional critics to review becomes easier when the potential audience – and their readership – increases.

This is why so many fringe venues relocate to larger premises after building a reputation; they recognise that, however well respected they may be, greater capacity can only strengthen their standing. The same is true of playwrights. Put simply, the bigger the venues that premiere your plays and the longer the runs, the more money and attention you are likely to receive (not necessarily 'earn'; it's as much hard work to write for a studio of one hundred seats as for an auditorium of one thousand).

This doesn't mean that writing for smaller venues is looked down upon; writers of all statures may relish creating something intimate, and some of our best new-writing theatres are also our smallest. But if a writer doesn't manage to present plays on bigger stages, their career – and income – will stall. Nearly all writers learn their craft in tiny studios or rooms above pubs, but only those who can land, and handle, a transition to bigger stages are likely to earn a living in the long term.

There's no cause for alarm if your first few plays are mounted at one or more 'fringe' venues (which tends to mean venues of up to one hundred seats, with limited or no in-house producing capacity, often neither commercially viable nor commanding much if any regular subsidy). Operating on this scale is almost inevitable at the start of a career, as craft is honed and reputation forged. There is a risk, however, of becoming trapped; many promising writers (and directors, designers and actors) never break out of this loop. Perhaps they don't want to, preferring the close relationship with an audience and strong collaboration of pulling together against low budgets. Certainly, there's no shame in writing plays that continue to draw audiences and develop strong relationships with collaborators. It is unlikely, though, to constitute a living. There comes a point when any playwright aspiring to live by writing must recognise that it's time to move to the next level. And in turn, there will come a time to move on from there. Beware stagnation.

This is why writers need to curate where their work goes on, to continually challenge their practice and bolster their earnings. James Graham, for instance, made his breakthrough at the estimable but tiny Finborough Theatre, and his subsequent plays have gone on at the National Theatre, the Donmar Warehouse, the West End and at a range of excellent regional venues like Hull Truck and Theatre Royal Plymouth. The Finborough, meanwhile, has continued seeking out other talented playwrights in need of a platform. You are well advised to map out what venues or companies will be the next reasonable step.

There's no single pathway. It's not simply about size – reputation matters too. If you mount a handful of shows at a pub or fringe theatre, of the size of, say, the Hope Mill in Manchester, and then premiere at a significantly larger venue, say the Bolton Octagon or Theatre Royal Stratford East, then your next play could very feasibly go on at a venue of equal or lesser size yet greater reputation, like the Royal Court Upstairs, or be scheduled for a small run as part of a really outstanding programme, such as a season with Paines Plough.

It's not just about constantly striving to play to bigger audiences, but being programmed by more competitive and prestigious houses or as part of more daring or innovative seasons. The key thing is to understand why a venue or slot is appropriate, and what it signals about your ambition and quality, whether that is by size or reputation.

Know your needs

The size or reputation of a company should never be the primary consideration in whether you work with them. It's all about whether they are sympathetic to your work, whether there is a mutual trust that promises a good creative relationship, and what deal they offer and whether it's appropriate.

Sometimes, the bigger the organisation, the cheekier they are with their offer. It's not malevolent. Naturally, as budgets get stretched, canny operators trade on their brand rather than a financial commitment, offering writers opportunities that bolster the CV more than the bank balance. Many reputable organisations only offer behind-closed-doors opportunities to emerging writers, with almost no intention or capacity to produce them, preferring to programme better-known, more commercial names. Although this is often railed against as cynical lip-service to the notion of supporting artists, it's understandable; many companies argue, quite justifiably, that the pressure-free chance to develop out of sight is vital in nurturing early talent. Whatever your perspective, the question is, when should a writer make the leap from cycles of hidden writing to public performance?

For instance, if Papatango offered a seed commission to someone who had only penned a short fringe run, it would constitute a respectable opportunity; if offered to a writer of several hit productions, it would be uninspiring (we serve only early-stage writers, so this is hypothetical). A seed commission (explained in the 'Making Deals' chapter) requires much work, yet comes with no guarantee of adequate financial reward or production, so a proven playwright is better off seeking projects with a greater return, monetary or theatrical, however prestigious the company.

The point is that, once you have debuted, there is only one currency to build on that: further productions. That doesn't preclude seed commissions, residencies or R&Ds from having immense worth, both artistically and financially; it's just that if you start to accept too many, they can eat up all the time that could be spent pursuing an actual production. There is a risk this establishes you in the collective industry consciousness as unready for big commissions. That can be a hard nut to crack – so try to judge when you have moved beyond this stage. In effect, know your worth, and pitch for that level (without being ungrateful for or needlessly dismissive of other offers).

This can be very tricky; turning away any offer is a wrench. A rough way to balance development and support with continued production opportunities is to figure out what your writing capacity is, then allocate some of it to seed commissions or R&D and reserve some of it for projects that are more likely to reach production. Work out:

- How many hours can you devote to writing, without compromising any stable income on which you rely?

- How many stories do you have the wherewithal to work on?

- How many drafts will you undertake before a project is complete?

- Is a proffered seed commission or R&D project artistically exciting for you?

These will help to suggest the number of plays you can work on within your schedule. Allocate your resources to avoid being swallowed by behind-the-scenes development. This sounds like a nice problem, but many fledgling writers get stuck in a loop. There is surely a limit to how much development anyone needs; ultimately, careers are made by productions. Nonetheless, also appreciate the value of such opportunities and leave some room for them.

There is no fixed policy to follow as to when you should be due what level of offer, and sometimes smaller offers with no likelihood of production are designed not out of lack of trust, or penny-pinching, but to enable artistic experimentation. Assess each offer on its own merits. This takes us on to:

Collaborators and vision

Size isn't all that matters. Sometimes smaller, more flexible organisations may propose more exciting, higher-risk ventures. Even if the offer is only a seed commission, if it connects you with an exciting director, or backs you to experiment with a different kind of work, then it may be a great chance to push on artistically.

Always consider what vision underlies the proposal. Are there new challenges or fresh collaborations? Is there the chance to make work for different audiences or reach new communities? Start with these questions:

- Is the company larger, or better funded, than previous collaborators?

- Is the company well regarded for its work?

- Does the company reach new or significant audiences?

- Is a collaboration with an exciting artist mooted?

- Is the company offering other long-term benefits, such as a residency, or could this relationship generate further opportunities?

There are many reasons why an offer may be irresistible, and few reasons to spurn it. In general, the only really valid grounds to reject an opportunity are if the company has a poor reputation or isn't offering a fair financial deal, if you, happily, have too many projects, or if you fear being swallowed by endless R&D loops.

Always look for reasons to say yes to people who want to support your writing, but don't be afraid to say no if the vision doesn't convince you, however prestigious the organisation. And if that's the case, then proactively pitch to others; some writers prefer smaller companies who are better placed to pursue more personally ambitious work. The golden rule in continually pushing a career to new heights is not to seek productions with big neon signs, but to grow the quality of the work and know what each new project does to stretch or reward the playwright.

What Next?

Grizzled music producers speak in dread of second-album syndrome. It describes the struggle for a band to follow up a first album's success with something equally groundbreaking, while maintaining sufficient familiarity to keep the fans happy. This is compounded by the fact there was a lifetime to make the first album and only a year or two to make the second. The same is true of a playwright. After pouring your heart, soul and personal experience into one play, it can be bewildering to move on under pressure. Just remember, that's how gems form.

It takes more thought than simply choosing theme and subject. Your process might be the same but you should now be further along in your journey as an artist. Your next step therefore is probably more important, in terms of defining you as a playwright, than the debut you laboured so hard to get. Your early work can show potential, but what follows must deliver results.

To illustrate: can you name Caryl Churchill's first play? Chances are, no. It was *Owners*, and while promising at the time, it has since faded away, whereas her later plays like *Top Girls* have indisputably become modern classics. Hopping over the Atlantic, Tennessee Williams's first play *Battle of Angels* flopped on Broadway, but did enough to earn him the attention that made his second play possible – and that was the phenomenon of *The Glass Menagerie*. Careers may be launched by first plays, but they are built on second, third and fourth plays. How should you approach yours?

Showing range and building your voice

It is important, even imperative, to show range, especially at the start of a career when producers are weighing up whether to offer commissions and need to be convinced. A common pitfall is repetition. While continuing to explore themes is perfectly valid, and you must be true to your vision, writing essentially the same play again should be avoided at all costs. It sounds obvious, but many writers revisit the same material once too often. This is perhaps because they are told to write what they know – good advice provided what you know is interesting. Nonetheless, to prove your writing chops you will at some point need to tell stories beyond your own, conceiving and inhabiting a variety of worlds and characters.

This is vital, because with so many writers starting out on relatively small stages, it can be hard to transition to more prominent, financially rewarding venues. Convince programmers that your writing can scale up and carry more weight.

To work towards this, be strict in the planning. Look at your previous play in detail, the themes, the structure, the characters. This should help avoid retelling the same story. Then, look at your process. If you find yourself drawn to writing plays with few characters, then look at delivering the same level of detail over a larger ensemble. If prone to writing quick, short scenes, try writing longer, continuous acts.

This is not to say you should artificially reinvent your writing. Use the reflection discussed in the last chapter to understand what works for you. But look to stretch your writing, and convince commissioners that you can deliver a range of stories of different scales and for varied stages.

Writing for screen

Showing range can extend to working across other media. It's no secret that the big bucks lie in writing for screen. A quick roll call of theatre writers championed by Papatango reveals that many have gone on to work in TV and film. Quite right too. Why should writers be restricted to one form? Some stories work better on the visual, big-scale world of the screen, while some belong on the verbal, visceral and intimate stage. The best, or at least the savviest, writers learn to deliver both.

Of course, many, even most, TV or film projects never reach the screen, but paradoxically a screenwriter will probably be paid more for something that never comes off than a playwright will for a hit play that's the talk of the town. And when a TV or film does get made, it can be a pension in its own right – and reach a far bigger audience than plays possibly can.

It's worth thinking, therefore, about how to make a name as a screenwriter as well as a playwright. The first step is to invite screen executives and television commissioners to see stage work (which is where an agent can be useful; see the 'Going into Production' chapter). It's openly acknowledged by TV and film people that theatre is their training ground and their recruitment agency rolled into one.

In my experience, if you're pitching directly to a TV production company you need to go through an agent (unless the company states otherwise). Initially they will probably want to see a writing sample, or to gain familiarity with your work in some other way. If they're interested, then you're likely to be invited to chat with a development executive; it's a chance to feel each other out and talk casually about your work and ideas. If there's a good rapport, then this is where you start to develop a working relationship. You may be invited to share ideas as a one-page pitch, with the possibility of further discussion. All this potentially leads to delivering a longer, more detailed treatment.

Ideally you'd research the companies you want to approach, so that you have a sense of the kind of projects they make and whether your ideas are a good fit. Try to avoid pitching what you think they want. Instead, pitch what you're passionate about writing, something you'd really like to see – this passion is what will draw people in.

If you're very early in your career, lack credits or are without an agent, then obtaining access to production companies may be trickier. Nonetheless, there are other ways to connect with producers, such as networking events. Some companies will run initiatives to identify new talent and these may be open calls. Keep an eye out for these things on companies' social media channels. Another useful approach is to network across, rather than up; get to know the development assistants as, often, they will eventually produce their own projects.

Dare was Papatango's fourth Resident Playwright. She has written extensively for television, including EastEnders *and* Waterloo Road.

MOVING ON

As well as these practical overtures, develop your writing to suit the screen. Remember that these media are more visual, and offer scope for short, expositional or plot-heavy dialogue that would fall flat in theatre but can be carried by the intense realism and immersion of a screen image.

As an exercise, challenge yourself to develop your playscript into a screenplay; think about how the structure would change, whether the world would need expanding from the intimacy and focus of theatre, and how visual tricks and camerawork could refine the storytelling. It's a technical challenge, but mastering it may well make the difference to becoming a professional writer.

Writing for radio

Another platform with immense potential for playwrights is radio. This senior medium still commands millions of listeners, while the rise of podcasts means that appetite for fresh stories is strong. You should not, therefore, neglect to approach radio producers or commissioners. These people are accustomed to harnessing stage talent. A quick survey of the BBC Audio Drama Awards reveals that the winners are heavily drawn from the ranks of theatre.

BBC Radio 4 often commissions adaptations of stage plays for its vaunted Afternoon Drama slot series; Papatango's first Resident Playwright May Sumbwanyambe adapted our production of his play *After Independence* for this platform, with George directing the original cast, and has since written new plays especially for radio. Similarly, 2012 Papatango Prize-winner Louise Monaghan has written several radio plays in recent years.

Make sure to invite radio commissioners to a production; if they can't come, then share the script and any strong reviews or quotations. As with angling for screen opportunities, it is often in this regard that having an agent can prove invaluable, as they should have connections and know whom to target. If you are operating independently, then look up the names of producers and directors of recent plays on BBC Radio 4 or independent companies like Big Finish Productions. The BBC Writersroom and Writers' Guild of Great Britain websites contain some handy lists, while the Radio Independents Group website is also useful.

It is a more realistic prospect to have a stage play adapted for radio, or to receive a commission for a radio play, than it is to write for screen, as producers' overheads and risks are smaller and the platform is enjoying a resurgence, meaning new material is always needed. Decision-making tends to be less prolonged and the process of moving from pitch to writing to production less convoluted.

Do not take it for granted though. To work on radio many of the visual tricks or storytelling of theatre will need to be re-imagined, so try to emphasise your skills in narrative structure and dialogue if you share excerpts or pen sample scenes. Also bear in mind that a radio play will tend to be relatively short, usually forty-five minutes to an hour. To adapt stage plays can require telescoping storylines or compressing character arcs; it is also a chance to make changes to fit this different medium. Be aware of the skills you will need to demonstrate.

Not only can radio provide a vital source of commissioning income, it can build a writer's profile among audiences and creatives. Many brilliant artists, whom it would be nigh on impossible to secure for a prolonged stage engagement, will be able to squeeze a one- or two-day commitment for radio into their schedule. The connections a writer can make through radio often lead to other opportunities and boost the CV.

Whatever you write next, and for whatever medium, it is important that throughout the process you continue to build your voice. Leave your comfort zone, and keep pushing yourself to grow and learn. You have had work produced and are now officially a playwright; as pretentious as it might sound, the next step is to decide what kind of playwright you want to be, whether you also want to be a screen and radio writer, and how you therefore present yourself to collaborators and commissioners.

Pitching to New Collaborators and Growing Old Relationships

Playwrights' careers don't evolve in isolation. Knowing how to find new collaborators who can push your writing further, and how to nurture old partnerships so that they remain inspirational, will improve your chances as a professional playwright.

Seek new people out

Once you've had your work produced, you're on a new level. That means reaching out to agents, directors, producers or actors whom you admire is more likely to draw a response (especially if you have judiciously collected juicy quotations or hefty stats, as covered in the 'Reflecting' chapter). Without expanding your influences, your work is unlikely to grow.

Don't be backward in forging new relationships; sending an email with a request for a coffee is commonplace, and it's how even big stars find new opportunities. Vicky Featherstone first met John Tiffany when he was an intern at West Yorkshire Playhouse and volunteered to help her run a festival for free, as long as she didn't tell his mum what he was up to – a humble start to an enduring creative partnership that has led to huge hits at both the National Theatre of Scotland and the Royal Court.

That said, never fixate on whom you'd like to work with just on the basis of reputation. As discussed in the 'Working with Collaborators' chapter, find partners who respect your work and add something to it.

Don't abandon old colleagues

You should know who helped you reach this point. Appreciate them – well, those who meaningfully contributed to your work; the nightmares can be dispensed with! But, seriously, theatre is a small industry and disloyalty is frowned upon. An artist isn't obliged to work repeatedly with the same people, but respecting a relationship, retaining the potential to work together again, is easy and benefits everyone.

Moreover, often the best work in a creative relationship comes only after a long period of trial and error, so don't focus entirely on chasing bigger venues or more high-profile collaborators. If you know artists who can deliver your writing satisfactorily, cherish them. They should be people you continue to call upon (and whom you support in return). As the partnership develops, so should the work – constantly seeking brand-new collaborations may not achieve this. It's not unusual for members of a creative relationship to build careers in tandem. As well as Vicky Feather-stone and John Tiffany, one also thinks of Nicholas Hytner and Alan Bennett, or Josie Rourke and Kate Pakenham, pairs continually making important work across different companies.

So, the more experience you accrue, the more you should understand the collaborator you need: is a project suited to a known partner or would it be more rewarding in new hands?

Be prepared – yet flexible

Whether approaching new collaborators or rekindling old lags, a playwright should shrewdly assess what could be on the cards. It may simply be an introductory coffee, merely declaring an interest; it may precede a pitch; it may be an interview. It sounds obvious, but these are not always signposted as clearly as they could be, in what remains an industry driven by intuition, conversation and spontaneity more than formal process and transparent assessment.

Many projects emerge from chats that writers approach unassumingly; equally, sometimes an opportunity can be lost because, through no fault of theirs, a writer was insufficiently prepared. Research the individual(s) being met, even if you know them, and surmise what they might ask or what you might need to ask. Recognise the uncertainty that attaches to many meetings, and prepare discussion points that enable you to pursue different gambits. This is especially true when meeting to discuss bigger opportunities than you have hitherto encountered; it can be hard to know what to expect, so be armed with a range of ideas.

A writer needs plenty of 'product', with several pitches to suggest; don't stake everything on one script. You never know what might tickle someone's fancy – or land your biggest project yet.

Insider's View: Dawn King

When I look back into the mists of time to see what had been happening for me after my first play *Foxfinder*, and how I generated work, I remember feeling that *nothing* seemed to have changed and being very frustrated. Why wasn't I now 'a playwright' with multiple commissions? Why was I still working for minimum wage in a cinema? Rage!

I've since learned that it takes time for the ripple effects of productions or finished scripts to spread out. Someone who loves your play might not be in a position to commission you for a while, so you need a little patience [it was seven years between *Foxfinder*'s production with Papatango and its West End premiere with Bill Kenwright!].

That doesn't mean sit on your hands. After *Foxfinder*, I chased all the opportunities available. I was already trying to get into film, and I wrote another two plays, one of which, *Ciphers*, ended up touring with Out of Joint, the Bush and Exeter Northcott. The other play has never been staged but I had a ball writing it.

To keep yourself going as you slog through redrafts, and to keep part of your brain alive for generating new ideas, have a 'mistress project'. The script you're supposed to be writing is your marriage and the thing you really want to write but you're not supposed to spend time on, that's the mistress. A successful mistress might become the new marriage, of course, down the line...

Dawn won the 2011 Papatango New Writing Prize for Foxfinder, *Papatango's production of which was named one of the* Independent's *top-five plays of 2011, and won OffWestEnd and Royal National Theatre Foundation Playwright awards.* Foxfinder *has since premiered worldwide and in the West End. Dawn has premiered new plays with Out of Joint, Northampton Royal & Derngate, and the Bush Theatre, written for TV and film, and been nominated for a BAFTA and the Susan Smith Blackburn Prize.*

'To Thine Own Self Be True'

Polonius is often portrayed as a pompous ass whose only contribution to the Danish court was to ruin a perfectly good arras. In fact, he says some pretty astute things – and when Dawn concurs that we should pursue projects that are true to us, then that's definitely sound advice to end on.

The only thing left to say is: books like this can give useful tips, but playwriting is an idiosyncratic, artistic, profoundly personal vocation. Your journey will be completely your own. Never compromise your process, your vision or your stories, because they will be what ultimately determine your successes and, inevitably, failures. We just hope this book will give you a better shot at navigating a writer's way through the theatre world.

Be open, be full of ideas, be brave enough to embrace uncertainty – theatre is full of knocks, but if you can handle those, from the first day of training to opening a show to pitching a whole new project, then you belong in this world. You are a playwright.

Good luck, and remember: all you need is a story.

MOVING ON

APPENDICES

We hope that these lists will help make your playwriting journey a little easier and the industry a little more open.

None of the organisations or individuals mentioned on these lists are necessarily personally known to us; inclusion is not a recommendation. Nor are these lists exhaustive; the industry changes quickly, and some names may have been inadvertently overlooked or omitted. They are, therefore, simply a suggestion of where you might start your researches.

Happy hunting!

TRAINING OPPORTUNITIES

Remember that courses change more frequently than a reviewer's mind, so these are intended as starting points for research into training options.

Some of these, especially undergraduate degrees, are not solely focused on playwriting. We have nonetheless only included courses featuring some specific teaching of playwriting; there are many courses that offer creative writing but do not necessarily have this specialist provision.

Undergraduate Degrees

University of Bangor, BA Creative and Professional Writing:
www.bangor.ac.uk/courses/undergraduate/W890-Creative-and-Professional-Writing

Brunel University London, BA Theatre and Creative Writing:
www.brunel.ac.uk/study/undergraduate/theatre-and-creative-writing-ba

University of East Anglia, BA Scriptwriting and Performance:
www.uea.ac.uk/study/undergraduate/degree/detail/ba-scriptwriting-and-performance

University of Greenwich, BA Creative Writing:
www.gre.ac.uk/ug/ach/w801

Lancaster University, BA Scriptwriting for Stage, Screen and Gaming:
www.blackpool.ac.uk/course/vm1he03?utm_source=whatuni&utm_medium=referral&utm_campaign=hotcoursesgroup

University of Northampton, BA Creative Writing:
www.northampton.ac.uk/study/courses/creative-writing-ba-hons

University of Wales, Trinity St David, BA Creative Writing:
www.uwtsd.ac.uk/ba-creative-writing

University of Warwick, BA English Literature and Creative Writing: www.warwick.ac.uk/fac/arts/english/applying/undergraduate/courses/qw38

University of York, BA Theatre: Writing, Directing and Performance: www.york.ac.uk/study/undergraduate/courses/ba-theatre-writing-directing-performance

Postgraduate Degrees

Bath Spa University, MA Scriptwriting:
www.bathspa.ac.uk/courses/pg-scriptwriting

University of Birmingham, MA Creative Writing:
www.birmingham.ac.uk/postgraduate/courses/taught/fcw/creative-writing.aspx

University of Central Lancashire, MA Scriptwriting:
www.uclan.ac.uk/courses/ma_scriptwriting.php

Central St Martins, MA Dramatic Writing:
www.arts.ac.uk/csm/courses/postgraduate/ma-dramatic-writing

City University of London, MA Creative Writing (Playwriting and Screenwriting):
www.city.ac.uk/courses/postgraduate/creative-writing-playwriting-and-screenwriting

University of East Anglia, MA Creative Writing Scriptwriting:
www.uea.ac.uk/study/postgraduate/taught-degree/detail/ma-creative-writing-scriptwriting

University of Edinburgh, MSC Playwriting:
www.ed.ac.uk/studying/postgraduate/degrees/index.php?r=site/view&id=775

Edinburgh Napier University, MFA Playwriting:
www.napier.ac.uk/courses/mfa-playwriting-postgraduate-fulltime

University of Essex, MA Playwriting:
www.essex.ac.uk/courses/pg00722/1/ma-playwriting

Falmouth University, MA Writing for Script and Screen:
www.flexible.falmouth.ac.uk/_lp/masters-in-writing-for-script-and-screen.html?gclid=Cj0KCQiAus_QBRDgARIsAIRGNGjKO
XxOXRT9HEmLILJc4xUKXVYtlIBjrdKynFmpttgLaeRuFYmoq
0MaAhtAEALw_wcB

University of Glasgow, MLitt Playwriting and Dramaturgy:
www.gla.ac.uk/postgraduate/taught/playwritingdramaturgy

Goldsmiths College, University of London, MA in Dramaturgy
and Writing for Performance: www.gold.ac.uk/pg/ma-dramaturgy-writing-performance

Regent's University London, MA Writing for Stage and Screen:
www.regents.ac.uk/study/postgraduate-study/programmes/ma-writing-for-screen-stage

Royal Central School of Speech & Drama, MA Writing for Stage
and Broadcast Media: www.cssd.ac.uk/course/writing-for-stage-and-broadcast-media-ma-mfa

Royal Holloway, University of London, MA Playwriting:
www.royalholloway.ac.uk/dramaandtheatre/prospectivepostgrad
uates/maplaywriting.aspx

University of St Andrew's, MLitt Playwriting and Screenwriting:
www.st-andrews.ac.uk/subjects/english/playwriting-screenwriting-mlitt

St Mary's University, MA Playwriting:
www.stmarys.ac.uk/postgraduate-courses-london/playwriting

University of Wales, Trinity St David, MA Creative and Script
Writing: www.uwtsd.ac.uk/ma-creative-script-writing

Unaccredited/Private Courses

Arvon Playwriting Courses:
www.arvon.org/genres/genre-theatre

The John Burgess Playwriting Course:
www.playwritingcourse.co.uk

Playwriting for Beginners, Central St Martins:
www.arts.ac.uk/csm/courses/short-courses/journalism-pr-media-and-publishing/play-writing-for-beginners

Industry Courses

Brockley Jack Writers' Workshop:
www.brockleyjack.co.uk/whats-on/writers

Criterion Theatre New Writing: www.criterion-theatre.co.uk/cri-trust/new-writing

Freedom Studios Street Voices:
www.freedomstudios.co.uk/projects/street-voices-6

HighTide Workshops: www.hightide.org.uk/get-involved/playwriting

Kali Theatre Writer Development Programme:
www.kalitheatre.co.uk/writer-support/writer-development-programmes.html

Live Theatre's Online Playwriting Course:
www.beaplaywright.com

National Theatre, How to Begin Playwriting:
www.nationaltheatre.org.uk/content/how-begin-playwriting

National Theatre Playwriting Course:
www.itunes.apple.com/gb/course/playwriting/id555641659

Papatango Theatre Company GoWrite Playwriting Courses:
www.papatango.co.uk

Royal Court Theatre Young Writers' Programme:
www.royalcourttheatre.com/playwriting

Royal Exchange Theatre Workshops:
www.royalexchange.co.uk/adults

Soho Theatre Writers' Lab: www.sohotheatre.com/young-people/soho-young-company/writers-lab

Tamasha Theatre: www.tamasha.org.uk/new-writing

The Student Guide to Writing: Playwriting:
www.thestudentguidetowriting.com

The Writing Squad: www.writingsquad.com

The Young Everyman Playhouse Writers Programme:
www.everymanplayhouse.com/making-theatre/yep-writers-programme

THEATRICAL LITERARY AGENCIES

This list includes some of the more reputable literary agencies with provision for playwrights.

42M&P Ltd: www.42mp.com

The Agency (London) Ltd: www.theagency.co.uk

Alan Brodie Representation Ltd: www.alanbrodie.com

Andrew Mann Literary Agency: www.andrewmann.co.uk

Berlin Associates: www.berlinassociates.com

Casarotto Ramsay & Associates Ltd: www.casarotto.co.uk

Curtis Brown Group Ltd: www.curtisbrown.co.uk

David Higham Associates Ltd: www.davidhigham.co.uk

Elaine Steel: www.elainesteel.com

Felix de Wolfe: www.felixdewolfe.com

Gemma Hirst Associates: www.gemmahirst.co.uk

Independent Talent Group Ltd: www.independenttalent.com

Jill Foster Ltd (JFL): www.jflagency.com

Judy Daish Associates Ltd: www.judydaish.com

Julia Tyrrell Management: www.jtmanagement.co.uk

The Lisa Richards Agency: www.lisarichards.co.uk

Kitson Press Associates: www.kitsonpress.co.uk

The Knight Hall Agency Ltd: www.knighthallagency.com

MacFarlane Chard Associates Ltd: www.macfarlane-chard.co.uk

Macnaughton Lord Representation: www.mlrep.com

MBA Literary & Scripts Agents: www.mbalit.co.uk

Micheline Steinberg Associates: www.steinplays.com

The Production Exchange: www.theproductionexchange.com

Rochelle Stevens & Co: www.rochellestevens.com

Sayle Screen Ltd: www.saylescreen.com

Troika: www.troikatalent.com

United Agents LLP: www.unitedagents.co.uk

THEATRICAL LITERARY AGENCIES

NEW-WRITING VENUES AND COMPANIES

This is a (partial) list of new-writing venues and companies that accept submissions.

Arcola Theatre: www.arcolatheatre.com

Birmingham Repertory Theatre: www.birmingham-rep.co.uk

Boundless Theatre: www.boundlesstheatre.org.uk

Box of Tricks: www.boxoftrickstheatre.co.uk

Bush Theatre: www.bushtheatre.co.uk

Curve Leicester: www.curveonline.co.uk

Everyman & Playhouse Theatres: www.everymanplayhouse.com

Finborough Theatre: www.finboroughtheatre.co.uk

Graeae: www.graeae.org

Hampstead Theatre: www.hampsteadtheatre.com

HighTide: www.hightide.org.uk

Leeds Playhouse: www.leedsplayhouse.org.uk

Live Theatre: www.live.org.uk

National Theatre: www.nationaltheatre.org.uk

National Theatre of Scotland: www.nationaltheatrescotland.com

National Theatre Wales: www.nationaltheatrewales.org

Out of Joint: www.outofjoint.co.uk

Paines Plough: www.painesplough.com

Papatango: www.papatango.co.uk

Pentabus: www.pentabus.co.uk

Royal Court Theatre: www.royalcourttheatre.com

Royal Exchange Theatre, Manchester: www.royalexchange.co.uk

Soho Theatre: www.sohotheatre.com

Theatre503: www.theatre503.com

Traverse Theatre: www.traverse.co.uk

NEW-WRITING VENUES AND COMPANIES

THEATRE PUBLISHERS

These publishing houses either exclusively specialise in or have an imprint that specialises in publishing plays.

Aurora Metro: www.aurorametro.com

Bloomsbury Methuen Drama:
www.bloomsbury.com/academic/academic-subjects/drama-and-performance-studies

Faber & Faber: www.faber.co.uk

Josef Weinberger Plays: www.josef-weinberger.com

Lazy Bee Scripts: www.lazybeescripts.co.uk

Nick Hern Books: www.nickhernbooks.co.uk

Oberon Books: www.oberonbooks.com

Playdead Press: www.playdeadpress.bigcartel.com

Samuel French: www.samuelfrench.co.uk

Smith Scripts: www.smithscripts.co.uk

PLAYWRITING COMPETITIONS

Increasingly, playwriting awards are supplementing, sometimes outright replacing, traditional submission opportunities. These are a list of the major competitions in the UK, all of which offer different rewards and have different requirements.

Bread and Roses Playwriting Award:
www.breadandrosestheatre.co.uk/playwriting-award.html

Bruntwood Prize for Playwriting: www.writeaplay.co.uk

Kenneth Branagh Award for New Drama Writing:
www.windsorfringe.co.uk/the-kenneth-branagh-playwright-competition.html

Papatango New Writing Prize: www.papatango.co.uk

Theatre503 Playwriting Award:
www.theatre503.com/writers/playwriting-award

Theatre Uncut Political Playwriting Award:
www.theatreuncut.com/award

Verity Bargate Award: www.sohotheatre.com/writers/verity-bargate-award

INTERNATIONAL COMPANIES

These are a few of the foreign companies with an interest in producing new English-language plays.

Butrini 2000 International Festival of Theatre, Albania: www.butrinti2000.com

Deutsches Schauspielhaus, Germany: www.schauspielhaus.de/en_EN

Escapade Theatre, Spain: www.escapadetheatre.es

Esplanade, Singapore: www.esplanade.com

Goodman Theatre, USA: www.goodmantheatre.org

Gothenburg International Studio Theatre, Sweden: www.gest.se/en

International Theatre Festival of Kerala, India: www.theatrefestivalkerala.com

Ja International Theatre, Portugal: www.jait.pt

Macao Arts Festival, China: www.icm.gov.mo/fam/27/en

Magic Theatre, USA: www.magictheatre.org

Milan Playwriting Festival, Italy: www.milanoplaywritingfestival.it/en

Münchner Kammerspiele, Germany: www.muenchner-kammerspiele.de/en

Queensland Theatre, Australia: www.queenslandtheatre.com.au

Roundabout Theatre, USA: www.roundabouttheatre.org

SEST, Sweden: www.sestcompany.com

Short + Sweet Theate Festival, Australia:
www.shortandsweet.org/festivals/shortsweet-theatre-sydney-
2018

Singapore Repertory Theatre, Singapore: www.srt.com.sg

STET, Netherlands: www.theenglishtheatre.nl

Talisman Theatre, Canada: www.en.talisman-theatre.com

Toneelgroep Amsterdam, Netherlands: www.tga.nl

Woolly Mammoth, USA: www.woollymammoth.net

POTENTIAL FUNDERS

There are a range of funders who may be interested in supporting an individual playwright or company making new plays.

Arts Council England: www.artscouncil.org.uk

Arts Council of Ireland: www.artscouncil.ie

Arts Council of Northern Ireland: www.artscouncil-ni.org

Arts Council of Wales: www.arts.wales

British Council: www.britishcouncil.org

Carne Trust: www.carnetrust.org

Creative Scotland: www.creativescotland.com

Fenton Arts Trust: www.fentonartstrust.org.uk

Fidelio Charitable Trust: www.fideliocharitabletrust.org.uk

K Blundell Trust: www.societyofauthors.org

Lionel Bart Foundation (bursaries for training/study): www.beta.charitycommission.gov.uk/charity-details/?regid=1086343&subid=0

MacDowell Fellowship: www.macdowellcolony.org/application-guidelines

Peggy Ramsay Foundation: www.peggyramsayfoundation.org

Royal Literary Fund: www.rlf.org.uk

Wellcome Trust: www.wellcome.ac.uk/what-we-do/our-work/arts

INDUSTRY RESOURCES

There are a multitude of helpful resources for playwrights, most accessible online. Spend some time trawling through the below, to glean pretty much all you'll need to know about rates, contracts, contacts and funding, as well as advice and tips from other playwrights or those working in talent development.

Arts Council England: www.artscouncil.org.uk

Arts Council Ireland: www.artscouncil.ie

Arts Council of Northern Ireland: www.artscouncil-ni.org

Arts Council of Wales: www.arts.wales

BBC Writersroom: www.bbc.co.uk/writersroom

Creative Scotland: www.creativescotland.com

Equity: www.equity.org.uk

Independent Theatre Council: www.itc-arts.org

London Playwrights' Blog (national opportunities despite the name): www.londonplaywrightsblog.com

New Writing North: www.newwritingnorth.com

New Writing South: www.newwritingsouth.com

Playwrights' Studio Scotland: www.playwrightsstudio.co.uk

Radio Independents Group: www.radioindies.org

Society of London Theatre: www.solt.co.uk

Writers' Guild of Great Britain: www.writersguild.org.uk

LIST OF CONTRIBUTORS

Many thanks to all who so generously contributed to this book.

Dare Aiyegbayo. Dare was Papatango's fourth Resident Playwright. She has written extensively for television, including *EastEnders* and *Waterloo Road*.

Matt Applewhite. Matt is Managing Director of Nick Hern Books, a specialist theatre publisher.

Tristan Bernays. Tristan is a playwright and winner of the OffWestEnd Award for Best New Musical. His work has been performed at Shakespeare's Globe, Soho Theatre, Southwark Playhouse, Bush Theatre, National Theatre Studio and the Roundhouse, and toured the UK. www.tristanbernays.com

Tom Brennan. Tom co-founded The Wardrobe Ensemble, for whom he has written and co-directed several plays which have toured nationally. As a director he has worked at the National Theatre, Almeida Theatre and Soho Theatre among many venues in the UK and US.

Sharon Clark. Sharon was formerly Literary Producer at Bristol Old Vic, and previously worked at the National Theatre, Watford Palace and Theatre503, before becoming a full-time playwright, dramaturg, and creative director of immersive theatre company Raucous. She was runner-up in the 2017 Papatango New Writing Prize and won a Judges Award in the 2017 Bruntwood Prize.

Rachel De-lahay. Rachel's plays have premiered at the Royal Court Theatre, Birmingham Rep and the Tricycle Theatre. She has also written for radio, TV and Netflix. Her plays have won the

Catherine Johnson Award, the Alfred Fagon Award, the Writers' Guild Best Play Award and the Evening Standard Most Promising Playwright Award, and her TV work has been nominated for a BAFTA. She is a trustee of Papatango.

Fiona Doyle. Fiona won the 2014 Papatango New Writing Prize for *Coolatully*, which Papatango produced at the Finborough Theatre and which has since been performed in the USA. Her next plays, *Deluge* and *The Strange Death of John Doe*, premiered at Hampstead Theatre, and she joined the National Theatre Studio on attachment. She has also written for NT Connections. She has received a MacDowell Colony Fellowship, won the Eamon Keane Full Length Play Award, and been nominated for the Susan Smith Blackburn Prize.

Kirsten Foster. Kirsten is an agent at Casarotto Ramsay & Associates Ltd.

Sarah Grochala. Sarah is a multi-award-winning playwright, dramaturg and academic. Her work has been produced at the Finborough Theatre and in Sydney and Toronto, and she was Associate Artist at Headlong from 2012 to 2016. She teaches playwriting and supervises PhD candidates at the Royal Central School of Speech & Drama.

Alex James. Alex is a Theatre Relationship Manager at Arts Council England.

Dawn King. Dawn won the 2011 Papatango New Writing Prize for *Foxfinder*, Papatango's production of which was named one of the *Independent*'s top-five plays of 2011 and won OffWestEnd and Royal National Theatre Foundation Playwright awards. *Foxfinder* has since premiered worldwide and in the West End. Dawn has premiered new plays with Out of Joint, Northampton Royal & Derngate, and the Bush Theatre, written for TV and film, and been nominated for a BAFTA and the Susan Smith Blackburn Prize.

Luke Owen. Luke won the 2013 Papatango New Writing Prize, and has since developed new plays with Headlong. His winning play *Unscorched* was translated into Italian and performed in Milan.

Sam Potter. Sam was Papatango's second Resident Playwright. Her first play, *Mucky Kid*, premiered at Theatre503 and was nominated for an OffWestEnd Award for Most Promising Playwright, and her play *Hanna* toured with Papatango across England and Wales. She has been commissioned by the Tricycle Theatre and Oxford North Wall, and was formerly Literary Manager at Out of Joint and Creative Associate at Headlong. As a director she has worked at the National Theatre, the RSC, Hampstead Theatre and Glyndebourne Opera.

Stewart Pringle. Stewart won the 2017 Papatango New Writing Prize and Papatango's production of *Trestle* saw him nominated for an OffWestEnd Award for Most Promising Playwright. He was previously Artistic Director at the Old Red Lion Theatre, for which he won the OffWestEnd Award for Best Artistic Director, before joining the Bush Theatre as Associate Dramaturg. He recently became Dramaturg at the National Theatre.

Moses Raine. Moses's first play, *Shrieks of Laughter*, premiered at Soho Theatre, and his second, *Donkey Heart*, premiered at the Old Red Lion Theatre and transferred to the West End.

May Sumbwanyambe. May was Papatango's first Resident Playwright, and won the 2016 Alfred Fagon Audience Award for Papatango's production of his play *After Independence* at the Arcola Theatre, which May then adapted for BBC Radio 4. He has received a BBC Performing Arts Fund Legacy award, been extensively commissioned across theatre, TV and radio, including for National Theatre Scotland, Theatre Royal Stratford East, Scottish Opera, and the BBC, and is a trustee of The Writing Squad.

SELECT BIBLIOGRAPHY

Frances Babbage, *Adaptation in Contemporary Theatre: Performing Literature* (London: Bloomsbury, 2017)

Michael Billington, *One Night Stands: A Critic's View of Modern British Theatre* (London: Nick Hern Books, 1993)

Michael Billington, *State of the Nation: British Theatre Since 1945* (London: Faber & Faber, 2007)

Mike Bradwell, *The Reluctant Escapologist: Adventures in Alternative Theatre* (London: Nick Hern Books, 2010)

Peter Brook, *The Empty Space* (1968; London: Penguin, 2008)

Marina Caldarone and Maggie Lloyd-Williams, *Actions: The Actors' Thesaurus* (London: Nick Hern Books, 2004)

David Edgar, *How Plays Work* (London: Nick Hern Books, 2009)

Richard Eyre, *Talking Theatre: Interviews with Theatre People* (London: Nick Hern Books, 2009)

Helen Freshwater, *Theatre and Audience* (London: Palgrave Macmillan, 2009)

Malcolm Gladwell, *Blink: The Power of Thinking without Thinking* (London: Penguin, 2006)

Lisa Goldman, *The No Rules Handbook for Writers* (London: Oberon Books, 2012)

Simon Gray, *The Smoking Diaries* (London: Granta Books, 2005)

Simon Gray, *The Early Diaries* (London: Faber & Faber, 2010)

Sarah Grochala, *The Contemporary Political Play: Rethinking Dramaturgical Structure*, (London: Bloomsbury, 2017)

David Hesmondhalgh, *The Cultural Industries* (3rd ed., London: SAGE, 2013)

Nicholas Hytner, *Balancing Acts: Behind the Scenes at the National Theatre* (London: Jonathan Cape, 2017)

"'I challenge them to leave but force them to stay": Playwrights on their Audiences', *Guardian*, 12 December 2017 (accessed February 2018): www.theguardian.com/stage/2017/dec/12/i-challenge-them-to-leave-but-force-them-to-stay-playwrights-on-their-audiences

Margherita Laera, ed., *Theatre and Adaptation: Return, Rewrite, Repeat* (London: Bloomsbury, 2014)

John McGrath, *A Good Night Out – Popular Theatre: Audience, Class and Form* (London: Nick Hern Books, 1996)

Katie Mitchell, *The Director's Craft: A Handbook for the Theatre* (Abingdon: Routledge, 2009)

Lucy Neal, *Playing for Time: Making Art as if the World Mattered* (London: Oberon Books, 2015)

John Osborne *Looking Back: Never Explain, Never Apologise*, (London: Faber & Faber, 1999)

Peggy Ramsay, *Peggy to her Playwrights: The Letters of Margaret Ramsay, Play Agent*, ed. Colin Chambers (London: Oberon Books, 2018)

Mike Rose, 'Rigid Rules, Inflexible Plans, and the Stifling of Language: A Cognitivist Analysis of Writer's Block', in *College Composition and Communication* vol. 31, no. 4 (December 1980), pp. 389–401

James Seabright, *So You Want To Be A Theatre Producer?* (London: Nick Hern Books, 2010)

Dominic Shellard, *British Theatre Since the War* (Trowbridge: Redwood Books, 2000)

Aleks Sierz, *In-Yer-Face Theatre: British Drama Today*, (London: Faber & Faber, 2001)

Barbara Simonsen, *The Art of Rehearsal: Conversations with Contemporary Theatre Makers* (London: Bloomsbury, 2017)

Sam Smiley, with Norman A. Bert, *Playwriting: The Structure of Action* (rev. ed., Yale University Press, 2005)

Simon Stephens, *Simon Stephens: A Working Diary* (London: Bloomsbury, 2016)

Heidi Stephenson and Natasha Langridge, *Rage and Reason: Women Playwrights on Playwriting* (London: Bloomsbury, 1997)

Katalin Trencsényi, *Dramaturgy in the Making: A User's Guide for Theatre Practitioners* (London: Bloomsbury, 2015)

The Diaries of Kenneth Tynan, ed. John Lahr (London: Bloomsbury, 2001)

Dennis Upper, 'The Unsuccessful Self-Treatment of a case of "Writer's Block"', *Journal of Applied Behavior Analysis* 7.3 (Fall 1974), p. 497

Steve Waters, *The Secret Life of Plays*, (London: Nick Hern Books, 2010)

Writers' & Artists' Yearbook (London: Bloomsbury, annual publication)

John Yorke, *Into the Woods: How Stories Work and Why We Tell Them* (London: Penguin, 2013)

'Remarkable unearthers of new talent.'
Evening Standard

Papatango discover and champion new playwrights through free, open-application schemes and opportunities.

Our flagship programme is the Papatango New Writing Prize, the UK's only annual award guaranteeing an emerging playwright a full production, publication, 10% of the gross box office, and an unprecedented £6,000 commission for a second play. The Prize is free to enter and assessed anonymously, and all entrants receive personal feedback on their scripts, an unmatched commitment to supporting aspiring playwrights. Over 1,300 entries are received each year.

Writers discovered through the Prize have received OffWestEnd and RNT Foundation Playwright Awards and BAFTAs, made work with the RSC, BBC, Hampstead Theatre, National Theatre, Out of Joint and other leading organisations, and premiered in over twenty countries.

Papatango also run an annual Resident Playwright scheme, taking an emerging playwright through commissioning, development and production of a new play. Our first Resident, May Sumbwanyambe, won the 2016 Alfred Fagon Audience Award for our production of *After Independence*, which we then adapted and produced for BBC Radio Four. Our second Resident, Samantha Potter, won a place on the Channel 4 Playwright's Scheme with our backing, and Papatango toured her play *Hanna* nationwide.

Papatango launched a new arm in summer 2017 called GoWrite. GoWrite delivers an extensive programme of free playwriting opportunities for children and adults nationwide. Children in state schools write their own plays which are then professionally performed and published, while adults take part in workshops, complete six-month courses at a variety of regional venues culminating in free public performances, or join fortnightly one-to-one career-facilitation services. GoWrite delivered face-to-face training for over 2,000 budding writers in its first year, with £5,000 available in bursaries to enable in-need writers nationwide to access our opportunities.

10% of seats at our productions are donated to charities for young people at risk of exclusion from the arts.

All our opportunities are free and entered anonymously, encouraging the best new talent regardless of means or connections.

Papatango's motto is simple. All you need is a story.

www.papatango.co.uk

Artistic Director
George Turvey

Executive Director
Chris Foxon

Resident Playwrights
May Sumbwanyambe
Samantha Potter
Sam Grabiner
Dare Aiyegbayo

Funding and Development Manager
Ruth Tosha Mulandi

Board
David Bond
Rachel De-lahay
Sam Donovan
Nicholas Rogers

Artistic Advisors
Colin Barr
Matt Charman
Tamara Harvey
Catherine Johnson
Dominic Mitchell
Con O'Neil
Tanya Tillett

www.nickhernbooks.co.uk

facebook.com/nickhernbooks

twitter.com/nickhernbooks